More Praise for Hank Wesselman's
MEDICINEMAKER
Mystic Encounters on the Shaman's Path

"Hank Wesselman is that rare combination of visionary and scholar whose message has the ring of truth, clarity, and urgency. *Medicinemaker* is anchored in personal experience, not fantasy. It is a thrilling journey that challenges our complacent assumptions about reality."
—Larry Dossey, M.D., author of *Prayer Is Good Medicine*

"An engaging personal narrative of spontaneous nonordinary experiences bridging 5,000 years by paleoanthropologist Hank Wesselman, whose earlier book, *Spiritwalker*, set the stage for sharing his new inner adventures."
—Michael Harner, author of *The Way of the Shaman*

"*Medicinemaker* is Hank Wesselman's eloquently written, courageous true story about a scientist turned shaman who travels 5,000 years into the future. It is a powerful testimony to the timeless connections between spirit and the intuitions that bind us all together with love."
—Judith Orloff, M.D., author of *Second Sight*

"Wesselman's dramatic story continues and unfolds in a way to inspire us all."
—Sandra Ingerman, author of *Soul Retrieval: Mending the Fragmented Self* and *A Fall to Grace*

"Wesselman makes a dramatic case for environmental activism."
—*Publishers Weekly*

ALSO BY HANK WESSELMAN

Spiritwalker: Messages from the Future

MEDICINEMAKER

Mystic Encounters
on the
Shaman's Path

Hank Wesselman

BANTAM BOOKS

New York   Toronto   London   Sydney   Auckland

This edition contains the complete text
of the original hardcover edition.
NOT ONE WORD HAS BEEN OMITTED.

MEDICINEMAKER
A Bantam Book

PUBLISHING HISTORY
Bantam hardcover edition published 1998
Bantam trade paperback edition / December 1999

BOOK DESIGN BY GLEN EDELSTEIN

Library of Congress Catalog Card Number: 97-50139

ISBN 0-553-37932-1

Published simultaneously in the United States and Canada

Bantam Books are published by Bantam Books, a division of Random House, Inc. Its
trademark, consisting of the words "Bantam Books" and the portrayal of a rooster, is
Registered in U.S. Patent and Trademark Office and in other countries. Marca Registrada.
Bantam Books, 1540 Broadway, New York, New York 10036.

PRINTED IN THE UNITED STATES OF AMERICA

BVG   10 9 8 7 6 5 4 3 2 1

This book is dedicated to the medicinemakers
of all traditions and all times . . .
for all those courageous men and women who
develop from the negative,
embrace the positive,
and live in service to others.

In their hands and hearts
rest the equilibrium of humankind
and its continuance.

When heaven is about to confer
A great office upon a man,
It first exercises his mind with suffering,
And his sinews and bones with toil;
It exposes him to poverty
And confounds all his undertakings.
Then it is seen if he is ready.

—MŌSHI

CONTENTS

Contents

INTRODUCTION

I am an anthropologist who works with a team of scientists investigating the eroded, ancient landscapes of eastern Africa's Great Rift Valley in search of answers to the mystery of human origins. My academic training lies in the fields of environmental and evolutionary biology, geology and anthropology, and much of my research involves reconstructing the paleoenvironments of the prehistoric sites from which the fossilized remains of humanity's earliest ancestors have been recovered.

In *Spiritwalker: Messages from the Future*, I have written about how my life took a decidedly different turn in the early 1980s, while I was finishing up my doctoral work at the University of California at Berkeley. One foggy summer morning just before dawn, I experienced a full-fledged altered state of consciousness that occurred spontaneously, without the catalyst of any spiritual practice or mind-altering substances. While deep in this expanded state, I had a close encounter with what a tribal person might call a spirit. This episode was followed by several other vivid experiences accompanied by ecstatic feelings of force or power that rendered me physically paralyzed yet hyperaware. I was at a complete loss to explain these strange occurrences. I was not one of those who had spent decades studying at the knees of the wisdom masters, practicing meditation and yoga, hoping for visions and transcendent experiences. In those days, I worshiped solely at the altar of science.

Several years later, my family and I moved to a farm on the Kona Coast of Hawai'i, where I experienced another series of spontaneous altered states. In the first, my conscious awareness was brought into contact with that of another man in a most dramatic fashion. It was as if I were inside his body as an invisible visitor or witness. I could see what he was seeing and hear what he was hearing. I could perceive his thoughts and emotions almost as if they were my own, and yet there were two separate personalities, his and mine, existing simultaneously within the one physical aspect.

When I recovered from my astonishment, I discovered that I could tap into this man's memory banks, receiving information as a multi-layered complex of thoughts, emotions, impressions, memories, and judgments. I learned that his name is Nainoa and that he is an individual of Hawaiian ancestry who lives somewhere on the coast of California roughly five thousand years from now in a world profoundly different from that of today. To say I was surprised by this incredible experience would be an understatement of vast proportions.

I had heard about such things as telepathy and clairvoyance, channeling and trance mediumship, but up until that moment my reaction to these psychic phenomena had been one of amused skepticism. Now here I was, a trained scientist, experiencing the awesome jolt of the real thing myself. My initial response was confusion mixed with disbelief, and I shakily branded the episode an extremely lucid dream. I say shakily because part of me suspected that what I had experienced was not a dream at all.

Much to my astonishment, the altered states continued, becoming an ongoing series of episodes that occurred roughly in sequence over the next four years. They were largely spontaneous in that I could not deliberately induce them through my intentionality alone, yet in each, my conscious awareness was merged with that of the same man.

Within these states, I had learned a lot about him and his world visually through his eyes, experientially through his actions in his level of reality and time, and cognitively through the veil of his culturally determined perceptions, judgments, interpretations, memories, and opinions. His thoughts and feelings had an alien quality, a foreignness, that was very distracting at first. I came to realize that this was due to the profoundly different "shape" of his mind, determined largely by his experiences since birth in his own slice of reality and within his own culture.

When I opened my eyes in Nainoa's body the first time, I tried to control his movements. His body responded with confusion to two separate sets of commands. Somehow, despite my own confusion and excitement, I managed to figure out the problem, and so I became completely passive. I merely "sat within" and observed. I believe that my limited experience with meditation proved invaluable, as I was able to discipline myself to become completely still, yet fully watchful. In the process, I discovered that if I wished to look at something, Nainoa would very shortly walk over and look at it. If I wanted to know something, it would obligingly appear in my mind . . . and in his. Although Nainoa's language is different from any that exists today, I was able to receive the gist of meaning of his thoughts and words as the shape of his knowing was translated into mine, a process I am still trying to understand fully.

In response to this amazing experience, my carefully constructed scientific paradigm of reality began to come apart, and at that time I had nothing with which to replace it. Although I didn't know it, I was in the throes of a classic initiation crisis, a mental and spiritual crossroads well known to the shamans of traditional tribal peoples and the mystics of our modern state level societies. But unlike the tribal shaman or contemporary spiritual seeker, I was not prepared for such a life-changing and ego-shattering event.

Yet within the expanded-state connections with Nainoa, a most amazing story began to unfold. In the initial episode, I had learned that his people are the descendants of Hawaiians who reached the North American coast in a fleet of double-hulled oceangoing canoes about 130 years before. Upon their arrival, they had found no people, no cities, and no evidence of the once-great American civilization. They had established a chain of settlements around the western edge of an inland sea—large, planned, self-sufficient slices of landscape with a fishing community on the coast and a farming community a day's travel inland.

From Nainoa's memories, I learned that the settlers' society is stratified by rank and privilege, much like that of the precontact Hawaiians of the past, with a political leadership derived largely from a ruling class with various ranks of "commoners" below them in the hierarchy—laborers, farmers, fishermen, stockmen, artisans, servants, and so forth. If I was, in fact, seeing a slice of the future, it seemed that humanity's destiny lies in a system of balanced feudalism.

On that first day, Nainoa left his community to engage in a journey of geographic exploration of the largely unknown interior of the continent. But where were the oak-studded grasslands, pines, and other evergreens of the California that I knew so well? The land I saw was covered with tropical rain forests, and the climate was most definitely tropical and wet. If this was indeed California, a dramatic climate shift had occurred, possibly on a planetary scale, bearing out contemporary science's worst-case predictions associated with the current greenhouse theory of global warming.

The adventure deepened as Nainoa crossed the inland sea, presumably a marine inundation of California's central valley, and traversed the forested regions and the mountains beyond. During this solitary trek, he himself began to have expanded-state experiences—psychic episodes in which he started to receive his own initiation at the hands of the spirits.

It was during this journey that Nainoa began to experience the time-shift phenomenon in reverse, on occasion finding his conscious awareness merged with mine. His reaction was to hypothesize that I was his ancestor, an insight that threw the whole affair into an entirely new light. As an invisible participant observer to these incredible events, my own investigations began to extend far beyond the ordinary nature of reality, into the inner realms of the human mind and spirit.

Upon achieving the comparatively drier wooded grasslands beyond the mountains, Nainoa found a group of indigenous hunter-gatherers of possible mixed Inuit–French Canadian descent and spent most of a year living with them. During this interval, he became romantically involved with a woman named Kenojelak, whose father, William, functioned as shaman for his people when the need arose.

Toward the end of my stay in Kona, Nainoa's growing awareness of me and his wish to make contact was facilitated by William, who began to instruct him in the ways of the traditional shaman. The two men visited a place of power where Nainoa and I finally conversed directly for the first time. It was also in this place that we were taken on a visionary voyage into the heart of the great mystery of existence by an immensely powerful spirit.

These experiences were documented in *Spiritwalker,* but my journeys did not end with that book's publication. On the contrary, they had only begun.

I know this sounds quite fantastic, even unbelievable. In my dark moments, I wondered often if I were going mad. Yet this fear was balanced by the intuitive sense that through these journeys, I had stumbled into something of considerable significance—something that was providing me with entirely new insights into what it means to be human.

CHAPTER I

Reentry

M Y FAMILY AND I departed from our farm in Hawai'i in the summer of 1989. We took up residence in a suburb of San Diego for the next academic year while I served as a visiting lecturer in anthropology for the local branch of the University of California.

When our children entered school in the fall, my wife, Jill, joined an all-women team of doctors, nurses, and health-care professionals, working as a physical therapist. We juggled our schedules to meet the needs of our children, our days revolving around school dropoffs and pickups, teaching classes and commuting on freeways, shopping in supermarkets and visits to the zoo, professional seminars and PTA meetings. It seemed as if we were constantly rushing, never quite completing one responsibility before the next would be upon us.

I reacted to being back in California with strong feelings of foreboding. The prosperity of the Reagan years had abruptly come to an end, and millions of people were unemployed, with millions more caught in the crunch of escalating medical and property costs. The newspapers were filled with accounts of yesterday's disasters and stories of dishonesty, fiscal mismanagement, violent crime, and abuse. The population of southern California had grown exponentially. Formerly open expanses of countryside were now filled with subdivisions and shopping malls, and the traffic was stifling. It was quite a change from the quiet life on our farm in rural, upcountry Hawai'i.

In the midst of all this, the visionary adventures I had experienced in Kona were always there, right behind my eyes. In the evenings, with the children in bed and the next day's lectures prepared, much time was spent contemplating what I had learned.

First and foremost, I had discovered the presence of some sort of inner doorway within myself, one that opened periodically, giving me glimpses into levels of reality and experience I had not thought possible. The opening was usually accompanied by visual hallucinations, spots of light, labyrinthine lines, zigzags, vortexes, and grids that some cognitive investigators have called "phosphenes." There was almost always a buzzing, roaring rush of sound accompanied by overwhelming bodily sensations of force or power that rendered me paralyzed for the duration of the experience. The intensity of the experience could have been quite frightening were it not for its exquisite nature. I now understood why the word *ecstasy* is associated with religious trance.

Something else of note had happened during our time in Hawai'i. I had become the *kahu*, the honored caretaker, of a *pohaku kupua*, a "spirit stone" that I found in the waves below the tideline at Kealakekua Bay, where I swam daily with my family. On the day that I found it, I recognized it with shock, for I had seen it in a vision more than a year before in the possession of the chief of Nainoa's settlement. The stone took up residence in a rock garden near my front door, and in time I began to suspect that it was part of the causality for the connection between me and Nainoa, for the stone had been there, unseen among the other rocks at the interface of the beach and the bay, when my visionary connections with Nainoa had commenced. Toward the end of my days in Kona, I received a clear impression that it wished to accompany me to the mainland of America—an intention in keeping with its formal name, Kapohaku'ki'ihele, the stone that travels.

When the shipping container containing our household goods arrived in San Diego, I located the crate containing the stone and unpacked it first. The dark boulder looked rather dry, and I wondered uneasily if it were still "alive" after its trip in the hold of a ship. It had always stood outside in our garden in Kona, so we placed it under a scraggly fig tree in the backyard of our rental, a postage-stamp-sized piece of sun-baked clay that had been neglected by the former tenants.

Interestingly, as soon as the stone was in place, the whole yard seemed to come to life. The grass staged a dramatic comeback, several untended clumps of Cape honeysuckle erupted into clouds of orange-red flowers, and a large dracaena burst into fragrant bloom. A stand of sickly-looking banana trees actually began to produce bananas. It was the fig tree, however, that underwent the greatest change. Once the stone was placed beneath it, the tree started to throw out leaves and fruit at a truly impressive rate that continued unabated even throughout the coldest part of the next winter, when the tree dropped its leaves and frost killed some of my bonsai. During the year and a half that the stone remained under the tree, the flow of figs never ceased.

Despite the stone's presence, I had no new altered-state experiences for almost a year, perhaps because I was so busy with ordinary reality concerns. I taught several anthropology classes at the university, including one focused on religion and magic in the lives of traditional peoples. My daily office hour continually lengthened as students dropped in to discuss aspects of this course, and I found myself listening to young people tell me their own stories of startling, life-changing experiences. Several had met the "shadow," the dark, monolithic spirit that both Nainoa and I had encountered at the onset of our visionary adventures. Many had had déjà vu experiences, clairvoyant or telepathic perceptions not regarded as valid or "real" by Western culture at large. When I counted up the number of individuals who had had some sort of mystic experience, I was amazed. More than 10 percent of the students fell into this category.

Many had also been badly damaged by life and were emotionally scarred. Within myself, I felt a growing sense of compassion, and I began to wonder how I could help them. Through my experiences in Hawai'i, I had become aware of the connection that exists between knowledge and power. However, it's one thing to teach a class about shamanism and magic. It's quite another to practice it.

In Western society, we tend to think of a magician as one who performs incredible illusions before amazed audiences. In tribal societies, magic involves accessing the realm of the sacred in order to persuade, control, or influence supernatural power to assist in manifesting something in the ordinary, everyday world. What is manifested is determined largely by the intentions and personality of the practitioner as well as the needs of the client or community. As I listened to my students, I was very much aware that I had no training, nor any tradition from which to operate in this capacity.

When the semester came to an end, I decided that part of the final examination would include ritual in which I would expose my students to the sound of the rattle for the first time. Many traditional people say that the rattle helps them connect with mystical power and that the sharp, dry sound is like a telephone call to the spirit world. But I knew this only from my reading when I gathered the class for the final meeting.

We pushed the desks back against the wall and sat on the floor in a circle. I drew the shades, darkening the room, and lit a single candle in the cleared center, a minimalist ritual I remembered from a shamanic workshop I had attended years before with the anthropologist Michael Harner. The rattle I used was a commercial object made of plastic that belonged to my children, but it had a nice sharp sound. I instructed my students to close their eyes and listen to the sound of the rattle, to just let their conscious awareness follow it and pay attention to anything that might come up.

As the dry, rhythmic whisper filled the classroom, I followed the traditional custom of addressing the spirits of the four directions to ask for protection and support—for myself and for all those gathered. I closed my eyes and felt my consciousness shift sideways as the familiar, dreamy state descended. Abruptly the feelings of power invaded my body, and I was momentarily staggered. As I wondered with some concern if I was going to go into a full, paralytic trance, the sensations stabilized at a level in which I could continue to rattle. I suddenly felt a familiar presence. I cracked open my eyes and got quite a shock.

There, against the darkness of the blackboard, a curious swirl of sparkling lights appeared. Within it, a cluster of spots took form and coalesced into a shape I knew well. It was my old ally the leopard man, an imaginary friend from childhood who had reentered my life during the Harner workshop. The leopard man had functioned as a spirit helper to both myself and Nainoa during my visionary episodes, and I suspected that he had played a pivotal role in bringing the two of us together.

I quickly glanced around the classroom to discern if anyone else could see him, but my students were all sitting quietly, their eyes closed, as I had instructed. I shot another look at my feline ally. He was standing bipedally, like a human, and seemed roughly as tall as me. His rosettes swirled with light as he alternately merged into and separated out of the darkness surrounding him. This was the first time I had seen him since leaving the islands, so I gathered my wits and offered a Buddhist bow while I endeavored to continue rattling.

I then mentally explained what I was doing and asked him for assistance. In response, he did something quite catlike. He closed his luminous eyes in that distinct squint that cats express when they are feeling good. His eyes closed, then opened slightly, then closed again, conveying ease. I glanced at his paws, or were they hands and feet? No, they were definitely paws, and his claws were retracted, a good sign.

As I walked around the circle, rattling above and around each student's head, the leopard man's eyes followed, witnessing the ritual, testifying to the beginning of my transformation from academic teacher in the Western sense into . . . what? I suddenly realized that a tribal person would say I was functioning as a medicine man.

As I concluded the ritual and the rattle subsided into silence, my awareness shifted, and the leopard man evaporated, dissolving into the swirl of light very much in the same way he had arrived. I sat down at my place in the circle feeling somewhat overwhelmed. Fortunately, the students then took over and made their final presentations. Throughout, the feelings of power remained, just below the surface. Both the scientist and the mystic within me were most impressed.

When the year's teaching was over, I suddenly found myself with large blocks of free time. In the mornings, with Jill at work and the children at school, I began to sit under the fig tree with the spirit stone whenever I paused to have a cup of tea, and my attention came to rest on my "field notes" from Hawai'i. One day I sat down at the computer and began to put together the first full-fledged version of *Spiritwalker*. Perhaps it was coincidence, but that night, an hour before dawn, something awakened me.

As I lay in bed in the darkness, I heard a coyote howl from the hillsides beyond the edges of the suburb. I looked out the window at the starry sky, and memories of the future moved through my mind. I felt quite awake, and as I watched the thoughts that flew through my mind like birds, I came to a decision. I formed a strongly focused intention to journey again to Nainoa.

I waited, but nothing unusual happened. I focused again. Nothing. After a while I decided to cancel the attempt. My attention shifted and I thought about the fact that I had failed to find a job for the coming year. I felt feelings of extreme disappointment mixed with fear. What was I to do? I had a family to support. Was I in the process of losing my profession as an anthropologist?

Long moments of soul searching followed, but no immediate solutions were apparent as I tossed and turned, unable to get back to sleep. Jill awoke and we talked in the dark until almost dawn and then made quick, intense love. Our lives were filled with work and responsibilities now, and rare were the moments we had alone together.

I felt very relaxed in passion's aftermath and looked out the window once again at the stars. I began to drop off to sleep when the sensations of power appeared abruptly within me, sweeping up my back and into my brain. I shut my eyes tightly, but the stars remained, points of light dancing in the dark. The exquisite paralysis commenced, accompanied by the familiar soaring feelings of bliss and the roaring rush of sound. I had been waiting for this for a year.

I formed an image in my mind of the spirit stone in the backyard and invoked its help. The sensations increased enormously. Flashes of light coalesced into bright spots that became lines as my eyes looked this way and that. As the brilliant grid took form within and around the lines, the transparent, flickering arc appeared and began to open, blinding me and flooding me with ecstatic force. As I struggled with the effort of breathing, feelings of outward movement began. The journey had begun.

There was no fear. This was familiar now, a known experience. I focused strongly upon my destination as my body shook and the roaring in my ears increased. I plummeted into the arc in a flash of fiery sensation; then the sound and the visuals abruptly diminished to nothing as the zone of darkness and silence was traversed. The smell of wood smoke and furs heralded the restoration of my sensory perception.

I had once again achieved contact with Nainoa. My excitement was immediately countered by an emotion I had not expected. I was flooded by a sense of deep and personal grief.

CHAPTER 2

First Journey:
The Mountain

NAINOA OPENED HIS eyes and stared out through a break in the mist and clouds at a patch of starry night sky. Something had awakened him. He shivered and drew his wet fur cloak more tightly around him, then glanced across the embers of the fire at his feet toward William and William's youngest son, Zaki. Their cloak-wrapped shapes and the furry forms of their dogs were almost indistinguishable, huddled against the cool, damp mountain air. He felt distaste for the wet fur and resolved to make them all proper rain capes once the correct plant types were found.

The three travelers were in the mountains on their way back to Nainoa's settlement and were currently traversing a forest with a lush understory dominated by tree ferns, bromeliads, and mosses dripping with moisture. He glanced again at the stars as the clouds closed in. Only two days ago they had left William's band at the base of the scarred mountain, and Nainoa felt a pang of loss. He thought of William's daughter Kenojelak, and his grief intensified.

He remembered the day they had met, almost a year ago. The Ennu woman had found him camped in a riverine forest, severely injured from a close encounter with a longhorn. She had become his lover in that same forest several months later, and the two of them had subsequently lived together as husband and wife. The hollow feeling in his chest grew deeper. He missed her.

His year with the people he thought of as the Ennu had finally come to an end when the stars and the onset of the season of migrating birds revealed that he had only two or three lunar cycles in which to return to his settlement before the rains resumed. Images of large crocodiles lurking in the semiflooded lowland rain forest around the inland sea filled his mind's eye. He shivered again. Unwary humans had been taken by them.

He thought about the Ennu and what he had learned about their lifestyle during the time he had lived with William's band. The Ennu were nomads, the descendants of people who had been migrating ever southward and westward from their point of origin in the far north for a long period of time, possibly since the collapse of the American civilization. Unlike his own people, the Ennu grew no crops. They were ambush hunters, following the endless herds of game upon which they preyed with great success.

Nainoa folded his arms behind his head and glanced across the smoldering fire at the Ennu dogs. Large and lean with pale eyes, upwardly curved tails, and short fur, these animals had an important relationship with their human masters. Large carnivores tended to avoid the Ennu because of the presence of their dogs. Also, the dogs were trained to drive game toward the hunters waiting in places of concealment. A series of gestures and indistinct hisses seemed to communicate what was required in any given instant. Nainoa suspected that both the Ennu and their dogs had worked this game plan out millennia ago.

Nainoa recalled his profound disappointment when he had realized that these hunters were all that remained of the civilization of North America. Gone forever were the mythic marvels of the Americans' knowledge and technology. Gone also were their machines, objects made of metal and recorded by the histories of his people to have been things of great power.

Nainoa's thoughts shifted then to focus upon the man he thought of as "the American."* Twice before, his conscious awareness had journeyed through time in some inexplicable way to find itself merged with this man's mind. In the first incident, the American had been in Hawai'i, the ancient island homeland from which his own ancestors had emigrated more than a century before. In the second, the American had seemed to be in California, but in a California profoundly different from that of today. And, marvel upon marvel, the man had actually been operating a machine at the time he had connected with him.

Both experiences had been much too real to have been dreams, providing him with amazing glimpses into the past, during which he perceived things and places that were clearly not within his own memories. The mythology of his people contained stories of individuals who had made such dreamlike voyages backward in time. Often the dream travelers connected with the spiritual essence of an ancestor, allowing them to recover lost knowledge. This had led him to conclude that the American could very well be one of his ancestors. The thought of the knowledge that might be recovered from these unsought and apparently spontaneous connections had subsequently taken a strong hold on him.

Nainoa remembered the day when he had discovered that the American had been connecting with him, a revelation that had shaken him to the core. It was also about this time that he had become aware

* Author's note: As has been mentioned, when I journey to Nainoa, I both perceive and understand through his mind-body complex. I have total access to his thoughts, memories, desires, and knowledge while we are in connection, and so I record the events of his life and time from his perspective. Therefore, when I relate Nainoa's thoughts about me—for he is sometimes as fully aware of me as I am of him—I do so in the third person. He knows me as "the American" and thinks of me in those terms.

that William was a mystic, or, as the Ennu said, "a spiritwalker." He had subsequently sought out the older man for advice on how to improve his contact with the American. William had then taken him to the spirit hills to enlist the help of the *dorajuadioks,* the immensely powerful spirits that resided in that place.

And the trip had borne fruit. For the thousandth time, he perused his memories of that event from beginning to end. Again he heard the strange roaring sound that seemed to come up out of the ground itself. Again he detected the unmistakable presence of the American within his mind, the presence that now seemed so familiar.

Abruptly Nainoa's awareness shifted back into the present. Something or someone was nearby. He could feel it. As he wondered if the American was in connection, an indistinct sound caught his attention and he came fully awake. His eyes scanned the dark forest.

William stirred in his sleep. The old hunter had decided to accompany him back across the mountains, saying that he wished to meet the Hawaiians and see the settlements of which Nainoa had said so much. Nainoa knew that the Ennu typically avoided the wet, foggy mountain forest with its tigers and bears, and he suspected that William had come with him because Kenojelak had discussed her prophetic dream with him.

A water spirit had approached her in a vision, telling her that William would return with him and that she would remain with her people to become a medicine woman. The spirit had also said that she would bear Nainoa a child . . . a daughter who would someday have a great gift for her father. Nainoa recalled the intense and protracted lovemaking that had followed this revelation and felt his blood sparkle in response. He allowed this memory to flow within his mind, feeling his connection to Kenojelak. He wondered if their daughter had been conceived.

Suddenly something alerted him again, and once more he came fully awake. There was a presence, something watching him. Again his eyes searched the darkness of the trees. He felt vulnerable sleeping on the ground in the forest, but his sleeping hammock had not survived a year's worth of play with the Ennu children, and William had said there was nothing to worry about, that the dogs would alert them to any danger from large predators. Nainoa glanced at them now. They were asleep. Yet the sense of presence remained.

He recalled having this same feeling during his long walk through the mountains the year before. Maybe he had once again attracted the attention of spirits—the spotted tiger man or the forest spirit, perhaps, or some other entity who had taken an interest in him. There was another possibility, too—the American.

William abruptly sat up, disrupting his thoughtline. The Ennu glanced at him, then reached over to put several damp pieces of wood on the fire. They smoked excessively before bursting into flame. The older man looked at his sodden furs, and the corners of his mouth turned down. Everything was wet.

"I feel something," William said, gesturing. He looked around carefully, then grinned. "There are spirits in this forest," he whispered. "They are curious about us and are thinking, 'Who are these strange humans who have come into our domain?' " He chuckled.

Nainoa was about to speak when he saw William become immobile and bring his fingers together in the hunters' curt gesture of warning. "There is something out there in the trees," he said quietly. "Something big." He glanced at the dogs and made a small, breathy sound that immediately alerted them.

Zaki raised his head, looking at them wearily and causing his father to chuckle again. "The young need their rest, and here we are, older men talking about spirits before breakfast."

Zaki caught something in his father's gaze and shook off any residue of sleep, picking up his bow in an easy flow of movement. Holding his quiver of arrows in his mouth, he used both hands to string the bow while he kept his eyes on the forest. Nainoa rose to his feet and took up his spear, noting that William's spear-thrower was already held loosely in his fist, with the javelin notched. The spear's tip bore a wide, sharp point made of flaked black stone.

Nainoa became still, allowing his awareness to expand with the flare of adrenaline that surged through him. It was there. He could feel it just beyond the nearest trees. His sense of being watched surged. William's glance moved in the same direction. The dogs picked it up and rose silently, fanning out, two in front and two at flank. William put more wood on the fire, then picked up the tightly bound bundle of dry rushes he had prepared for just such an opportunity.

As the dogs' threatening snarl emerged from the darkness, the tiger's answering roar stunned them all with its force. William touched the torch tip to the fire and rose as it burst into flame. The tiger was there among the trees, its reflecting eyes revealing its presence. Nainoa moved out to the left, grasping his spear with the leaf-shaped iron point. Zaki went out to the right, notching an arrow and holding two more in his teeth.

The dogs held their distance, containing the tiger as William advanced slowly, holding the torch aloft. The carnivore backed up a step. Being set upon by dogs in the company of several large beings, one of whom was holding fire, was a new experience for it. The three men became immobile, weapons ready, each poised to act. William's whisper held the dogs still. The tiger remained where it was and stared at them impassively. The stripes broke up its outline, rendering it almost invisible in the foliage. Perhaps it was just curious, checking on the trespassers in its territory. Nainoa locked eyes with the tiger.

For long moments there was only that gaze and the sense of tension that flowed along it. He looked deeply into its eyes and formed intentions in his mind, offering respectful greetings, explaining the need to travel through its territory, asking permission. He told the tiger that they were just passing through and would take little food, only what they needed. On impulse, he added that he had heard once that the tiger spirit had an interest in scholars because of their similar mind shapes. Scholars, like tigers, were hunters, but hunters of knowledge.

Something shifted in that moment, and the tiger looked away. Nainoa felt the sudden release of tension and, glancing at William, saw the older man slowly transfer his spear to the hand that held the torch. Then he suddenly struck the spear with the shaft of the spear-thrower, making a sharp report and causing a shower of sparks to fly from the torch. The tiger opened its eyes wide in alarm and sat up. William continued to strike the two pieces of wood together, producing a series of loud, rhythmic clacks that made the torch vibrate and crackle. Then he took a step forward.

The tiger rose, turned, and with a long backward glance at the three men melted into the trees. The dogs began to follow until a hiss from William stopped them. He continued to strike the sticks together, indicating by gesture that Nainoa and Zaki should join in, matching his rhythm. Nainoa leaned his spear against his shoulder and clapped his hands together sharply. Zaki struck his bow with an arrow shaft. Their staccato cadence rang through the forest, sending the tiger on its way.

After a time, William halted and laughed with delight. Glancing at Nainoa, he said, "The tiger is *unkayorak'nobordalek*, the master of the forest. He is also *unkayorak'amayok*, the master of the game animals. He came to look us over."

The hunter laughed again, then dropped his voice to a conspiratorial whisper. "When you're dealing with tigers, it's best to appear powerful. That particular tiger will not wish to approach us again." He gave Nainoa a long look. "Its spirit aspect, however, makes a powerful ally as a *dordok*, a spirit helper." Then his look sobered as he glanced at his son thoughtfully. "Let's break camp and get ourselves beyond this soggy place."

They climbed out of the wet forests and ascended steadily through the mountain woodlands of curious needle-leaved trees toward the highest of the mountains, retrekking Nainoa's original route of the year before. At midmorning Zaki killed a sheep with large curled horns. They hung it in a tree, dressed it, cut the meat into strips, and filled their game bags. They gathered several bundles of firewood along the way and refilled their water bottles from a stream before climbing the peak on which he had camped. Nainoa had told them of the spirit flight he had experienced at this place, and William was curious to see it.

They arrived at the rocky ledge near the summit in the midafternoon. The sun-warmed platform was large enough for the three to sleep with a fire at their feet, and they decided to stay the night. They stacked the firewood and their personal gear while Zaki took all their furs down to the south-facing rocky slopes below, pinning them down with stones in the sun to dry in the warm wind. William stared out at the grand vista of endless mountains capped by the immensity of the sky, then turned and grinned at Nainoa. "*Blasbitorek* . . . nice spot."

The hunter extracted a chunk of the morning's firewood from a bark container and brought it to life with his breath. He piled twigs around a twist of dry grass, got the fire going, estimated how much wood they might need, and dispatched Zaki in search of more. Then the two men sat and fed the fire, preparing it for cooking the meat as they gazed out at the view.

"Tell me more about how the Ennu experience the spirits, William. Why do they approach us, for example?"

The older man's eyes widened as he considered the question. "The spirits come in different kinds, different types. Some represent the spiritual aspects of nature, the spotted tiger spirit, or Zilatu, the spirit of the air. Others, like the *dorajuadiok,* have no physical counterpart. Some are the spirits of humans who are not currently embodied. Then there is our own personal spiritual aspect. All exist at a certain level of awareness and have qualities and abilities that distinguish them from each other. All possess a certain capacity for action as well.

"The spirits approach us because we are part of their world. They are curious about us and are always about, watching, listening. They are everywhere, in everything. Through interacting with spirits, we humans can receive information as well as assistance in accomplishing certain things here in the everyday world—like finding game animals or good stone for making tools.

"The spirits are the carriers of mystical power. Humans with the ability to spirit-walk can access this power through them." The older man's gaze swept the rocky cliff into which their campsite was tucked. "We have talked about the earth spirits before. They live inside the rocks and rarely come out. Most are gentle and shy. Their minds are much like human minds, although they don't have to think about things like we do. They simply know. They possess vast knowledge of history and the universe."

As he spoke, William picked up an angular shard of stone and carefully etched a drawing of a long, linear humanoid form on the dark rock wall of their shelter. It had spidery arms and legs and a small, nondescript body and head with a wide-eyed expression. The older man's gaze became serious.

"One must be careful in dealing with spirits, however. Sometimes rocks of curious appearance are really hostile entities that have been transformed into stone by something more powerful than they. These spirits can attack humans who pass too close, invading their dreaming or inducing them to act in a malevolent manner. Sometimes they are powerful enough to kill people. It usually happens slowly, a wasting illness in which the unfortunate person's life force is consumed. Some places beyond the spirit hills to the south and east are avoided because they are known to harbor malevolent rock spirits of this sort."

The older man glanced around at the walls of their shelter, then smiled as Zaki returned with more wood, which they stacked along one side of the ledge. "But this place feels fine. Perhaps we can connect with its power tonight. Let's cook all this meat first, though."

Zaki was William's son with a wife who lived in another band, separate from the one in which Nainoa had been associated for the past year. In late adolescence, Zaki was still unmarried and had come with them on their journey to Nainoa's people for the adventure of it. He was a good hunter and spoke little, listening in silence to the older men when they spoke.

The afternoon passed in the cooking of the meat. It had fat in it and tasted good. Nainoa boiled some in his cooking pot with salt, creating a hot soup that the three men consumed with relish. They fed the dogs as they roasted and smoke-dried the rest, eating as much as they pleased. When the day faded, they settled into their now dry furs for the night. The four dogs fended for themselves, finding sleeping places elsewhere on the rocky slopes.

The sky was clear at their level, and when the moon rose, it illuminated the sea of clouds that hung in the valley far below. The mountain peaks seemed to float on this sea, creating the illusion of islands. The view was truly magnificent. Nainoa looked up at William's drawing of the rock spirit. The firelight flickering over the uneven surface created a sense of motion.

"I have mentioned the spirit stone in the care of Chief Kaneohe, the director of my settlement," Nainoa mentioned. "It appears in my thoughts from time to time. Could this stone harbor one of these earth spirits, William?"

"It may," said the older man. "You have said it came from the lands of your ancestry across the ocean. It may be in connection with that land's collective awareness and power. You said it came from a volcano that is awake. There are several such mountains to the south and north. I have camped on them while visiting relatives. My dreaming is always interesting there."

William's eyes gleamed as he surveyed their rocky niche. "Perhaps our dreaming here will reveal something." He reached over to his pack and detached his drum, the one he'd made for a recent healing ceremony of a kinsman. The dampness of the cloud forests below had loosened its head, and it now produced no more than a soggy thud. He propped it near the fire, where the heat might dry it.

"As you know," he said, "the drum is quite useful in assisting the shifting of awareness, but I don't know if this one will ever sing again. It was too wet to use at our meeting with the tiger this morning."

Nainoa thought about this statement, then asked, "Would the drum have driven the tiger off?"

"We Ennu use the method successfully out on the plains when we meet *liobi*, the lion, but we usually have several hunters drumming together. Whether or not a single drum will work with tigers remains to be discovered." William looked thoughtful, then he took up his javelin and spear-thrower and struck them together a dozen times in quick succession. "This sharp sound worked well. It may serve us better in your wet forests. We also use it in our songs."

The older man established a beat of steady, rhythmic clicks, then spontaneously broke into a song Nainoa recognized. It was about a man who went out to hunt horses one day and met another man on the grassy plains to the east of the mountains. It was a long song with a repetitive refrain that creative singers could keep going all day with endless verses. Zaki joined his father, and Nainoa settled back to listen. It would be some time before the two exhausted the various possibilities.

He let his mind drift on the cadence of the song, his eyes unfocused in the flames of the fire. It had been a long day and he was tired from the climb. He took a deep breath. The air was very thin here, too.

He thought about his return to the Hawaiian settlements near the coast and of his reason for leaving them. A year before, civil war had broken out between two of the land divisions. When it looked like the aggressors in the struggle were about to fall upon his settlement, Chief Kaneohe had sent all the food surpluses into storage in neighboring land divisions, redistributed the human population to places of safety, and withdrawn to the capital to petition the governor for use of the *koa*, the governor's warrior force.

The chief had sent Nainoa on a quest, an expedition of investigation into the unknown interior of the continent to see if open-country grasslands existed beyond the mountains. The Hawaiian settlers had not been able to bring horses with them on their great transoceanic voyage to the coasts of America 131 years before, and the chief wished to possess and breed horses once again, as had his ancestors back in the home islands.

Nainoa was a servant in the chief's household and had accepted the mission without question. He had crossed the inland sea and traversed the great lowland rain forests beyond. He had penetrated further into the interior than had any previous party of explorers. His mystic encounters along the way had made this journey an extraordinary experience. He had crossed the mountains, beyond which he had indeed found open grasslands inhabited by horses. He had also discovered the Ennu, the apparent descendants of the once-great North American civilization.

He glanced at the two singing men. The Hawaiian voyagers had found no one when they arrived on the coast six generations ago. He would arrive back at his settlement with Ennu ambassadors accompanying him. It would be a first, a discovery without precedent. But the horses had presented a problem. The long-legged grass-eaters were wild. The Ennu were hunters and had not domesticated them. From the little experience he had had in dealing with livestock, Nainoa knew it would be far easier to bring back a small herd than a single horse. But how?

He glanced up at a long, curiously shaped basket with a wide woven carrying strap hooked around a rocky prominence. It contained his compromise: the sun-bleached skull and skeleton of a young horse, tied in a bundle. This would provide proof of the animals' existence and create the impetus for a return expedition to the Ennu lands with a party of stockmen skilled in animal husbandry. He thought about the barrier to the west, the great cliff between the mountains and the lowland forests below. A route would have to be found, one that horses could negotiate.

William and his son had warmed to their song and were now enjoying themselves immensely. Nainoa's mind drifted, his consciousness punctuated by the rhythmic clicks. He gazed at William's drawing, which still seemed to move in the flickering firelight. He thought of the spirit stone in the custody of his chief.

As his eyes closed and he slipped sideways toward his dreams, Nainoa suddenly felt the sensations of power appear within him, and he awoke with excitement. The percussive rhythm was carrying him into an expanded state of perception. A sudden rush of power roared into him. The surge was exquisite. It was carrying him . . . carrying him . . .

All at once, words in Old English appeared in his mind's ear. "Greetings, descendant."

A shock wave ran through him. The American.

His mind's eye filled with an image, a memory from a previous visionary connection when he had seen this man's face as a reflection in a wall of glass. Amazement surged within him, amazement that was somehow distinctly his. At the same time, he could feel the other's emotional state as well. How was this possible?

"I'm not certain myself," came the thought in Old English, expressed with a flash of wry humor. Old English was a literary language among his people, the language in which the oldest histories were written. Because Nainoa was trained as a scholar, he could understand it.

"I've come to accept the reality of the connection between us," came the thought. "Although I don't fully understand the nature of it, or even how such a thing is possible, in some way you and I are able to establish periodic connections across space and time—about five thousand years of time, if your estimations are correct."

As Nainoa wrestled with the unfamiliar vocabulary and pronunciation, he was aware that his struggle was almost instantaneously relieved by a rapid series of thoughts that appeared in his mind, illustrating the terms with visual imagery and emotional associations. He could understand the meaning of the words.

"The *kahuna* mystics would say," Nainoa ventured, "that we share an *aumakua*, you and I. We are both manifestations of the same spiritual source. You and I are ancestor and descendant in a lineage, animated as well as connected by our common spiritual essence. I do not understand the nature of it, but there are stories of others who have had such connections."

"When I am in connection with you," the American responded, "I can perceive through your thoughts and emotions to some extent. I know that you can do this too, for I have been merged with you during several of your visits with me here in my own level of reality and time.

"I have thought a great deal about this strange phenomenon. From my standpoint, the experiences seem to be largely spontaneous, triggered by events or circumstances here in my level that are entirely random, yet synchronous in some way with similar events or circumstances occurring there in yours—times I have been in bed with my wife, for example, when you were abed with yours."

The beginnings of embarrassment were quickly replaced with a flash of humor, mutually felt. The thoughtline continued, "More important, there are concerns that both you and I share. Both of us are deeply immersed in the investigation of history, although our specialty areas are somewhat different. You are interested in the time before the fall of my civilization. I am also interested in the past, but the remote past. I am concerned with the very earliest humans, the ones that separated off from their ape cousins and evolved in their own direction, changing and becoming human in the process."

"Ape cousins?" came Nainoa's query.

Thoughtforms and concepts flowed within their merged minds. These were richly illustrated with imagery of arid landscapes, curiously shaped bones, and people with very dark skin. Abruptly the imagery shifted into perceptions of forests and the hairy forest people—what the American called "apes"—that resided there. "The story of human evolution began many millions of years ago in the continent called Africa. I want to know when it happened, why it happened, and how it happened.

"But I have another historical interest of equal or greater importance. I am deeply concerned about the immediate future of my people. As you have correctly surmised, I live in the time before the collapse of my civilization. I have no idea *when* this event will happen, but the sense of *how* it will occur is becoming clearer. We have much to discuss, you and I."

There was a long pause, and then a new direction. "I have thought often of the moment when you and I would converse again."

"I too," Nainoa offered.

There was a hesitancy and a sudden shyness between the two. In the awkward intimacy of this moment, feelings of strong friendship and affection flowed along their connection. There was a relationship, yet what was its nature? Was it like a father-son dynamic? Teacher-student? The bond between brothers? What was an ancestor-descendant relationship like? "There is much I wish to learn and much I need to understand," Nainoa began.

"The same is true for me," replied the American. "It is possible that this mutual need is part of the causality for the connection between us. So let me assure you that you are welcome to visit my world and time through my body and my mind. There is much within my memories you will find interesting. My knowledge of history is deep."

There was another long pause, and then an overwhelming feeling of genuine astonishment, shared by both and articulated by the American. "The experience is simply amazing. 'We' are actually a singularity within which two separate selves exist in two separate time frames. Both of these selves have the ability to achieve expanded states in which we can see and hear in a manner not possible in ordinary waking consciousness. We both can spirit-walk."

"Are there others among the Americans who can do this?" Nainoa asked.

"There are," came the reply, "although they tend to keep a low profile."

"Low profile?"

"Mystics are not highly regarded in my culture and time. They tend to keep their abilities and knowledge to themselves. There was an unfortunate incident that occurred about four hundred years before my time, an event in which the descendants of the old European tribal shaman-healers were almost completely wiped out—murdered because their mystic abilities brought them into conflict with the official state religion and with the medical establishment of that time. As a historian, you will find this episode interesting.

"It began in the societies of England and Europe during a period of history called the Renaissance. This was a time marked by great change. It was a time of emergence, of flourishing, in the realms of art and architecture especially." Colorful imagery began to move through their minds, impressions of Florence, cathedrals and icons, paintings and sculpture, Venice and Rome; Nainoa was staggered by what he perceived.

"It was also an age of geographic exploration, a period of discovery enabled by an advance in the technology of shipbuilding. European people expanded out into the larger world for the first time, circling the planet and sailing to America much like your ancestors did one hundred thirty years ago. During the Renaissance period, the expansion of human knowledge extended even out into the cosmos, where a master stargazer named Copernicus perceived that the vast complex of the universe was in motion. He found that the earth was moving around the sun. Another master stargazer named Galileo invented an instrument through which the distant stars and planets could be clearly observed, proving that Copernicus's ideas were valid. This caused a crisis in the state religion, an early branch of Christianity whose old creation myth was being assailed by the expanded horizons achieved during this age of exploration.

"It is worth noting that the Church, as we called it, was also being badly shaken by various messianic movements, and several major branches broke off; the Church of England, for example, and Martin Luther's group. It was a difficult time. Great plagues of epidemic illnesses devastated the population, and rebellions among the peasants created chaos."

Nainoa's mind wrestled with many unfamiliar terms and concepts, and registered a query about the lifestyles of the people of this time. Imagery flowed in response: impressions of medieval Europe, the rural farmlands under the care of the commoners, the towns and cities dominated by the landlords, merchants, and the Church. There were scenes of castles and churches, vignettes from paintings and woven tapestries, scenarios re-created as bas-relief sculptures mixed in with memories of things known and places seen.

"During the great plagues, the people died like flies, nobles and commoners alike. Neither the official priests nor the physicians and surgeons were able to have any effect, and the populace turned to the folk healers and medicinemakers in the towns and countrysides. The Church found this a political threat. So did the physicians and surgeons, who subsequently bound themselves into a professional guild with acts of incorporation that clearly defined who could and could not practice medicine.

"Both the newly formed organization of Physicians and Surgeons and the Church were dominated by men. Many of the most powerful and effective healers were women. In this time of trouble and change, these women, known collectively as the witches, became the societal scapegoats at whom the accusing finger was pointed."

There was a long pause, and then the thoughtline went on. "It has been estimated that somewhere between three hundred thousand and nine million women were murdered during the 'great witch hunt,' an appalling event that reached its greatest intensity during the hundred-and-fifty-year period between 1500 and 1650.[1] When a family's crops failed, a witch was blamed. When a physician's patient died, a witch was accused. There were economic factors involved as well. The women's estates, especially those of highborn families—their wealth, possessions, and land—usually became the property of the Church upon their demise. It was a ghastly, shameful business that the people of my time have yet to fully understand and acknowledge. Despite the great achievements of Western civilization during the Renaissance, the political and religious leadership reached unparalleled capacities for evil."

There was silence in the minds of both as the scope and implications of these events sank in.

"The persecution and near extinction of the European shamans and medicinemakers has forever put a restraint on our current medical establishment's attitudes toward healing using the ancient, mystic method of utilizing the power of the mind. As you know, the relationship between the mind and the body is critical to the healing process, yet the ability to access expanded states to discover the spiritual aspects of disease is not generally regarded as valid in my time and has fallen into disuse.

"Despite this, I suspect that there are many who still experience it spontaneously, as you and I do. I sense there are many who can access the inner worlds . . . many who can spirit-walk. In my time and place, some use the term *journey* to describe the experience."

There was silence within their minds as this concept was considered by both. The experience was, indeed, a journey.

William and Zaki stopped singing to watch a spectacular falling star streak across the southern horizon. Nainoa felt his awareness shift, and he saw the tail end of the meteor's death as he opened his eyes. He sat up and looked around. He had crossed some sort of boundary, made some form of transition. The primary focus of his awareness had suddenly been reestablished in his own everyday level of reality.

William turned and looked speculatively at Nainoa. As Zaki began to sing again, the older man silenced him with a gesture. Nainoa took time to run the entirety of what he had just experienced through his mind. When he was sure he had it, he turned to the two men and gave them a shortened version of what had happened, recalling blocks of the conversation and reconstructing them into a coherent whole. When he finished, William was watching him carefully.

"Is the American still in connection with you?" he asked.

Nainoa waited. There was silence within. "I don't know. During the expanded state, it was as if we could communicate directly. Now I do not perceive him or his thoughts. There is silence in my mind."

William said, "Your awareness shifted back into this level when I stopped clicking. You are no longer in the visionary state. Perhaps the two of you can only talk together when you are both expanded at the same time." The Ennu hunter thought about it for long moments, then added, "I cannot advise you. I have not experienced a connection like yours."

William smiled and threw up his hands. "And what an interesting adventure. Imagine. There are two of you, one here, one there. Heeeee . . ."

Nainoa thought about what the older man had said and asked, "Why does the rhythmic sound assist in achieving the expanded state, William?"

The hunter looked around carefully as though to see if anyone was listening before answering in a whisper, "No one knows for sure. It is thought that the sound attracts the spirits who assist us, and that the power we feel during our expanded moments is achieved through them."

Suddenly Nainoa heard a strange noise, like a bell ringing, but very far away. He looked at William and said, "What is that sound?"

The old Ennu looked at him curiously. "What sound?"

CHAPTER 3

Training

T HE ALARM CLOCK went off at dawn, drawing my awareness rapidly back into the present and terminating the contact. What a moment for technology to interfere! I had finally reachieved connection with Nainoa after almost a year's hiatus, and it had been interrupted by a mechanical device for measuring time.

The irony of this suddenly struck me, and my rising irritation evaporated into amused relief, which in turn grew into exhilaration. I had managed to accomplish something I had been highly desirous of doing ever since I left Hawai'i: I had been able to converse directly with Nainoa. My elation was immediately tempered by the realization that we could apparently do so only when both of us were in the expanded state simultaneously. When Nainoa's awareness had shifted back into his ordinary state of consciousness, I had tried to communicate, but he hadn't been able to receive.

Jill rose from bed and jumped into the shower. I remained where I was and mentally replayed the entire episode. As before, the experience was not at all like my ordinary dream states. It had been as if I was really there, and I mean *really there*! As before, I found upon my return that only moments had passed in my own time.

I spent a while reviewing the dialogue between William and Nainoa. I had been able to grasp the meaning of what was said as a flow of thoughts, direct translations, associations, imagery, elicited memories, emotions, and judgments. The phenomenon occurs rapidly, in bursts of thought-feeling and pulses of meaning that appear in my mind as percepts are translated into concepts in Nainoa's mind. I have little time to think about what I have just perceived before the next complex of thoughts, feelings, and meanings arrives.

I finally got out of bed, pulled on a robe, and went to the kitchen to make a large pot of tea. I opened the patio door and went out to the spirit stone under the fig tree in the backyard. I picked some ripe figs and ate them as I regarded the black chunk of lava in the growing light. On impulse, I squatted and placed both hands on the stone. In Hawai'i, I had on occasion received jolts of sensation similar to bursts of electricity when I touched it. I was now in my ordinary, everyday state of consciousness, however, and felt nothing unusual. I stood up and surveyed its grim visage with affection. Instead of eyes, a diagonal groove traversed its flat face. There was no nose, and the mouth was only suggested by a natural layering of the stone. As its sculptor, I had brought out the "mouth" and "chin" with minimal modification, so that the stone now resembled a slablike head. Most of the block remained untouched, just as I had found it. A couple of white shell leis were wrapped around its pointed apex, providing a pleasing contrast to the dark stone and giving it the appearance of a ritual object.

At this moment my children appeared at the door asking for breakfast, and the day began.

This first reconnection with Nainoa happened in late May of 1990. As the days stretched into summer, the contact did not resume, perhaps because I was preoccupied with more pressing concerns. As the rejections to my applications for a teaching position piled up, I became aware of the great pressure on academic departments to diversify their faculties. As a Euro-American male over forty, I was as politically incorrect as one could get. I realized that I was unlikely to get a full-time academic position, and that I was in the process of losing my livelihood.

Jill was also in conflict over her own profession. She was working in private practice and was finding it impossible to get reimbursed by the medical insurance companies of her clients. In the first six months of work, she didn't get paid a dime. Our savings and cash reserves were dwindling. Concerns over the family's financial security were growing daily.

It was during this time that I began to feel the need to talk about my episodes with others who were more experienced than I from whom I might acquire some more training. Unlike people in traditional tribal societies, I had not engaged in years of directed exercises with an experienced older shaman, and I keenly felt my lack of expertise.

This insight was strongly reinforced one day by an encounter at the San Diego Zoo, where my daughters had become quite fond of visiting the animals. On this occasion, it was around noon, and Jill and the children had gone to the refreshment stand to buy food and drinks while I lingered before the Chinese leopards, admiring them as they patrolled their enclosure with graceful strides. They are without doubt among the most handsome of creatures.

"Do they remind you of the leopard man?" a voice said from behind me. I turned to find one of my former students watching me, a young woman who had come frequently to talk during my office hours at the university. I had hung one of my oil paintings of my spirit helper on the wall of my office, and she had asked me about it one day. I had, in turn, revealed to her only that it was a picture of one of my old childhood imaginary friends. Her question now prompted one of those instantaneous mental flashes, a memory of a weekend in the early 1980s when this curious being came back into my life during a shamanism workshop led by Michael Harner.

On that day, I had found myself in a group of fifty or so people of varying ages and backgrounds, listening with interest as Harner discussed core concepts held in common by traditional tribal shamans the world over. He had shared that the methods used for achieving altered states are strikingly similar everywhere, suggesting that the ability to access these states might be part of the biological heritage of a substantial portion of the human species. He had revealed further that the ability to experience trance is not determined by ethnicity, nor is it the exclusive property of any cultural group. He had speculated that with a minimum of training, even nontribal Westerners like ourselves could achieve what he calls "the shamanic state of consciousness."

In the experiential work that followed, Harner had introduced the workshop participants to the classic shamanic journey, a disciplined way of making contact with the spirits in nonordinary reality and acquiring knowledge from these inner sources of wisdom. To facilitate the process, he had used monotonous and repetitive drumming, a powerful physical stimulus to which the human subconscious mind responds. In one of the many exercises, the participants were encouraged to work in pairs, each attempting to access the mythic Lower World to find a helping spirit for the other. I was highly skeptical of all this at that time but had decided to reserve judgment. I was an anthropologist, after all, and part of me was equally curious to see what would occur.

I had found myself paired with someone I didn't know, a young woman with long, dark hair named Sandra Ingerman. The lights were extinguished except for a single candle, and the drumming session began. I lay down on my back on a blanket on the floor next to this woman, half of me wondering what I was doing there, the other half feeling guarded enthusiasm. When the drumming concluded, Sandra sat up, leaned over me, placed her cupped hands on my chest, then blew her breath into my sternum. An interesting heat penetrated directly into the center of my thorax. When she gently raised me to a sitting position and blew into the apex of my cranium, a second surge of warmth invaded my being.

Sandra then sat on the floor facing me and proceeded to describe her journey in a quiet voice. I listened politely, maintaining my professional sense of distance until she described meeting a spiritual entity who said it knew me from my past and wanted to resume a relationship. As she described what this spirit looked like, shock ricocheted around inside me. It was the leopard man; there could be no mistaking it. There was no way she or anyone else could have known about my secret pal.

All this passed through my mind in a flash as I stood there at the zoo talking with my student. We engaged in a light conversation for several moments as the spotted cats stalked back and forth in their cage next to us. When our dialogue came to a natural end, her last words to me were, "I really enjoyed your class. A lot of the students thought of you as a sort of Western medicine man." Then she went on her way with a cheery wave, while I remained rooted to the spot, lost in thought.

A medicine man. Most anthropologists I know would go to great lengths to avoid being categorized in this way. Was this what I was destined to become?

I emerged from my ruminations to find one of the leopards observing me with a flat stare. I locked eyes with it, looking into its pale gaze, and thought of the leopard man. In the next moment, my youngest daughter, Anna, thrust a cold drink and a hot dog into my hands, changing the mood. Jill looked at me speculatively, then glanced at the leopard and grinned. "Having a chat with the animals, eh?" Her perception prompted a memory of something I had heard the mythologist Joseph Campbell say at a lecture years ago in San Francisco. He said the old tribal shamans were the last human beings who could talk to the animals.

I glanced at the spotted cats. They looked well cared for but bored.

I bade them a mental farewell and followed Jill and the children up the shady ravine, pausing to admire a large eagle in its small enclosure atop a fabricated rock outcrop designed to emulate an authentic African habitat. Memories emerged, and in my mind's eye I saw the eagle soaring above me in the vast, pale sky over eastern Africa's arid, thorny deserts.

I had spent many years out there among tribal peoples. I thought about what it meant to be a tribal medicine man and shook my head. I was not a tribal person, nor could I aspire to be. I was also very much aware of the negative feelings aroused in many traditional people in response to the New Age movement's enthusiasm for things tribal—especially ritual or ceremonial procedures that these people consider to be their own. I too felt misgivings as I perused the advertisements published in New Age magazines by well-meaning individuals presenting themselves as shamans. In my experience, that was not the way traditional shamans operated.

I recalled a fragment of conversation between Nainoa and William, a moment when Nainoa had asked the older man if he was a shaman. William had smiled and glanced at one of his sons, who had looked uncomfortable as he answered. "There is something you must understand, Nainoapak. The spirits are always about, and they despise spiritual arrogance. For persons to announce out loud that they are *ungagok* [a shaman] would displease them greatly. It would be regarded as boasting, and so no *ungagok* worthy of the name would ever do so. It would be a quick way for even the most powerful *ungagok* among our people to lose their power."

The young man had then looked at his father and concluded, "My father is acknowledged as *ungagok,* as a spiritwalker, among our people." And that was the way it was done. Traditional shamans do not claim the title; they are given it by the people of their communities on the basis of their demonstrated abilities.

In attempting to understand my own expanded states of awareness, I had learned that the shaman is a universal figure in all the world's cultures. In many, shamans are highly regarded and are central to the daily life and well-being of their communities. In others, people with shamanic abilities live on the fringe, functioning as computer programmers or bank tellers in their daily life and quietly providing their extraordinary skills to networks of friends and associates on the side. The shock waves generated by the systematic genocide practiced by the witch hunters are still being felt four hundred years later.

As my family and I drifted past enclosures occupied by African ungulates, I thought about the curious phenomenon called "channeling" or trance mediumship. In this situation, the medium is said to be able to relinquish voluntary control of his or her physical body while in a trance state, thus allowing a spiritual entity to enter and work directly through them. I had seen cases of spirit possession in Africa and knew of Westerners who had experienced it directly.[1] But Mircea Eliade, the esteemed scholar of comparative religions, has made it clear that this is not an activity that typically distinguishes the shaman.[2]

The trance medium is a passive instrument, usually unconscious of what is occurring at the time it is happening and generally without memory of the events that transpire during the time of possession. The spirits come to the medium, while the shaman, conversely, is a person who journeys to the spirits, approaching them in their own level of reality. The shaman is not a passive instrument, but interacts as an autonomous individual, remaining fully conscious of what is happening at all times at all levels of awareness. Shamans are thus able to recall what took place during their journeys in great detail.

Given these distinctions, I felt convinced that I was not channeling Nainoa, nor was he channeling me. To the contrary, each of us journeyed to the other, fully conscious and aware of what was occurring in both levels of time and reality simultaneously, but with a primary focus established in one slice of reality for the duration of the contact. Both of us remained fully awake and remembered everything that had taken place afterward.

I thought again about the term "medicine man." It is very common for people to confuse shamans and what they do with the kind of work done by medicine people in tribal societies, because every shaman is a kind of medicine person, but not all medicine people are shamans. In fact, most medicine men and women are not shamans, but fill social roles more like those of priests.

What distinguishes shamans from all other religious practitioners is their ability to journey into the spirit world, where they then do their main work while in an expanded state of consciousness. The priest typically does not journey, but accomplishes his or her tasks here in ordinary everyday reality, functioning mainly as a ceremonialist for their community on a regular calendrical schedule. Although traditional tribal medicine people may have many shamanic experiences—while on a vision quest, for example—they too tend to function more as ceremonialists, conducting culturally important rituals and making offerings or prayers to the spirits, or as herbalistic healers, treating patients from their extensive knowledge of plant medicines. Some, of course, perform both shamanic and priestly roles.

As we continued to walk past the animals, I thought of the curious mix of Old World and New World fauna that I had perceived in the future through Nainoa. The tropical forests of the lowlands to the west, the mountain cloud forests and coniferous forests at high elevations, and the wooded savanna east of the mountains were filled with a diversity of animal species that had originated in many different parts of the world. I wondered if they were descended from animals in private collections, circuses, and zoos such as this one, released to survive on their own at civilization's end.

The end of civilization. This was an issue that was always on my mind now. My family and I waited in a densely packed crowd for a gondola ride back to the other side of the zoo, and when we were high in the air at last, I looked out at the urban sprawl of San Diego in the distance. I remembered the open freeways and the clarity of the light that had existed in California when I first visited, back in the 1950s. Now the freeways were clogged with cars, and the sky was filled with a dirty haze that concealed the distances by day and the stars at night.

Shortly before our departure from Hawai'i, Jill and I had gotten to know an emeritus professor of biology from Stanford University who had retired to a beautiful home above Kailua-Kona. I recalled a conversation one evening when the professor had stated flatly, "In my opinion, Western civilization is going into collapse phase."

His insight echoes the concern felt by many scientists who have watched the world population double in the last twenty years. Studies of contemporary species have revealed that creatures who indulge in catastrophic overpopulation usually crash, with extinction being a real possibility. There seems to be no built-in evolutionary mechanism to keep individuals from maximizing their reproductive potential, and so it is possible to say that therefore there exists no evolutionary safeguard against extinction.

Maybe, I thought, we need more medicine people—modern ones with full knowledge of the issues facing us and the ability to help humanity achieve the necessary shift in priorities and worldview so that we can avert (or survive) the ecological catastrophe that is just about to happen.

I thought about my ability to access expanded-awareness states and wondered if animals could also experience them. I recalled going out on the African savannas to shoot gazelles to provide meat for the expedition I was working for back in the early 1970s. Whenever I had the rifle with me, I couldn't get closer to them than 250 or 300 yards, but when I was just out driving on my way to a site, I could approach to within 50 yards. How had they known?

My own experiences had revealed that the expanded state is accessed through the subconscious mind, or *ku,* as Nainoa thought of it. Animals lack the developed intellect of humans and at the level of mind could be thought of as mostly *ku.* Could the ability to access expanded states be a natural one, possessed by all living creatures to a greater or lesser extent? Could it be that humans, in divorcing themselves from their former intimate association with nature, are in the process of losing it?

I had discovered quite by accident that I possessed it. As I thought about these issues, I again felt the need to discuss them with others who were more experienced than me. Michael Harner came to mind. I knew that he had established an educational and research foundation devoted to preserving shamanism and helping revive it throughout the world, and that he and his associates had developed specific training courses in what he calls "core shamanism."[3]

The "core" includes what's left when all the symbols, costumes, ceremonies, and rituals that are distinctive to one culture or another are stripped away, leaving only the bare bones—the central concepts and methods found within all of the world's shamanic traditions. A trained anthropologist, Harner had been most respectful of traditional peoples and had not usurped or taken on any other culture's symbol system or rituals. He did not teach his students to "play Indian." He had drawn on his anthropological knowledge, presenting the ancient time-tested techniques in ways that would be meaningful to Westerners within the context of their lives in Western culture— techniques that would bring them into direct contact with the spirit world.

In the last decade, Harner had emerged as a central figure in the current revival of interest in shamanism in the West. As my family and I entered the reptile house, I paused to observe a magnificent rattlesnake and decided it was time to acquire more training.

When I received the current newsletter and schedule of course offerings published by Harner's foundation, I learned that Sandra Ingerman had become a credentialed psychotherapist and was now one of the foundation's teachers. I saw she was leading workshops in several different subject areas during the next few months, and since I had some unexpected free time on my hands, I decided to apply. In addition to acquiring information and experience, I was curious to meet her again and to see what a Western medicine woman was like.

In August I drove north to participate in a week-long workshop being offered at a small conference center on a private ranch in the wine country of northern California.[4] It was late afternoon when I arrived. I parked the car, found Sandra Ingerman on the patio near the main building checking people in, and reintroduced myself. She was as I remembered her, a slender, soft-spoken woman with long, dark hair and expressive eyes. She had just finished her first book on soul retrieval and conveyed a sense of friendly warmth with a touch of shyness.[5] It had been eight years since we had met at the workshop in Berkeley. I guessed that she had had thousands of clients and students by this time, so I did not ask her if she remembered me.

As more participants arrived, I went to find a bed in the men's communal bunkhouse, then set off to explore the environs. The rambling paths between the buildings revealed inviting places to sit and read under spreading oaks. There was a pool to swim in and a hot tub and sauna. One path led across a grassy meadow and up into the hills covered with trees. I took it and found myself staring out across long wooded ridges in the fading light of the day. There was something—was it familiarity, perhaps, or presence? I couldn't be sure. I had not been to this place before. Maybe it was just my old feelings of connection with nature.

A sense of community began to grow within the group as we worked together. I became aware that the ability to access expanded states was expressed variably among the participants. There were those with a strong grasp of it and the knowledge of how to use it. Others had had a glimpse and wanted more.

During the week's activities, I had several strong experiences with the classic shamanic journey, facilitated by the drum. It had become easier for me to shift my level of awareness into the light trance state, because I knew now what I was reaching for. I use the term *light* because these journeys into the inner worlds of nonordinary reality were experienced at a different level of intensity than the psychosomatic totality of time traveling, accompanied by the incredible sensations of power and bodily paralysis, that I felt when I made contact with Nainoa.

I sensed this was a beginning, the start of a new way of life for me that would reveal itself by degrees as I allowed myself to be drawn further down what the Native American peoples call the "path of power." My notes from this workshop contain a quotation someone offered over dinner one evening: "The mystic is the exploratory consciousness of our species."

I thought about this quote as I drove back to San Diego at week's end. My investigations of the outer world in the remote, tribal regions of Africa had taken a new direction. I was now exploring the inner worlds, and I was doing this through the vehicle of my own consciousness. This was very exciting and helped offset my growing anxiety and despair at not being able to find a job within my chosen profession.

It was close to midnight when I returned home. Jill and the children were asleep. I quietly slipped into bed and sank into slumber, tired from the long drive. I awoke several hours later and began to toss and turn, unable to get back to sleep. I realized that I was energized by all I had experienced during the previous week. I wondered if I could induce an expanded-state connection with Nainoa. I formed the intention to do so and waited, but nothing happened. After fifteen minutes I decided to see if I could enlist the assistance of the spirit stone in the backyard.

I got out of bed and pulled on a robe, went downstairs, and stepped out into the darkness. The air temperature was warm, almost tropical, and the summer stars were blazing away overhead as I squatted under the fig tree and placed my hands on the stone. I conveyed friendly greetings and let my mind drift over all that had occurred recently, then formed a mental image of Nainoa and expressed my intention to reconnect with him.

Nothing happened. I waited, but there were no power pulses, no paralysis, no phosphenes dancing in the darkness. I was puzzled. I lay down on the grass next to the stone and tried again, focusing my attention. Nothing. My ego was somewhat put out. What about my newfound experience and expertise?

Disappointed, I went back into the house and turned on a light in the living room. I stared thoughtfully at my painting of the leopard man, wondering how to proceed. I lay down on the floor and went over some of the exercises I had learned at the workshop. Again I focused my intentionality and waited. Nothing appeared in my mind and body. Maybe I was trying to force it. I decided to cancel the attempt and went back upstairs.

As I eased into bed, Jill awoke and turned toward me, throwing a long leg across my body and drawing me into her embrace with a whispered endearment. We had a joyous marital reunion, renewing our bond through the expression of our affection for each other in the exquisite physicality of lovemaking.

It was close to dawn when our dance was done. As I drifted in passion's aftermath, my fingers entwined with my lover's, I was struck again by the power of what had just been manifested, and I understood quite clearly that only by surrendering to that power could it be experienced fully. This was the key: not control, but surrender.

With that thought, the sensations suddenly emerged within me. I felt excitement as the sparkling phosphenes appeared in my visual field and the rushing sound filled my ears. The state expanded, intensifying, as my body became paralyzed with the force that was filling me. As the glittering grid took form in the darkness, I perceived my own fibers of light in connection with it, drawing my conscious awareness toward it. The brilliant crescent appeared and began to open, whereupon the sense of movement commenced. The roaring in my ears increased. Once again I was off to the future.

CHAPTER 4

Second Journey: The Great Forest

THE HEAT OF the lowland tropical forest was welcome after the cold nights in the mountains, but it came with a price. Water dripped constantly from above as the travelers walked down the game trail through the early morning mist. All around them loomed the dark shapes of enormous tree trunks and thick lianas. The rich aroma of decomposing leaf litter and damp earth permeated the air. The absolute stillness was broken only by the sound of dripping water and by occasional birdcalls filtering down from the canopy far above.

Nainoa thought about their journey as he walked. His Ennu companions were enthralled by the abundance of new animals revealed at every turn in the trail. While descending the long canyon from the highlands above, he had located the enormous snake that he had seen the year before. It was in its pool in the grove of trees. William and Zaki had gazed at it in wonder while he told them stories about the serpent from the mythology of his people. "Most commonly, the snake is thought of as the symbol of wisdom," he had said.

Always the hunter, William had chuckled and rejoined, "Among my people, snakes are good to eat. But today our game bags have food in them, and this serpent looks like one to avoid."

When they entered the great lowland forest, Nainoa had spent a morning making rain capes, weaving stripped palm fronds into a loose netting to which broad leaves were attached, providing acceptable substitutes for the well-made *bonsho* available in the settlement markets. William and Zaki had watched him as he worked, acquiring the craft so that they could make and restore their own. Nainoa had told them that their furs would never dry in this humid forest, so they had stashed them in a crevasse protected by an overhang in the sunny south-facing rock wall of the canyon to await their return. Nainoa looked at his companions now, striding down the indistinct path, their torsos covered by leafy rain capes and their hair festooned with parrot feathers under makeshift hats. He had become very fond of them.

He suddenly sensed something and paused, letting his awareness expand outward. One of the Ennu dogs stopped and looked back at him, bringing William to a halt. The Ennu's eyebrows rose inquiringly. Nainoa made a gesture signifying that it was nothing, and the trio resumed walking in silence, their eyes scanning the forest floor for serpents and the spoor of game.

Nainoa wondered what had alerted him. Whatever it was, he did not detect it now. Perhaps it was not in the outer realm; perhaps it had come from within. As his mind shifted in that direction, he was distracted by animal calls in the distance. William glanced at him again.

He refocused his attention on the hunt, held the other's eyes, and shook his head almost imperceptibly. They were the calls of the *ganakolao*, the hairy forest people.* The Hawaiians never hunted them

* Chimpanzees.

or ate their flesh. It was thought that the manlike beasts were inhabited by the spirits of humans who had committed evil deeds during their lifetimes, and so there was a *kapu* against killing them.

They resumed trekking. They would find other meat, and with luck they would reach the ruined *siti* by day's end. His attention reached outward down the trail, recalling the way he had taken the previous year, remembering a grove of giant timber bamboo ahead and a steep streambank covered with butterflies where they might find fresh turtle eggs buried in the sand.

Nainoa thought about his recent visionary reconnections with the American. The first incident had occurred fourteen days ago on the mountain peak, an extraordinary experience in which the American's words had suddenly appeared in his mind, enabling them to converse directly. The second had happened only a few nights before, at their camp on the rim of the great cliff called the barrier, the same place where he had made the very first dream contact with the American the year before.

Just before dawn, something had awakened him in the darkness, and as before, the sensations of power had rushed into him, taking him by surprise. He had shut his eyes tightly as the ecstasy filled him, wondering if he might use this opportunity to reconnect with the American. With that thought, the expanded state had deepened, and abruptly he had found himself first falling and then flying through the darkness of what seemed to be a great vortex filled with sparkling lights swirling past him. His body had soared on the sensations of power as his mind achieved a state of intense clarity. A luminous emptiness had appeared within him, one within which an image had suddenly appeared. He had recognized it instantly. It was the spotted tiger man.

His amazement had increased as he perceived that the image was a static form—unmoving, nonliving. He realized that it was a painting—one depicting his spirit helper staring across time and space, straight into his eyes. The *kupua* was portrayed standing upright like a human among some stylized trees that seemed to merge into abstract borders around the painting's perimeter. There was something very familiar about the image.

He had drawn back from the picture and glanced down at his hands, his pulse racing. There was no doubt. His conscious awareness was once again merged with that of the American. So this was the American's painting. He looked at it again and realized suddenly why it seemed familiar. The scene symbolized his very first encounter with the spotted tiger man, the one that had happened in the canyon the year before. The American must have been merged with him when it happened.

He had looked to his right and seen a finely crafted wooden table and several chairs. Beyond was a large window covered by a single piece of clear glass through which he had perceived a clump of banana trees growing outside. To his left he discerned the rest of the room. There were more paintings on the walls, furniture of an odd design, and bookshelves filled with books. Another wall of glass at the end of the room revealed more trees outside and parts of another house nearby. It was a different house from the one he had seen during his connection with this man in Hawai'i. His mental query had provoked a response from the man's mind, and he had learned that the American was now residing in California.

The American had been alone when he arrived and seemed unaware of his presence. As Nainoa's astonishment began to settle, something interesting had happened. In response to his curiosity, the man had walked slowly through the house, studying everything with focused attentiveness while mental imagery had flowed through their minds, illustrating and explaining what was seen.

The indoor kitchen had contained miraculous machines, most of which he did not understand. He remembered the lights vividly. They were simply astonishing. They apparently utilized a kind of power that flowed like water through ropes of metal that linked every house to a central source where the power was produced by machines. This discovery was most exciting because the earliest histories of his people contained vague descriptions of such a power.

He had been treated to a detailed examination of an indoor bathing room, illustrated once again by mental imagery explaining how water was heated using this same power, how water was conveyed from one place to another, how human waste was disposed of. There had been a large rectangle of reflective glass on the wall, and within it, he had studied the American's face once again.

In this way, he had learned the truth of what the man had told him on the mountaintop. As a visitor within his body, Nainoa could observe and acquire knowledge, perceiving the American's world while receiving information through the man's thoughts and memories— visual impressions, emotional feelings, mental judgments, and inter- pretations that came together as rapid pulses of meaning that he was able to understand.

Something truly remarkable had happened next. The American had walked out of the house and looked around a small piece of land delimited by a high fence. The air temperature was chilly, and few plants were in bloom. In one corner, Nainoa had seen a familiar shape in the shade of a small fig tree. As he looked again at the object, his mind had reeled. It was Chief Kaneohe's spirit stone!

Before he had a chance to recover, another stream of thoughts, memories, and feelings had appeared in his mind. In this way, he had learned of the stone's origin, of its discovery and subsequent journey to the mainland of America in the care of this man. So the legend of Kapohaku'ki'ihele, the stone that travels, was true, and the American, his ancestor, had been the stone's first *kahu.* The pattern of their linkage was becoming clearer. Nainoa recalled the painting of the spotted tiger man and felt pieces of the puzzle falling into place.

His attention was abruptly drawn back into the present as his companions became immobile. The dogs had picked up something. He watched William and Zaki, whose noses seemed to quest forth like those of their dogs. With a glance, William invited Nainoa to join them. As he approached soundlessly, William pursed his lips and pointed, indicating fresh scat on the trail ahead. Flies were just discov- ering the acrid pile. Nainoa recognized it as the dung of a spotted tiger. It was the second time this morning that this had happened. "We are being followed," he whispered.

"Or escorted," William offered. "You have a relationship with the spirit of this animal, do you not?" Nainoa nodded. "And you have discovered that your ancestor also enjoyed its companionship, right?" Nainoa remembered the American's painting and nodded again. "Escorted," William asserted with satisfaction. "See if you can request assistance. Perhaps some of those small forest deer could be driven to cross our path."

This thought hung in Nainoa's mind as they resumed trekking. He watched the trees, wondering if he would see the spotted tiger looking back at him through the greenery. The big cats were very elusive and were rarely observed by humans. He resumed thinking, and impressions of the American's world passed through his mind.

Nainoa had been merged with the American for most of a day and part of a night. During this time, the man had apparently been completely unaware of his presence. Despite repeated attempts to communicate directly, there had been no dialogue. He had discussed this with William, and they had concluded that their earlier assumption must be correct: Only when both were in the expanded state of awareness simultaneously was direct communication possible.

The episode had provided him with a dramatic look at the American's world and the time in which he lived. He had accompanied the man as he left his home and drove his machine at great speeds along huge roads, filled with uncountable numbers of other machines, to the center for learning where he served as a teacher. An amazing distance was traveled in a very short time in this manner. The landscape had looked dry and open, and Nainoa had wondered where the great lowland forest was.

The center for learning was a large community of huge buildings on a plateau near the ocean. The American had been there for most of the day, during which his invisible guest was astounded again and again by all that he saw. The vast library had surpassed his wildest imaginings, and the place where books were bought and sold was equally astonishing. As he observed the sheer number of the bound volumes, he was able to conceptualize, as never before, the amount of knowledge that had been lost with the collapse of the Americans' civilization.

Everything he had seen during that long day had fascinated him: the cars and books, the "students" and the "university," the food the American ate, and the machines called "computers." At each instance, the American's mind had released quantities of information about all these wonders in response to his need to know. His thoughts about cars, for example, had included rough outlines of how they were designed and built and how they were powered. Nainoa's mind was literally quivering with excitement at these recollections as he followed his companions down the forest trail. When he returned to his settlement, he would transcribe all that he had seen into written accounts that would be added to the histories.

The travelers were traversing a fern-covered hillside when the dogs became immobile once more, their posture alerting the men to the presence of game. Nainoa watched the dogs slip into the undergrowth, fanning out as the men readied their weapons and took up position. Long moments passed, and then a crashing in the bush revealed that the dogs were driving something toward them. As Nainoa brought up his bow, a blurred shape arched across the trail, then plummeted to the ground where it lay kicking, pierced by Zaki's arrow. It was a small forest deer.

Another rushed by before him, and another, heading for the stream below. He heard the muffled twang of Zaki's bow and saw another fall to the ground, an arrow embedded low in the chest. The dogs brought down a third, their jaws clamped on its throat. The remaining deer scattered and disappeared. The entire event had happened in an instant.

The wounded animals were dispatched quickly as William looked into their eyes and muttered a short prayer to the deers' spirits, apologizing for ending their lives in such an abrupt manner. He added that this was done to satisfy hunger, and that their spirits would be honored as their flesh was eaten. Then the older hunter looked up approvingly at his son. Breaking into laughter, he glanced at Nainoa and said, "You and I are not getting much practice on this journey, but we are eating well."

With artistry, the men hung the animals by their back legs from the branches of a fallen tree and went to work, dressing the carcasses and feeding the dogs as they filled their game bags with fresh meat cut in strips. At their evening camp, they would cook as much as they pleased and smoke the rest for the days to come. The Ennu ate some of the organ meat raw and cracked open the long bones with stones, sucking out the raw marrow.

In a short time the task was done. They tied what remained—the antlers, bones, skin, and feet—in bundles and affixed them to a tree limb well above the ground. William uttered another prayer of thanks to the animals for providing them with sustenance. Then they moved on in silence, walking with care into the brightening morning. William smiled at Nainoa and said softly, "Please express our thanks to your spirit helper."

In the late afternoon, they encountered the first remains of fern-covered chimneys at the edge of the ruined *siti*. Walking deeper into the site, they discovered the tree-covered mounds stretching into the hazy distance. They decided to camp between the flaring buttresses of a cotton tree, erecting between the slablike roots a rough shelter thatched with broad leaves to ward off the drips. More leaves were quickly woven into sleeping mats to protect them from the damp earth. Firewood was gathered while Zaki made racks of green saplings on which to cook the meat. Then the younger man settled down to feed the fire while Nainoa and William wandered through the ancient site, examining the mounds with interest.

The forest floor, padded by millennia of rotting leaf litter, revealed nothing despite their careful search. At Nainoa's suggestion, they examined the root balls of trees that had been toppled by wind, looking for artifacts that had been pulled up from below. In one, they found a few glass shards as well as several chunks of masonry.

Nainoa told William about the metalworkers who lived in the settlements, describing them as a class of artisans who mined the ruins of *siti* sites like this one for the metals they needed to make tools, weapons, wagon fittings, cooking pots, and personal ornaments. He described how the placement of new settlements around the inland sea was now determined both by the availability of suitable agricultural land and by proximity to a *siti* site.

"We don't know why the American civilization came to an end," he said, "but our historians think it likely that their population simply exhausted the ability of their lands to feed them. Our histories reveal that such disasters happened in the past in our home islands, and in each instance, much of the population died in these terrible catastrophes. This finally led the surviving chiefs to impose strict laws designed to control the population size. These laws applied to everyone, chiefs and commoners alike. They remained in effect for thousands of years, until the great voyage that brought the Hawaiians to America.

"After our arrival, the production of children was considered to be of great importance, and the laws were relaxed. There are now almost a hundred thousand of us living around the inland sea, so our survival here in America is ensured. Unlike on our islands, there is endless land here."

William appeared lost in thought for some moments. His language had no words for numbers that large, and Nainoa had improvised, using terms that conveyed multiples of ten. He still wasn't sure the older man understood. The Ennu's eyes were serious, however, as he replied, "Perhaps it is good that the high mountains and this great forest separate your people from mine. I used to think of the game animals in our hunting lands as inexhaustible, but with that many people . . ." He let the thought trail off.

As the twilight deepened, they returned to their camp and built another fire between their sleeping place and whatever might come in the night. Zaki continued to cook the meat, keeping the fire beneath the racks just high enough. They began to eat as William filled his son in on their survey of the ruins, adding his own commentary on what was seen. As Nainoa listened, he realized that these Ennu did not fully understand what a *siti* used to be. As nomads, they had simply no experience of a permanent, year-round established settlement, let alone a *siti*. He wondered how they would react to his own community, and how the community would respond to them.

He felt concern. His society was rigidly hierarchical, and his people were intensely status-conscious. The Ennus' diminutive height and lack of chiefly manner would be apparent to all. They were hunters, and among the Hawaiian settlers, hunters were commoners.

His thoughts were interrupted by William, who began to sing a particularly bawdy song about a man and a woman who were attracted to each other but were never alone, so they couldn't do anything about it. Zaki joined in and the two traded verse for verse, recounting the hilarious exploits of the pair as they tried again and again to celebrate their feelings for each other. Nainoa had heard this song many times, and settled down on his sleeping mat to listen.

Memories arose in his mind, vivid recollections of his love life with Kenojelak. He saw the flash of her smile in his mind's eye as her merry laugh echoed in his mind's ear. His senses expanded as his body remembered hers and his nose recalled the scent of her hair and skin. Deep inner stirrings were activated in response. Those feelings brought forth more recollections of the startling things he had experienced while merged with the American.

That day in which Nainoa had seen so much had finally come to an end when the man returned to his home in the early evening. His wife and children were awaiting him. They had two daughters now, and from the size of the elder, Nainoa got a rough idea of how many seasons had passed in the American's level of time since their connection in Hawai'i—three, perhaps four years. He also noticed that the woman had some gray in her hair, and that her body seemed fuller. She was very beautiful, and he had felt the American's response to her as she kissed him.

The man and his wife had then prepared the evening meal, giving him firsthand experience of American food preparation and cuisine. There had been chicken marinated in lemon juice, garlic, and salt and cooked on a metal rack over charcoal in a curious round metal container on three legs. There had been leafy vegetables with a sour, salty sauce, and a starchy food called rice cooked in a polished metal pot. He had been delighted with the food, especially a soft substance served last that was both incredibly cold and unbelievably sweet.

The machine used for cooking indoors was quite amazing in that it did not produce fire. Rather, pots of food were placed on areas of its surface shaped like coiled snakes that became red hot, apparently utilizing the same power that caused the lights to shine. Nainoa had found this simply miraculous.

Throughout the meal, he had been privy to the intimate details of the inner life of the family. He had overheard conversations about daily work. Issues of concern going on in American society as a whole were discussed with great seriousness. There were also interactions suffused with humor and laughter. He had watched as the man's wife told a story, her teeth flashing in a wide grin as her dark eyes sparkled with glee. She was very funny and had a quick, incisive mind that missed nothing. Nainoa suddenly recalled he had once told William that the American's wife resembled Kenojelak. He had thought about this statement later, wondering how he had come to this conclusion after only having seen the woman once. Now he had to concede that his earlier insight was valid. The two women were indeed somewhat alike.

Soon after, the American had retired to bed with his wife. Nainoa remembered vividly what had happened next, for he had been there during their lovemaking. Had he been simply an observer or had he participated? He was not sure. For long moments he savored his memories of that delicious encounter, his body becoming aroused in response.

Then he redirected his attention toward another issue. Perhaps this experience of connecting with his ancestor was what the Hawaiians called *noho,* an ancient word associated with spirit possession. There were historical accounts of people who had made connection with the spirits of deceased ancestors, merging with them as he had done, usually receiving information or lost knowledge from the past. There were also individuals in the settlements who were accomplished *haka*—mediums through whom someone else's spiritual aspect was able to speak. Sometimes the bitter drink called *awa* was prepared, ritually offered, and drunk by both the *haka* and the client in order to reach the state of awareness in which the connection occurred.

Occasionally ordinary people like himself, without prior experience in *noho,* were temporarily possessed by their *aumakua,* their personal spiritual aspect, usually without warning. Sometimes this happened when the person was seriously ill or in danger of dying in some accident. Under these circumstances, the person sometimes experienced the miraculous avoidance of some peril, or received bursts of extraordinary energy that allowed them to recover from their illnesses. Often these people became medicinemakers with the power to heal others.

He recalled a comment that William had made about medicine people several days ago. "To be a medicinemaker, one must have *shumonadok*—well-formed ethics. One must also have *oma*—a generous and well-formed heart." The older man had thought for a moment, then concluded, "People can acquire great power in life, but if they have poorly formed ethics and an underdeveloped heart, they can't be a medicinemaker."

Nainoa's reflections were interrupted as the old hunter abruptly stopped singing and turned to look at him, causing him to wonder if the Ennu had perceived his thoughts.

"Nothing like a little deer meat to stir up the blood, and here we are in this endless forest, without our women to comfort us." William smiled wistfully at the thought, then fell silent as he looked around, surveying the night carefully. Nainoa noticed his nostrils flare as he focused all his senses on their immediate surroundings. He wondered if the older man could see in the dark.

Nainoa's ongoing concern about his settlement suddenly appeared in his mind. Had it been destroyed by the invaders from the land division to the south, or had Chief Kaneohe managed to convince the governor to send her soldiers to save it? He made a mental estimate of the distance between their current position and the settlement on the other side of the inland sea to the west. With luck, they would be there in twelve to fourteen days. He wondered what would await them on their arrival.

He listened to the impressive chorus of insect and frog sounds that filled the night around them. There was a rhythmic quality that ebbed and flowed, emerging from and dissolving into the dark wall of noise. He felt his mind begin to drift, and his eyes began to close. He saw William give him a long look. Then the old hunter reached over, took up his javelin and his spear-thrower, and began to click them together, following the rhythm of the throbbing flow of sound. As Nainoa's eyes closed and his body relaxed, he felt his mind moving into cadence with the sharp, dry clicks.

Then something curious happened. As William's clicks continued, the background sound of the forest began to decrease. It definitely seemed to diminish . . . to diminish . . . until it became almost silent.

Within that silence, a voice suddenly appeared within his mind.

"Greetings, descendant."

This time there was no shock, no surprise. Nainoa smiled as his awareness returned to full wakefulness. He formed the mental words of response in Old English.

"Greetings, ancestor."

A thought came through. "I have been visiting since this morning. The experience has been rich, as always."

The voice ceased at this point, as though expecting some response. Once again Nainoa felt a sense of shyness come over him. The American must now know that Nainoa had been present during a very private moment with his wife.

Humor suddenly filled his mind, and he felt his concerns lift.

There was a dry chuckle followed by a statement. "You and I have shared some great moments together, and there will be more."

A new thoughtline began. "I am aware of your concerns for the well-being of your community. I too feel them. Let us try something together. Do you remember your spirit flight from the mountaintop last year, when you found your mind merged with that of a bird? There are traditional people who live in my time—people like the Ennu. They have accomplished *kahunas* who can spirit-walk. Our general term for persons with such abilities is *shaman*. These individuals are said to be able to achieve spirit flight at will, although sometimes they use mind-expanding extracts from powerful plants to help them."

"Like *awa*?" Nainoa thought, his mind wrestling with unfamiliar words.

"Yes, but much more powerful. I have never experienced them myself, but I have read about them. But here is something interesting. Most accomplished shamans do not use such substances. They train until they are able to achieve the expanded state and fly free of their bodies through their intentionality alone. The rhythmic sound of the drum or the rattle is sometimes used for assistance, however."

The sound of William's clicks pervaded their merged consciousness, providing presence and promise. "Let's see if we can detach from your body so that we can go and have a look at your settlement," came the thought.

Nainoa's mind raced at the prospect. Perhaps they could do it. "But it is dark," Nainoa thought. "And it is far. How will we find our way?"

"You have a rough idea of where you are now in relation to your settlement. Use your mind to create a pathway back. Go back the same way you came here. Hold the image of your town firmly in mind, and we will see if we can find our way. But we need a helper who is at home in the dark—one who can fly. I have always been a great admirer of the owl."

"I once knew a hunter named Nagai, an old man who befriended me as a boy," Nainoa thought. "He also admired owls. He told me once that the owls sometimes provided him with protection and guidance when he took dream journeys to faraway places at night."

With that thought, a surge of euphoria rushed through him as some shift occurred. On impulse Nainoa stretched out his arms and felt as if his fingers were growing into feathers. The power sensations roared into him, accompanied by the familiar rushing sound. Nainoa gasped for breath as he felt something pulling at him. It seemed to originate in his back, high up between his shoulder blades. Then there was a distinct sense of release accompanied by a soft pop as he detached from his body at that spot and rose into the shadowy sky, lifting on the night wind, riding on the spirit of the air. The darkness faded as his vision expanded. It was as though he could see through it into vast distances.

As Nainoa ascended between the great tree trunks, he could see his Ennu companions sitting beside the fire below. He could see his own body lying on his mat. William was looking upward. Nainoa saw the flash of his teeth and knew that the old man could see him.

Abruptly the American made a suggestion, reminding Nainoa of his continued presence. "I've got an idea," came the thought. "I've been doing some training. Hold tightly to your image of your settlement. . . ."

A curious arc took form in the air directly before him—a curved line of light that extended downward on both sides until it formed a circle. Shortly the circle's interior became opaque, then darkened. The darkness took on a sense of depth that resolved itself into a curious vortex that hovered in their field of vision. Nainoa looked into its depths, into the darkness filled with points of light, and remembered experiencing it before. "Let us go," came the thought. "Keep our destination clearly in mind and do not fear."

The vortex began to swirl to the left, and Nainoa allowed himself to be drawn into a long, dark tube filled with lights. A sense of movement began, one that accelerated rapidly, and he began to fly with great speed through the darkness, the lights racing by him into the unimaginable distance. Almost immediately, one of the points of light ahead became larger, and he found himself heading right for it. Suddenly he emerged from the tunnel and found himself floating in the night sky once again. Below him was the sprawling inland settlement of the Kaneohe land division.

Nainoa was stunned. On the one hand, the mode of travel and the speed with which the distance had been covered was simply amazing. On the other, he had never seen his community from the air before. The houses were illuminated by the tiny lights of lamps and cooking fires forming rows of brilliant dots that radiated from the central administrative hub, giving the town the appearance of a great wheel. Smoke from the cooking fires hung over the community like a cloud. Through it he could dimly make out the paths and roads that extended beyond the town's edge across the fields and plantations that, in turn, were surrounded by the darkness of the forest.

The community appeared to be inhabited and looked well cared for. So it had not been destroyed after all. Relief surged through him, then anxiety returned. The settlement was occupied, but by whom? Had it been taken over by the invaders? Were there new masters living in the high chief's residence?

Nainoa saw the tall cotton tree growing from the courtyard at the hub and swooped down, part of his mind marveling at his ability to travel and perceive in this way. He perched in the branches, looking avidly around, noting that the director's roof had been newly thatched. His own cottage was still there. He rejoiced. His home was safe.

At that moment he heard an indistinct noise and saw a man emerge from the back entrance of the director's house. His gaze sharpened as he recognized him. It was one of Chief Kaneohe's advisers, a priest named Paleko. The man was a subchief with strong political connections to one of the most powerful families in the community. Nainoa had never liked him.

A memory from his boyhood emerged, a recollection of the day he first met his friend Nagai in the open-air marketplace where the old hunter had a stall. Nagai had been showing a spotted tiger skin to several young nobles and had looked thoroughly bored with their persistent attempts to bargain the price down. Nainoa had drawn near and was watching curiously when Nagai saw him.

"Tell me, young sir," the old man had addressed him. "How much do you think this magnificent tiger skin is worth?" Silence had fallen as the young men turned and saw him. As a servant, he should have responded with a modest demurral and looked away, but something in the old hunter's manner had encouraged him to speak up. "I do not know how much it is worth now, sir," he had replied boldly, "but I suspect it was worth considerably more to its original owner."

Nagai had found this answer hugely amusing, much to the young chiefs' discomfort, and they had abruptly left in a huff. Paleko had been one of them. That day had marked the beginning of his friendship with Nagai, as well as the inception of the enmity between him and Paleko.

Nainoa watched the priest leave Chief Kaneohe's house and walk around a corner. Nainoa followed, landing lightly on the peak of a roof. Paleko looked somewhat stooped and paunchy. His hair had grown thin in the last year. He was carrying a bundle partially concealed beneath his cloak.

Nainoa dropped silently from the roof and swooped close to the priest before landing on a post. The man paused, looking at him curiously for long moments before turning and disappearing down the path toward the town. In those brief moments, he had seen only an owl. But Nainoa had gotten a glimpse at what the priest carried. It was an article of Chief Kaneohe's clothing, an old shirt with a plant design stenciled on it that he sometimes wore when visiting the farmers. This was most curious. Perhaps the shirt was to be mended.

Nainoa turned then and headed for the men's house, alighting on the roof next to the smoke hole. A meeting was in progress below. A project was being discussed—the clearing of a new section of the forest so that the fields could be extended. He knew everyone in the room. His community was intact. And what of Chief Kaneohe?

He flew upward, landing lightly on the windowsill of the chief's bedroom, but nobody was there. Perhaps the director was visiting with one of his wives. He made the rounds of the women's residences, but the chief was not there either. On impulse, he checked the chief's personal *heiau.* The door of the thatched *hale mana,* the house of power, was slightly ajar. A light came from within. He drifted lightly down onto the stone platform.

The director was there, seated in deep meditation on a woven mat before the spirit stone, its fierce expression illuminated by the glow of a small stone lamp. There was an offering wrapped in a *ti* leaf on the small altar in front of it. Nainoa looked quickly around. The woven baskets containing the bones of the chief's ancestors had been returned from their places of safekeeping elsewhere. Feather capes hung from hooks on the walls. More objects wrapped in black *kapa* cloth were stacked in the corners.

A sense of urgency made itself known within his mind. "We must return," came the thought. "We must follow the sound of William's clicks back to the camp before he stops." Nainoa listened and realized he could still hear them, even at this distance. How was this possible?

"One more thing," Nainoa thought to his companion. He flew soundlessly across the courtyard to his cottage and darted through the window. The small one-room building was unoccupied, but Nainoa saw his possessions, kept safe during his absence, had been returned to their places. Even after his being away for a year, his chief still awaited him. This small display of faith warmed him immensely.

"Let us go back, then," he thought. Immediately the curved line appeared and resolved itself into the dark vortex swirling with lights. As before, he allowed himself to be drawn into it, his speed increasing until he found himself hurtling through the dark tunnel, following the sound of William's rhythmic clicks. His speed abruptly decreased as the light came up again, and, looking down, he perceived the camp below. There was Zaki, still turning the meat on the racks over the low fire. He could see William, his eyes closed and his body rocking back and forth as he clicked the two pieces of wood together. And there was himself, lying motionless between the huge roots of the tree.

63

As he began to descend, a last thoughtline appeared in his mind: "It has been a magnificent experience visiting within you once again. As I said before, feel free to visit within me when you feel the need."

For several minutes Nainoa lay still, eyes closed, marveling over what had just occurred. Then he opened his eyes and grinned at William. The older man sensed his gaze, opened his own eyes, and stopped clicking. Nainoa gestured weakly, then shut his eyes again and began to review what he had just seen. It had been wondrous, simply wondrous. He addressed a last question to the American, but there was silence within his mind now.

He emerged fully from the trance state then and propped himself up on one elbow. He looked at his companions and smiled to himself. He was going to return to his people in the company of a powerful medicine man and his son.

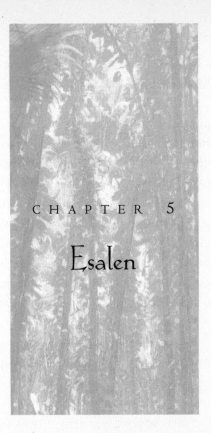

CHAPTER 5

Esalen

THE REVELATION OF my role in the dynamic between Nainoa and myself stunned me. I had become a source from which lost knowledge of the past could be recovered by humanity's descendants. When Nainoa's mind was in connection with mine, he could theoretically access anything in my memory banks, ranging from information that I'd just read in the daily newspaper to almost fifty years of accumulated life experience, including all my knowledge and scientific training.

Information about our high technology would be interesting, of course, but largely useless. With the exception of a few artifacts and weapons preserved in chiefly collections, Nainoa's people have no ferrous metals, nor do they possess knowledge of metal ores or their origins. Virtually all their metal objects are fashioned from copper, brass, bronze, and aluminum artifacts recovered from archeological sites. Iron and steel, with their propensity to rust, simply did not survive the five-thousand-year tropical interval.[1]

Although I could provide information about metals and metal-lurgy, this information too would be largely useless. There are no longer any low-grade ores at the surface of the earth, as was the case during the Neolithic period, when metals were first discovered. Ores today must be mined from deep within the earth's crust, utilizing machines and high technology to obtain them. Lacking ferrous metals and thus machines, Nainoa's people (and by implication, their de-scendants) will never be able to obtain these ores, and without the ores, they will never be able to reinvent machines or a machine-age technology. The implication: Once our high technology is gone, it will be gone forever. Humanity's descendants will never be able to re-create the world that we all take so much for granted.

So what information could I offer Nainoa's population that would better their world? As I thought about this issue, I came face-to-face with my own shortcomings. As an American raised in twentieth-century urban culture, I knew perilously little about livestock, agricul-ture, irrigation, weaving, leather working, wagon building, or any of the other things that make up the technology base of Nainoa's soci-ety. There was my knowledge of history, of course, but how would that better the life of the commoner who works the fields or the artisan who makes and barters rain capes in the marketplace?

These concerns chafed at me throughout the fall of 1990 while I continued to send out my résumé in response to job openings but got no response. Despair grew within me as the family's financial situation worsened, causing considerable tension in my household. Jill, realizing that she was going to have to give up her business for a salaried position "within the system," drove up to northern California in November and immediately found a job with an acute-care hospital. This was mainstream employment that would pay the bills and provide the family with medical benefits. We spent the rest of the month packing up the household and headed north just before Christmas. The spirit stone rode with me in the back of my car.

We took up residence in a rental house with an overgrown, woodsy backyard in a suburb of Sacramento. It was winter and everything was leafless. I placed the stone behind the house under a wooden arbor covered with a thick, untrimmed grapevine. The lava boulder looked powerful standing upright in this woody cave, its several shell leis wrapped around its apex.

Shortly after the December holidays, I attended another training workshop on shamanism with Michael Harner's foundation, a two-week affair held at the well-known Esalen Institute on the Big Sur coast of central California. This one was to be led by both Harner and Sandra Ingerman. I hadn't seen him since my initial contact back in the early 1980s and viewed this as an opportunity to reconnect.

Harner looked different from how I remembered him. He was thinner, but his dark, penetrating gaze was the same, though his beard had turned completely white. His serious demeanor was still offset by his wacky sense of humor, and as we waited in line for dinner the first night of the retreat, our discussions were continuously punctuated with his humorous asides and joint bursts of laughter. We shuffled through the self-serve line, mounding our plates with delicacies, then sat together at a long table, where I observed him with interest as I ate.

Harner has impressive credentials. He did his doctoral work in anthropology at the University of California at Berkeley and functioned as assistant director of the Lowie Museum of Anthropology while there. He taught at the New School for Social Research in New York as well as at Columbia and Yale Universities, and served as cochairman of the Anthropology Division of the New York Academy of Sciences. His field research had been wide and varied, taking him into the tribal lands of the upper Amazon Basin, Mexico, Lapland, and The Canadian Arctic. He was now directing and running the Foundation for Shamanic Studies, through which he had developed and fostered an international network of field associates and faculty operating on five continents—individuals who help to preserve and encourage traditional shamanism where it is being threatened by rapid social change.

When we met for our first formal session after dinner, I received an interesting shock. Although I had never been to a workshop at Esalen before, there was something very familiar about the long, dark-carpeted room that was to be our home base during the next two weeks. As we went through our introductions, each participant saying something about himself or herself for the benefit of the group, I suddenly realized what it was.

Two years before, while still in Hawai'i, I had had a visionary experience in which I found myself in the presence of the volcano spirit Pele. I had felt at a loss as to how to proceed, and in response to my need to connect with someone who knew a little more about dealing with spirits than myself, my conscious awareness had been transported to an unfamiliar room filled with unfamiliar people, among whom I had recognized Michael Harner. As my gaze swept the room now, I realized that this was the place I had seen in that vision. I didn't know what to make of this. Had I actually experienced some sort of short-term time shift in which I had been able to see through my own eyes in the future? Or had I actually "journeyed" to this place at that time, making contact then? It had been about this same time of year, and Harner could well have been there.

The initial goal of every shamanic aspirant is to learn how to enter nonordinary reality and go to a place commonly referred to as the Lower World, where traditional tribal shamans meet with spirits, connect with mystical power, and acquire information about matters of personal importance. The first objective of the neophyte is to enter this inner world and establish a relationship with a spirit helper from whom he or she can then acquire power and protection, assistance and information. An excellent book by Tom Cowan titled *Fire in the Head: Shamanism and the Celtic Spirit* has some words to offer on this subject:

> *The shaman is a master of escaping the mind-body matrix that*
> *characterizes ordinary consciousness and entering the shamanic or*

nonordinary state of consciousness. In this dream-like state, the imaginal realm reshapes itself, creating a placeless, timeless field in which the shaman can participate in the consciousness of other creatures. It is at this point that shamanic journeying and shapeshifting share a common enterprise. Shapeshifting requires reshaping the imaginal realm, and consciousness becomes objectified in some other thing. Journeying [also] reshapes the imaginal world, and consciousness becomes geographied; it becomes the spiritworld in which the shaman will travel. Shapeshifting is consciousness-as-object; journeying is consciousness-as-landscape.[2]

On that first evening, my goal was to both journey and shape-shift in order to access the Lower World and reconnect with my spirit helper. It was also an opportunity to obtain information about issues of current importance in my life. The exercise is, among other things, an ancient, time-tested method of divination, and I, a nontribal Westerner, was attempting to use it with a strong assist from Michael Harner and his drum.

While I distinguish my conscious, goal-oriented shamanic journey work from the deep, transtemporal visionary states in which I connect with Nainoa, they are experientially similar, and I suspect that both are expressions of the same phenomenon, though experienced at different degrees of intensity. My shamanic journeys are subjective and dreamlike in nature—vivid visualizations that often begin as thoughtforms produced by my creative imagination or as memories accessed through my subconscious mind. At some point there is a shift, and this inner imagery "comes to life," progressing into levels of experience and awareness that I have not created or remembered. Things happen then, and through practice, I have discovered both that I can act in these perceived realities and that they have an autonomous existence that is separate from myself. In the narrative that follows, I have decided to avoid terms such as *mythic* or *archetypal* as well as any particular framework of interpretation and just describe what I perceived.

As the first drumming session began, I lay down and darkened my visual field with a mask designed for that purpose. I relaxed my body as fully as possible, recalled the goal and the destination of my journey, and sank into the sound of the drum. I erased the screen of my thinking mind and became still.

After a short period, I refocused my attention and brought up the memory of the power sensations. This recollection was perceived through my body, through my *ku* or subconscious mind, producing a somato-cognitive process that could be called "think-feeling." I listened to the drum and reached for the sensations, and, much to my amazement, succeeded in eliciting them.

I felt my body stiffen as the exquisite rush began. Sporadic bursts of light coalesced behind my closed eyes into brilliant spots that, in turn, became lines and lightninglike zigzags as my eyes shifted this way and that. The light condensed into the brilliant fibers of the grid as my body continued to be flooded with the sensations of power. I was absolutely thrilled. With the assistance of the drum, I had finally managed to crack open the inner doorway at will! Although it had been my intention to do this, I have to admit that I was somewhat stunned when it actually happened.

I regathered my wits, recalled my destination, and "became the mirror." On one side lay the outer world of objective experience; on the other, the inner worlds of subjective reality. On one side was my body, on the other my mind—the two acting in relationship and serving, in tandem, as the interface, as the doorway between these two realms of experience. As my awareness expanded, the connection I was seeking occurred. A feeling of inward and outward expansion began. At this point, there was no longer a sense of the two being different. The thin crescent of light appeared among the curious phosphenic hallucinations before me. The rush increased, and I felt the presence of doors within doors, of passages opening into endlessnesses.

I accessed my memories to manifest an image in my mind's eye, a thoughtform of a location that I would use as a stepping-off place, like an airport or a train station. Then I went there. I simply kept the image of the place in mind and allowed the sound of the drum to carry me. It seemed only a moment later that the primary focus of my consciousness shifted from "here" to "there."

My senses kicked in one at a time. I smelled the salt tang of the sea and heard the ocean breaking on the beach. I could hear the birds singing and the breeze rattling the palms. I felt the sun-warmed lava rocks under my feet, and as I opened my "eyes," I found I was standing on the black stone platform of the *heiau* at Kealakekua Bay. To the west lay the sparkling cobalt vastness of the Pacific. Below me was the crescent of rocky beach and the old Hawaiian village site in the trees behind the pond. Above it loomed the dark cliff, stretching upward into the immensity of Mauna Loa. I had spent every morning here for years, swimming in the warm water with my family and walking through the ruins in the forest. I knew every tree, every rock. I scanned my surroundings with excitement. It looked different somehow.

I seemed to be the only person here. I stopped thinking and listened to the sound of the waves, feeling the peace and tranquility of the place slip into me. I glanced toward the tamarind tree in whose shade I had once placed the spirit stone, and much to my amazement, the dark shape of the stone was there. Curious, I descended the *heiau*'s lava steps and walked around the pond toward the stone. As I entered the forest's shade, I bent and put my hands on the stone's surface. I waited . . . but nothing happened. A connection had not been established. Something else was required.

I squatted down and focused my attention fully on the rock, feeling its roughness with my fingers. I could see the indistinct chisel lines I had made in bringing out the stone's form and marveled at the accuracy and realism of the vision. I greeted the spirit in the stone and offered a quick mental sketch of what was intended. I asked for protection and support, and for its blessing in my endeavors. Without warning, the connection suddenly occurred. I could feel it: a mindshape . . . an intelligence that felt utterly unlike a human mind, and yet I was aware that it could perceive. And at that moment I felt very clearly that it was perceiving me.

I was filled with wonderment. The fact that the stone was actually in my backyard in Sacramento gave rise to the suspicion that in this level of experience and awareness, distance does not exist, at least not in the same way we experience it in ordinary reality. Through my mystical experiences, I had come to understand that I was in the Middle World of dream, a level of reality in which everything everywhere is connected to everything else through the vast matrix I perceive as the grid. I suspect that this grid is energetic in nature, and that the energy within my physical body was at this moment connected with that of the stone because both are part of the matrix. I decided to see if I could tap into the greater energy of the matrix, using the stone as a vehicle. I formed the intention within my mind and—

Pow! Once again the muscle-numbing sensations of power flowed into me through my arms. My body (in the room at Esalen) felt as though it was being inflated with a blast of roaring, ecstatic force. As I stiffened, the clarity of my perception expanded enormously.

The sound of the drum drifted through the trees, reminding me of the objective at hand. I needed to find an entrance to the Lower World. I scanned my surroundings. I didn't see any obvious caves or lava tubes beckoning. Then an idea appeared within my mind. I stood up and looked closely at the pond's surface. Orange flowers from the *kou* trees were floating on the water. I could see the pastel reflections of the trees and sky above. I looked into the water, through the reflection and downward, and recalled a local story that the pond was the abode of a *mo'o,* a water spirit. Unease passed through me. Humankind had not been exactly beneficent to the environment of late. I watched the pond's surface and waited. Nothing happened.

Then, almost imperceptibly, the water began to stir. The surface began to move in a distinctly circular, clockwise direction. I watched, entranced, as the vortex of a small whirlpool appeared and drew an orange flower down into the depths. Was there a lava tube below connected to the ocean beyond? Was it the tide sucking the water out, or was it something else? The vortex widened and became somewhat tunnel-like in appearance. I felt certain of what it was: The pond, prompted by my intentionality, had revealed itself as the doorway. After another moment's indecision and hesitation, I invoked the *mo'o* and asked for permission to enter its domain. Nothing untoward occurred, so I filled my lungs with air and dived in.

As I broke through the surface, I seemed to achieve torpedo speed and rocketed downward into a dark underwater opening in a swarm of swirling bubbles. Did I feel slippery fingers flowing over my skin and through my hair in soft, watery caresses? A rushing, buzzing, whispering sound filled my ears, in which I could detect low-frequency murmurings and mutterings. I kept my objective, my destination in mind. I was going to the Lower World to meet my helping spirit.

As the myriad effervescent lights streaked by in the tunnel, I was aware that I didn't feel pressed for air. A blissful euphoria began to grow, one that filled me completely. Ahead in the darkness, I saw a point of golden light that grew larger by the moment. I flew through the sparkling tunnel of water toward it. Abruptly the light overcame the darkness, and, propelled like a projectile, I broke the surface in a fountain of brilliant bubbles.

I found myself in a tropical forest pool surrounded by massive trees and thick lianas. There was some momentary disorientation as I looked around. Outlines were softened by a drifting mist illuminated by golden light that seemed to come from everywhere. The landscape resembled the place where Nainoa had first encountered the leopard man in his vision. The tree trunks had that same, odd flickering quality. In the next moment, a familiar sound drew my attention to the right.

Tok!

It was the sound of wood being struck with wood. I slowly swam to the bank in the direction indicated, climbed out of the forest pool, and walked up the sandbar into the jungle. The illusion was very real. I studied the substrate carefully, identifying mosses and liverworts and interesting mushrooms with long stems. I looked down at my body and perceived it as luminous and naked. The air was warm and thick. Each tree, vine, and shrub glowed with a subtle inner radiance, creating an effect like a Maxfield Parrish painting. Birdcalls floated in the stillness. It was undoubtedly the most beautiful forest I had ever seen.

Tok!

The sound drew me. I walked slowly, noting everything with a razorlike clarity. I remembered that the clearing Nainoa had seen was up ahead somewhere . . . and it was. I walked out of the blue shadows into the circle of golden light, looking around for the leopard man, and he was there, watching me from the cover of the trees. His appearance was rather like that of the Cheshire cat in Alice's adventure—all spots and eyes, but bigger, much bigger. As I walked over to him he appeared entirely feline, looking much like a real leopard.

I ran my fingers through his fur and scratched along his face and chin. He relaxed and closed his eyes, his throaty rattle of greeting intensifying as he pushed his head against me. I pushed back, scratching his neck up behind the ears. Suddenly he seized my hand between his jaws and held it. I had to trust that he would not hurt me, that he was there as an ally. This strange connection produced another huge surge of the sensations, rendering my body virtually rigid as a stick.

The leopard slowly released me and stood up on his back legs. He looked me straight in the eye, his face assuming a distinctly human configuration as his transformation into the leopard man was completed. I stared into his pale green eyes and was very much aware that I was face-to-face with a supernatural being. Although he had assumed a humanoid shape in response to me, I did not perceive him as human, nor did he have a human mind. I understood quite clearly that "he" was the composite spiritual essence of a large species of cat, an ancient ambush hunter produced by the same ecosystems that gave rise to the earliest humans.

We turned then and walked together in silence through the forest, through the golden light between the great trunks, enjoying each other's company. I recalled childhood adventures, unthought of in almost forty years, and a sense of warmth flowed into me from my beastly companion. He had been there too. He remembered our secret places in New York's Central Park. We walked together through the forest, through the golden light, thinking of the past, the leopard man and me.

The dialogue that followed was more of an interaction than a conversation. I quickly reviewed my reasons for coming, and thoughts, feelings, and impressions flowed through my mind in response. It was much like being merged with Nainoa's mind, only this mind was utterly alien. There was never any hostility or sense of danger. The spirit exuded a neutral emotional state combined with polite curiosity. As the beast-man's pale green gaze fastened upon me, there was a quiet, intense watchfulness. There was absolutely no doubt in my mind that my spotted companion was an ally.

When I heard the drumbeat change, summoning me back to the workshop room, I explained that I was leaving and why, adding that I wished him to return with me, to provide company and assistance, power and protection during the next two weeks. He then did something completely unexpected: He leaped at me—and into me, merging with me in some unexplainable way. I felt incredibly energized by this merging and, looking down, perceived my body as distinctly leopardlike.

The drum beckoned. I began to run. Did I drop to all fours on that mad dash through the forest? I'm not sure, but it took only moments to reach the pond, dive in, and torpedo back through the tunnel of water, arriving in a burst of spray below the *heiau*. I loped up onto the stone platform and looked around. Where was the doorway? I didn't see the place through which I had arrived.

On impulse I closed my eyes and fastened my awareness on the sound of the drum. I visualized my body lying on the floor of the long room at Esalen. A sense of movement began, and within moments my primary focus reestablished itself there. As Harner drummed the finish, I slowly emerged from the altered state, then sat up and opened my notebook and recorded the journey. I felt powerful, supple, and relaxed. I looked across the room and wondered if I could leap across it in a single bound. I recalled that I was about to turn fifty and decided not to try.

• • •

One evening several days later, I returned from soaking in Esalen's natural hot springs and tumbled into bed, slipping into unconsciousness almost immediately. I awakened in the darkness in the middle of the night and was unable to get back to sleep. It was in this semiconscious state that a memory suddenly appeared in my mind without warning, a recollection of something that had happened late one afternoon in the northern part of Tanzania's Serengeti Plain almost twenty years before.

It had been November and the short rains had arrived, signaling the end of the long East African dry season. I had just finished a three-month field season with an expedition and was doing research at the Kenya National Museum in Nairobi. I had decided to take a break and drive down to the Serengeti to see the great migrations of the wildebeest. On the afternoon in question, I was out in one of the expedition Land Rovers, observing animals and driving with care, staying on the packed dirt road to avoid getting stuck in the soft earth.

It was getting on toward sunset when I began the long drive back to the lodge where I was staying. As sometimes happens, I was overtaken by a sudden rainstorm that arose out of nowhere. It seemed to take only moments for the sky to turn completely dark and the land to be inundated with water. The headlights made little impact on the swirling darkness, and it became difficult to see the route. My concern grew. If I strayed from the track, I would surely get bogged down.

About five miles from the lodge, the track crossed a low place between two long ridges, and as I descended the hillside, a lightning flash revealed that the low ground in front of the car had become a stream filled with rushing brown water. It wasn't very far across, but there was no way of telling how deep it was. The rain was coming down in buckets, and I didn't relish the idea of getting out to check. I put the car in low range four-wheel drive and eased into the swirling water in first gear. It was deep. The water rose to the tops of the boxlike fenders, and I felt the car slip sideways in the current. I came to a decision and powered across, but as the car lurched up the other side, the spark plugs got wet, the engine died, and it refused to restart.

There was no way I could dry the spark plugs. It was pouring. I had been out for much of the day and I was hungry. I had no desire to spend an uncomfortable night in the Land Rover, but it was a good hike back to the lodge and the night was filled with wild animals. I sat in the dark car and thought dark thoughts. The rain was coming down in a solid, steady roar of sound, and I could see virtually nothing. Should I walk back or should I stay? I had heard tales of tourists who had failed to return to the hotel and whose empty cars were found the next morning stuck somewhere in the park. There were lions out there in the night, and humans were well within the size range of the animals they preyed on. I had no gun or weapon except for a Maasai club in the dashboard. I elected to remain in the car.

About half an hour later, the rain began to let up. Experimentally I tried the ignition. To my delight, the engine caught and started. The heat of the engine block must have dried the spark plugs. I thanked whatever guardian spirit had provided this escape, put the car in gear, and drove out of the stream. Within a hundred yards, a flash of lightning revealed that the track led straight into a herd of Cape buffalo. There must have been at least thirty of them, and they were spooked by the thunder. As a flash lit up the landscape for a brief instant, I saw a bull with a massive, cancerous gall on one of his huge horns glaring straight at the car. Had I walked, I would have run right into him.

All at once the herd surged into motion, and the night all around the car was filled with snorting beasts and thundering hooves. Great shadowy bodies veered around the Land Rover and disappeared into the darkness. I opened the car window and leaned my head out. The night was silent once again. The storm had passed.

It was then that I heard the low, guttural sound. I heard it just once, but there was no mistaking what it was. There were lions out there in the grass. So that was why the buffalo were spooked. I waited tensely but did not hear them again. I shone my flashlight around but did not see them. I knew they were there, however, and felt great relief once again that I'd stayed with the car. I returned to the lodge, treating myself to a large whiskey before dinner.

The detail of this memory was so vivid, I could smell the wet grass as I lay in my bed at Esalen. Suddenly, without warning, the sensations of power appeared within me, and the exquisite paralysis had me in its invisible fist. The progression of phosphenic visuals occurred. The sound of the ocean waves outside the cabin merged with the familiar rushing, buzzing sound, then receded into the distance. There was a brief sense of transition, of floating through a vast hall in the darkness, whereupon I found myself standing outdoors in the night, barely able to make anything out.

A chill went up my spine as a flash of lightning revealed the landscape around me. In some impossible way, I had been transported back to that savanna in East Africa. I had thought often about that night in the game park and wondered just as often if the lion would have killed me—if that had been "my lion," so to speak. I felt a trill of fear; I wasn't in a Land Rover now. I stood immobile in the darkness, my ears straining to hear the slightest sound, my eyes waiting for the next flash so I could see. I could dimly make out a track snaking away through the grass and began to move in that direction. Simultaneously I wondered what I was doing there. Who or what had drawn me back to this place?

The fear lessened a bit as I walked across the grassy plain. At some level I sensed that I would just have to trust, to surrender to whatever happened next. My growing feeling of renewed confidence was abruptly replaced by shock as the next lightning flash revealed an animal approaching me through the grass. It was a lion and its head was motionless, held parallel to the ground, as it flowed soundlessly toward me.

There was no time for reflection. In the next moment, there was a sudden blast of its hot breath in my face, and a sense of incredible pressure as its stiff whiskers wrapped around my head and its jaws fastened on my throat. My arms went around its maned neck almost in an embrace as its body slammed into mine and I was borne backward to the ground. The impact was the last thing I felt. My conscious awareness disengaged from my physical body in that instant, the exit seeming to occur up high between my shoulder blades. With the transition, I could suddenly see in all directions at once.

I stood there astonished, watching, as the lion did what lions do. Years ago I had seen a trio of male lions stalk, kill, and eat a baby giraffe. This was no different except that the legs emerging from under the lion's massive shoulder were human, were mine. I felt full-fledged amazement as well as a curious detachment. There was no place to go, nothing to do, so I watched. When the huge carnivore was finished, it stood and roared into the night, again and again and again. Then the beast moved off, a deep rattle of contentment emerging from its massive throat. Before me lay all that was left, a scatter of bone fragments gleaming wetly on a damp place on the grass.

The red sun rose out of the east and dried the bones, bleaching and weathering them quickly. The hot, dry winds came and scattered them among the rocks, tinkling like a ceramic wind chime. There was a sense of time passing, but how much and how long mattered not at all. It was as if eternity was incorporated into that endless day, until, at last, the sun began to sink in the west. Throughout, something held me there, a silent witness at the place of my death.

With the fading light, I perceived movement on the savanna. I focused my senses fully in that direction but saw nothing. Then, as I looked away, I perceived movement again. Something was out there in the grass—a cluster of moving points that resolved themselves into a leopard approaching across the plain, a yellow ocher creature on a yellow ocher field. The beast came on in utter silence, heading straight toward me. When it arrived, it paused and looked at the bones scattered in the grass, then approached and sniffed them curiously. With a throaty sound, the leopard's spotted shape stiffened and abruptly shifted, becoming distinctly humanoid in configuration. It was my old ally, but he had come too late.

Stretching out a spotted, muscular arm, he extended his claws and gathered the bone fragments together in a pile . . . and from his thoughts and memories of me, an image formed, projected out of his green eyes into and around the osseous mound in the dry grass.

Haaa . . . haaa . . . haaa . . . His breath flowed in leopard coughs of sound across the bones as he blew life into the image forming around them. I could see it quite clearly. The sun's radiated heat shimmered in the air, warming and energizing the leopard's thoughtform. A sudden whiff of smoke appeared as wind arrived and the grass ignited, forming a brief fiery vortex, enlivening the image with life force. The leopard man smiled his alien smile, observing "me" with interest as a distinct and physical "self" took form once again.

I reached out then and merged with this new self. Suddenly there was a definite sense of being back in my body. I looked out through new eyes into those of the leopard man. For long moments I just stared into those pale green pools. Then the cat slowly closed his eyes, breaking the gaze, conveying greeting. I had a new body.

We turned then and walked away together along the track of red earth through the dry grass toward the horizon. This was a most curious and, at the same time, gratifying experience. I was aware that I had been taken apart and put back together again. I felt different somehow. I was also aware that I was walking across a part of the spirit world in the company of the leopard man. I felt the bond, the relationship between us, and perceived it as an ancient one.

My spotted companion glanced at me, then looked away, conveying nothing. Its tail twitched nervously, perhaps because of my intense scrutiny. I watched him with my peripheral vision. Although the leopard man looked humanoid, there was nothing human in its blank, detached stare.

It was then that I saw long, black shadows racing across the pale grassland toward us. I looked up. There were broad-winged raptors riding on the wind, reaching into it with their long primary feathers, gaining lift. They began to circle above us. I remembered my recent spirit flight with Nainoa, and on impulse I stretched my arms up toward them and felt my fingers begin to grow into featherlike elongations. The sensations in my body surged as I reached into the wind, then abruptly rose into the air, lifting on the thermals gusting off the shimmering land. Almost immediately, a sense of soaring began within me . . . the kind I sometimes have in flying dreams. I rose into the peach-colored sky, circling with the raptors, ascending higher and higher. Below me, I saw the leopard man looking up.

My attention shifted toward the zenith, and there I saw a vast, brilliant light in the distant apex of the sky. I knew now what it was. For long moments I stared into the heart of the golden light and felt great waves of emotion sweep through me. Then, closing my eyes like the leopard man, I brought my winged hands together and bowed.

This dream, if that was what it was, resembled a classic shamanic dismemberment experience. Among the Siberian peoples, such episodes are often associated with shamanic initiation. Usually the dreamer is attacked, taken apart, and boiled down until just the bare bones remain. Then the neophyte is put back together again, receiving a new spiritual body but with all the bad parts left out. For the uninformed, such an experience could be psychologically devastating, propelling the experiencer toward the psychiatrist's office. For the tribal person, such an experience would be expected under ritual or ceremonial circumstances. For me, it happened in the workshop I was currently involved in.

At breakfast the next morning, I related the story of my dismemberment to Harner, whose dark eyes gleamed behind his glasses. "Dismemberment is poorly understood by the academy," he said. Then he paused theatrically and added, "Now, tenure is something they do understand." Everyone laughed.

"Often, in beginning workshops, people go out on their first shamanic journey and have a dismemberment experience," he continued. "Psychologically, it's as if one is meeting a fear and discovering that everything is still quite okay. You come back with a new spiritual body. Very often, chronic physical symptoms disappear. It helps to have some idea of what is going on ahead of time so that you don't get freaked out."

I recalled the experience of being attacked and killed by the lion and shuddered, then realized that what Harner said was true. I had not been consumed with terror or immobilized by fear. At some level I had faced my fear. I had been almost at ease, observing my death with detached amazement and a deep inner acceptance of the rightness of it all in the eyes of the universe. This equanimity had been possible in part because I knew what was going on and was not afraid.

Toward the end of the workshop, I had a visionary visit with Nainoa. It began, as usual, in the hour before dawn and was accompanied by the paralysis as well as the visual and auditory phenomena. At that time of night, I was rested and my body was fully relaxed. The rhythmic sound of the waves facilitated the experience, I'm sure, as did the past ten days of directed inner work. But what initiated it?

As I drifted, paralyzed, in that shallow zone between wakefulness and sleep, I heard a distant rooster crow. Were there poultry at Esalen? I didn't think so.

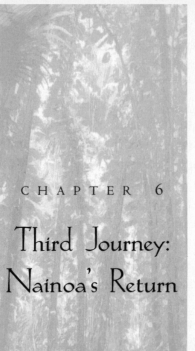

CHAPTER 6

Third Journey: Nainoa's Return

AINOA AND HIS companions looked down from the rocky outcrop that capped the hill shouldering above the canopy of the tropical forest. Below them lay his settlement, with the town in the distance beyond the cleared fields. A rooster crowed, to be answered by another, and another. He studied the administrative hub rising above the town, then glanced at William and Zaki. This was the first such settlement they had ever seen, and their faces reflected awe. He glanced down at their dogs and felt a pang of sadness. There were only three of them now.

When they had arrived at the river that would carry them down to the inland sea, he had found his canoe intact where he had left it the year before. He had decided to repair the strapping of the outrigger and the high sideboards before crossing the inland sea, and it had taken a day to find the correct type of palm, strip the fronds, and make the necessary cordage. It was during this time that one of the dogs was taken by a crocodile.

The animals had been catching fish, wading chest deep in the shallow water of the river, when a submerged log suddenly came to life and seized one of the females in a pair of immense jaws. The unfortunate animal barely got out a yip before the reptile killed it with a snap of its long head and disappeared, bearing its victim into the depths of the murky, brown water. This was the first big crocodile the Ennu had seen, and they had remained silent for the rest of the day, mourning the loss of their companion. The tragedy had been offset by their rising enthusiasm as Nainoa taught them the skills of paddling and sailing the outrigger. The Ennu did not have canoes, although they tied bundled reeds into floatable rafts for fishing and hunting water-fowl in their lakes.

They had set off down the river, the three men, their gear, and the dogs making a full load. They had cleared the stands of mangroves of the river delta the following day, and had then paddled up the marshy eastern coast to a location opposite the multipeaked island that the current governor's grandfather had designated as a place of refuge. The chiefs often met there for conferences, arriving with their retinues in long double-hulled canoes, residing in large houses erected in advance by their servants. Nainoa had been to this place with Chief Kaneohe and Nagai years before and was curious to see if anyone was in residence.[1]

He had made for the shallow bay on its southern coast but found the center deserted. They had spent a day hunting among the island's jungly green mountains and had killed three deer. While smoking and cooking the meat, they had enjoyed swimming in the warm waters of the bay, where the Ennu had seen their first dolphins. The breadfruit was ripe now, and he had found three large *ulu* and roasted them in the coals. As they ate the sweet and sticky delicacy with their fingers, Nainoa had explained how the Hawaiian voyagers had brought this tree from their home islands as living, rooted cuttings in leaf-wrapped bundles of soil.

The wind had been favorable the following day, and they had made an uneventful crossing, arriving on the western shore of the inland sea in the dusk. Two more days had been spent paddling and sailing through the myriad islands to the small cove from which he had embarked the previous year.

On making this final landfall, they had hidden the canoe and established a forest camp back within the trees, well away from the water. By chance, their evening fire was spotted by a band of hunters from his settlement. Among them were several of Nagai's old friends, and they were greatly surprised to see Nainoa. They knew that he had been sent into the interior the year before, but he had never returned and they told him that many presumed that he was dead. Nainoa had invited them to stay the night, to share food and information. The hunters, eager to hear his story and curious about his strange-looking companions and their equally alien-looking dogs, had readily agreed.

During that long evening, he had given them a rough outline of his adventures during the time that he had been away. The Hawaiians had been enthralled at his tale and had looked with increased interest at his Ennu companions when he revealed them as fellow hunters. Friendly bonds had been established right from the first, and Nainoa had breathed a sigh of relief. This meeting had been a good omen, a good beginning. It had also provided him with his first experience of being a translator, for the Ennu could not understand the settlers, nor the settlers the Ennu.

The hunters had related, in turn, what had happened during his absence. The civil war had been brief and the community spared. The governor had acted swiftly, sending the *koa*, her army of soldiers, to deal with the aggressors from the south. High Chief Shimoda had directed the operation, sending a fleet of long canoes filled with warriors to the port, while two more divisions of men approached from the land. The aggressors were trapped in the middle just as they were arriving to sack the community. A bloody battle had ensued, and many lives had been lost, but the *koa* had prevailed.

All members of the noble family responsible for the outbreak of the warfare, including anyone related by blood to the offending chiefs, had been arrested and taken to the capital. The governor had heard their case, after which almost five hundred people, from elders to children, had been executed, wiping out an entire lineage and providing a harsh example to any who decided to break the peace in the future. The land division of the aggressors had been confiscated and had since been redistributed to a new ruling family.

William and Zaki had looked blank as he conveyed to them what he had learned. The Ennu did not have soldiers, nor did they indulge in warfare, and Nainoa realized that the death of five hundred people would leave quite a hole in their world. He learned something else during that evening that disturbed him greatly. Chief Kaneohe was gravely ill, and it was rumored that he might not survive. The hunters suspected sorcery.

Nainoa thought about all of this as he looked down across the fields toward his settlement on the final afternoon of his journey. He was filled with excitement mixed with worried concern. He had sent one of the hunters to inform Chief Kaneohe of his imminent arrival and to give him time to arrange a reception. He knew that the man would spread the news, telling everyone he came across that Nainoa, secretary and clerk to the director, was returning from a year's explorations of the interior beyond the mountains, and that he was arriving with company.

He prepared himself for reentry, wrapping his last remaining *malo* around his hips, tying it securely, and rebraiding his hair. It was the first time in almost a year that he had adopted the Hawaiian style of dress. He slung his makeshift rain cape over one shoulder and arranged the rest of his gear carefully. He wanted to make a good impression. He looked at his companions, who had fastened long blue and green parrot feathers in their hair. He had asked Zaki to fashion collars for the dogs so that they could be tied if need be. They were ready.

They descended the hill through the last of the trees and approached the rocky streambed that bordered the cleared fields. Nainoa looked up as they passed under the massive bulk of the cotton tree near the forest's edge. Its fern- and orchid-filled crown high above was again loaded with green seed pods. On impulse he stopped, rested his hands on its thorny trunk, and closed his eyes. He cleared his mind and addressed the collective spiritual essence of the forest through the tree, expressing gratitude for his safe journey. There was no particular response, no falling fruits, no trilling birdcalls, yet he felt better for having done this.

William nodded approvingly as they left the trees and crossed the stream on the water-polished boulders. "These great trees have strong spirits," the older man commented, looking up at the towering giant. "They possess peculiar dreamlike minds that are very kindly."

Nainoa thought about this statement and replied, "There was a great spiritual teacher named Kotama who lived many thousands of years ago in a fabled land west of the great ocean who said something very similar. There is a quotation written in our histories that is attributed to him: 'The forest is a being of great kindness and benevolence. It offers shade to all, even to the timber cutter.'"

The older man laughed with delight as they climbed the steep bank of the stream, heading toward the fields. "The trees were aware of us as we passed through their realm," he said. "I felt their minds regarding us. They were attracted to you. You seem to have a way with trees, Nainoapak." When they reached the top, he looked back at the dark wall of trees and stopped to listen. The great forest was silent, as it had been on the day of his departure.

They turned then and set off across the fields, heading for the north road. On the way, Nainoa walked through a field of unpicked cotton, explaining to his friends how cloth was made from the coarse white tufts bursting out of their dark capsules. He pointed out the drainage canals and explained their usage in relieving the saturated soil of excess water during the rainy season, carrying it to the flooded paddies where the starchy *taro* was grown. He indicated the terraces on the cleared hillsides, directing their attention to a distant sisal plantation on a drier south-facing slope and giving a brief description of how rope was made. He gestured toward the pale green foliage of the long rows of candlenut trees, *kukui,* and described how oil from the trees' nuts was burned in lamps, how the soot from their burned shells was made into a black dye useful for patterning cloth, tattooing skin, writing, and brush painting. As they passed a banana plantation he tried to describe the relative merits of the different varieties grown.

William was silent as he digested this information. After some thought, he asked, "Did your ancestors bring all these plants from your home islands across the ocean?" Nainoa answered in the affirmative. "Our oceangoing canoes were like floating farms, filled with people, livestock, and plants. The crops were kept alive with rainwater gathered from the large scooplike sails. Often the people went thirsty so that the plants could live. When the voyagers arrived, they cleared land and planted. As you can see, our crops have done well. So have we."

He felt pride as he went on to describe how the descendants of the voyagers had extended their farms inland from the coast as more and more land was cleared. He revealed how the land divisions were organized, with a farming and fishing community on the edge of the sea, and a sister community inland, devoted entirely to farming and livestock, supplemented to some extent by hunting. The Ennus' ears perked up.

"The hunters usually live with their families in their own small villages at the edge of the fields or within the forest itself. They are very independent people and do largely what they want, although they are responsible to the chief of their land division. It is often they who discover new *siti* sites as they search the forest for game, medicinal plants, feathers, and timber."

As they walked down the north road toward the town, commoners began to wave and smile from their work in the fields as they recognized Nainoa. Some approached and greeted him warmly, taking his hand in both of theirs and bowing with respect. He knew them all. As clerk to the director, he had been responsible for much of the administration of the huge estate. As he asked for news of their families and the current year's harvest, the farmers looked at the Ennu curiously, regarding their big dogs uneasily. Nainoa informed them that his companions were visitors from the east, the descendants of the once-great North Americans. The peasants' eyes grew wide with surprise at these words, commenting to one another on the momentous nature of this discovery.

As Nainoa repeated these words for each new group of listeners, his explanation grew longer and more elaborate as he sought to invest his companions with status. By the time they reached the town's edge, he was describing William as the chief of his people and a powerful *kahuna* healer and Zaki as heir apparent. The commoners looked at the Ennu with respect and deference at these words, commenting that his return in such esteemed company was most fortuitous. Each group lowered their eyes as they revealed news of the director's illness. He felt their concern and their fear and recalled the hunters' suspicions. If the rumors were correct, there were dark forces at work—forces to be feared.

A considerable crowd had gathered at the town's edge, among whom Nainoa saw a group of servants from the chief's household. When they recognized him, they ran toward him, but stopped at an ominous rumble from the Ennu dogs. Nainoa asked Zaki to hold them, then walked to meet his friends, embracing each one warmly. Tears flowed copiously as their phrases of greeting and concern jumbled together in his mind.

"It is so good to see you. We thought you were dead. Have you heard the news of the civil war's outcome? We are finally rid of that rotten bunch from the south. Chief Kaneohe is overjoyed at the news of your return. He wishes to receive you and your visitors immediately. He is also very ill and has not responded to treatment. We are all concerned."

As his colleagues' eyes turned toward his companions and their dogs with interest, they slowly fell silent. Nainoa made the introductions once more, everyone within earshot hanging on every word. As he spoke of William's abilities as a medicine man, the people's expressions of interest sharpened and gained formality. *Kahuna* healers were most highly revered. They were also accorded a good deal of awe and social distance because of their abilities to access the supernatural realms, and Nainoa realized that he had found the perfect way to infuse William and Zaki with status.

A man named Koma, the highest-ranking servant present, spoke up. "It is a most favorable omen that you have returned at this time, Nainoa." His eyes shifted toward the Ennu as he continued, "And in such esteemed company." Nainoa translated for William and his son, the crowd gaping at the sound of his alien words. Then Koma smiled warmly and approached the Ennu, took their hands in his, and bowed. The others followed suit, bowing and welcoming the visitors with expressions of goodwill. The Ennu beamed in response and bowed awkwardly in return, thus committing their first social gaffe.

Nainoa was about to explain to William that one bowed only to those of equal or greater rank, then realized that the statement would mean nothing to him. Instead he turned to the assembled servants and raised his voice so that it would carry into the crowd. "Among the Ennu, these men are most highly regarded among their people. They are leaders who possess great knowledge and power. They extend their greetings and goodwill to you all."

The crowd around them heard every word, observed every gesture and facial expression. Nainoa saw those on the edge break off and run for the town, stopping to speak to any who would listen. The news was spreading. It was a good beginning. He turned to the servants and said, "Let us go to the director. Where will he receive us?"

It was at this point that one of the settlement dogs made the mistake of emerging from under a trellis filled with drying gourds and approaching the Ennu dogs curiously. By the time Zaki became aware of what was about to happen, it was too late. Without warning, the three dogs broke free of Zaki's grip and lunged for the unfortunate beast, which was half their size. They had the dog down in an instant, unleashing a collective snarl that scattered the crowd. William and Zaki simply laughed and whistled their beasts off the yelping animal.

Nainoa drew his knife and cut three lengths from the coil of rope around his waist, then asked Zaki to leash the animals before entering the town. It wouldn't do for the dogs to start killing the settlement's livestock. Then he turned to his colleagues and said, "Let us go to the director without delay."

As he spoke, he saw them all looking at his iron knife and spear in silence. "Gifts from the director before my departure," he informed them offhandedly. Something shifted in their eyes as they looked away. His possession of these objects implied much. Among the settlers, only chiefs carried iron weapons.

As they walked toward the hub of the administrative center, the streets of the town were lined with people calling out greetings and expressing gratitude for his safe return. William and Zaki looked with interest at everything they passed. As Nainoa stopped to greet a close friend among the weavers, he showed his companions how cotton yarn was transformed into long strips of cloth that were, in turn, sewn together into clothing. As they passed an odiferous two-wheeled cart drawn by two commoners, Nainoa explained that the human and animal waste it contained was being taken to the fields to be used as fertilizer. William said nothing but eyed the vehicle and its large plank wheels with great interest. As they walked along the edge of an outdoor market, the old hunter suddenly stopped and stared in blank astonishment. Nainoa began to describe the function of the sprawling market before a comment from William revealed what had actually stopped him: The Ennu had simply never seen so many people in one place before.

On their final approach to the hub, they encountered a party of chiefs descending the stone stairway that led to the administrative center above. Nainoa swiftly informed the Ennu of the necessary protocol and drew them aside, dropping his eyes and bowing his head to let the group pass. He felt distaste as he did so, realizing the effects of his year of freedom from the caste system that determined political and social rank in the settlements. As the chiefs passed, they suddenly halted, and a voice Nainoa knew well cut through the silence.

"Well, it is Nainoa, returned from the dead." He felt a chill as he looked up. It was Chief Paleko, the priest that he had seen in his visionary visit. He said nothing until invited to speak, as custom required. The priest glanced down at William and looked him over before glancing at Zaki, who was holding the dogs on their leashes. "Who are these people with you?"

"Visitors from the east, Chief Paleko," Nainoa replied, speaking with formal courtesy and saying as little as possible.

"Yes, I've heard," the priest replied, his voice expressing arrogant disdain. Nainoa glanced at his friends uneasily. William and Zaki had not dropped their eyes and were regarding the man and his attire with open curiosity. Although not as tall as Nainoa, the priest's crest of hair, bodily girth, and dyed cloak made him a most imposing figure. The other chiefs in attendance were silent, regarding the travelers with expressions that betrayed nothing.

"They look like commoners," Paleko observed, his sardonic tone conveying distaste. "But these dogs have possibilities." As he took a step forward and raised his hand to point at them, the three animals let out snarls that stopped the priest in his tracks. Prepared this time, Zaki held them easily as they lunged.

Paleko stepped back in haste, almost falling as he tripped on his own cloak. The other chiefs with him smiled in amusement, then quickly resumed expressions of studied indifference as the priest glanced at them in annoyance. Throughout, William continued his observations of the man before him, his dark eyes looking directly into those of the priest. Paleko evidently found this unsettling. He turned to his retinue and said, "Come, we have more important issues to deal with today."

Nainoa and his companions watched them depart, then William turned to him and said, "We talked once about people who have dark shapes to their spirits. There goes one." Koma, who had not understood William's words, said in hushed tones, "Paleko is a bad one. He is jealous of your close relationship with Chief Kaneohe. Watch out for him, Nainoa." Then the servant looked at the Ennu approvingly, adding, "But you have returned with allies, I think." The man's eyes dropped to include the dogs. "Powerful allies."

High Chief John Kaneohe received the travelers in the large anteroom of his personal residence. The sliding doors were open and the stone garden could be seen beyond the wide porch. Three of the chief's senior wives were present, as were a number of their older children. Also in attendance was his immediate staff, an entourage of subchiefs and senior servants almost sixty strong. Nainoa's eyes widened in surprise as he discerned the imposing figure of High Chief Kilipiano Kaneohe, the director's older brother, who lived in the port and who was in charge of the entire land division. Close to a hundred people were present, seated on platforms of varying levels. Nainoa knew them all. As their collective attention fastened upon him, their *mana* was palpable.

Chief Kaneohe was propped up on the woven mats and cushions of the large central platform. His skin had a waxy yellowish tint, his eyes were shiny, and his face was gaunt. He looked feverish. The seriousness of his condition was reflected in the presence of two renowned *kahuna* healers from the capital, High Chief Pita Wilipaki and his wife, High Chiefess Lowena Kahalopuna, the governor's oldest daughter and the highest-ranking person present. The director smiled as Nainoa prostrated himself in silence, touching his forehead to the floor. Then Nainoa rose to his knees and, as was customary, waited for his chief to invite him to speak.

"You have no idea how glad I am to see you, Nainoa," the chief exclaimed informally in a slightly breathy voice. Long moments passed as the two men assessed each other in silence. Then the chief smiled and said with more formality, "In anticipation of your accomplishments and in honor of our guests from the east"—he directed a weak smile at the Ennu—"I hereby formally adopt you into my lineage and raise your rank to chiefly status. Your *galana*, your rank, will be determined shortly. Your name will henceforth be recorded as Ali'i Nainoa Kaneohe." The director looked at his elder brother and received a nod of approval, then turned to the secretary to his left and said, "So let it be written." Then he raised his voice and addressed the room at large. "All who are gathered here are witnesses to my words. All of your names will be included in the account recorded in the histories of our people. Is there any who objects?"

Silence. The ailing chief then turned to Chief Wilipaki and said, "The ceremony will be carried out at a later time. You will see to it, Wilipaki, will you not?" The tall, lean gray-haired man with a trim white beard bowed his assent, directing an alert, friendly glance at Nainoa.

Nainoa looked around the silent room. All eyes were upon him. He felt light-headed as the full implication of the chief's words sank in. Again his eyes swept the assembly and saw smiles growing everywhere. He gathered himself and replied with formality.

"My gratitude for the honor you have given me is unbounded, sir. I shall continue to serve you in any capacity of which you might have need." Then he smiled and adopted informal speech. "My heart, too, rejoices at being in your presence after so long, sir. I have an interesting story to tell." Everyone relaxed.

"I could use a good story," the high chief replied. "But first bathe and refresh yourselves. You smell of the forest, Nainoa, of wood smoke and adventure. I'm envious. Go with your companions and restore your bodies. Take some food at the *mua;* the men's house has missed your presence, and the breadfruit are in season."

The chief looked queasy as he glanced at the servant Koma. "Chief Nainoa's cottage has been waiting for his return. Take bedding from the depository and make our adventurers comfortable there. Give them proper clothing befitting their rank—cloaks and pants from my personal stores." The chief's eyes flicked over the Ennu. "Convey my respectful greetings to your friends, Nainoa. They are honored guests in my household and under my protection for as long as they choose to reside here."

The cries of keening gulls could be heard through the open sliding doors. Chief Kaneohe smiled and said, "You see, the birds agree with these proceedings—a good omen." Everyone murmured approvingly. Then the ailing man spoke to the room at large. "Knowing this man as I do, I suspect that the account we are about to hear will be richly detailed. It will doubtless take many days to hear in its entirety. We will meet for the first session this evening at sunset." The chief suddenly looked ashen and exhausted.

Then he redirected his attention to the man before him and said warmly, "Welcome home, Chief Nainoa Kaneohe."

CHAPTER 7

The Kahuna

T HE KEENING OF seabirds came in through the partially open
sliding glass door of my cabin at Esalen, drawing my awareness
back across the interface. The first light of dawn was just
breaking. I got up, slipped on my clothes, and went down to the rocky
beach below the retreat center. For more than an hour I sat in meditation, watching the waves as memories of the future moved through my
mind.

I felt very emotional during the day that followed and sought
solitude in the hot springs between the training sessions, closing my
eyes as I steeped in the hot water, digesting all that I had experienced
the night before. Having had such intimate access to Nainoa's
thoughts and emotions, hopes and fears, and knowing how difficult
upward social mobility was in his society, I was aware of the magnitude of his achievement in becoming a chief. Now he would be able to

gather social and political power, enabling him to achieve far more in every direction. I was absolutely thrilled for him.

My celebratory thoughts were offset by the deep concern I felt for Chief Kaneohe. The man had looked seriously ill. I am not a medical doctor, but my many years in remote regions of Africa had allowed me to acquire a basic working knowledge of medical diagnosis and practice. I knew that the chief could have any number of things, from a parasitic infection to cancer. I recalled how he had appeared—his gaunt face, the yellowish cast to his skin, the fever, his barely concealed nausea, his obvious fatigue. I needed more information. I wondered if my subconscious *ku* had picked up something of which my conscious mind was unaware. I decided to ask it.

Knowing how responsive this aspect of my self is to nature, I opened my eyes and savored the wild seascapes of the Big Sur coast for long moments. It was midafternoon, and the hazy winter light was soft. I listened to the roar of the surf and watched the waves explode on the rocks below. There was a sea otter out there in the kelp, and pelicans were flying in formation over the waves. The sky over the wooded hills was a deep cerulean blue, and high overhead the turkey vultures were cruising the coast highway looking for roadkill. I inhaled the salty air and drank in the stark physical beauty of my surroundings while I simmered in the hot pool.

I closed my eyes and addressed my *ku* directly, asking for information about Chief Kaneohe's illness. Almost immediately an image arose in my mind, a rather horrifying one—a memory of my mother's lifeless body in a coffin in Zurich, her skin turned yellow by hepatitis. A surge of unease rocked me as I understood. It was a communication, a symbolic one, from this deeper level of myself. The implication was clear. I recalled the chief's physical appearance and admitted that it was possible that he had hepatitis. The man did look jaundiced. My feelings of concern mounted. If the man's liver suffered extensive damage and he went into a coma, as my mother had done, he was finished. This would leave Nainoa bereft of his sponsor, a most serious loss for him. I wondered if this was why the chief had elevated him to chiefly status before hearing the story of his walk. Perhaps he had had a premonition of his impending demise.

I got out of the pool, pulled on my robe, and left the baths to prepare for the drumming session that evening, filled with purpose. I concentrated on an interesting and unexpected discovery I had made earlier in the week: I had more than one spirit helper. While deep in the expanded state, they had come, one at a time, establishing contact and building relationships. Most had been animal spirits or some combination of animal and human, but several had seemed to be plantlike. I had learned that each was skilled at accomplishing different, specific tasks. I had sensed the spirit stone among them as well, its awareness remote but watchful.

When the session began that evening, I closed my eyes and induced the sensations of power within my body, then visualized myself traveling to the *heiau* next to Kealakekua Bay. Once there, I extended an invitation to all of my helping spirits to join me. As their watchful presences became manifest, one after the other, I could feel the sensations of power in my body increase by increments. When all were present, I explained why I had summoned them. I discussed the nature of the chief's illness, described his location in space and time, and asked for information on how to proceed.

The answer was immediate and unanimous. The chief's personal power supply had to be augmented. He urgently needed a strong infusion of *mana* to help his body overcome the illness and assist his *ku* in repairing and regenerating his damaged liver. My scientific side was monitoring all this, as always, and concurred that this course seemed logical. If the man's immune system could be enhanced, he had a chance. I addressed the presences within my mind and requested that they access such power and direct it in a healing capacity toward the ailing chief. I felt their agreement.

I decided to throw in my own efforts as well and drew on the *mana* that permeated the *heiau* and its surroundings, intentionally increasing the power sensations within myself to a level that I could just barely stand, causing my body to vibrate uncontrollably. I held the state for as long as I could, collecting as large a charge of *mana* as possible, then I formed an image of Chief Kaneohe within my mind and willed it to him with a whispered prayer on his behalf. The sense of release was perceptible. The sensations receded as the energy departed, allowing my body to relax once again.

I then turned my attention to the entities within my mind and asked with some anxiousness what else could be done. The leopard man approached and looked directly into my eyes, squinting catlike and pushing his head against me, projecting reassurance. I experienced a sense of relief, an emotional calming. The project of saving the chief was now in their capable hands. I sensed completion and thanked my spirit helpers for their participation, honoring them for their roles in this healing ceremony. Immediately I felt their withdrawal and shifted the primary focus of my awareness to my body, following the drumming sound back into the workshop room at Esalen. When the session came to a close, I felt much better.

I returned to Sacramento at the end of the week feeling very much empowered. It was as if I had gained something of great value—as though I possessed a great secret that only I knew about. This provided quite an ego boost for a short while. Unfortunately, the feeling dropped away precipitously as I remembered my dilemma once more. What of my own future? Could I take the knowledge and skills I had gained and use them to help me find a job?

I received a call from a local college shortly after my return. They needed someone to teach an anthropology class during the spring semester. By chance, the same institution was intending to hire a full-time physical anthropology instructor for the coming fall. The coincidence seemed synchronistic, and I applied, filled with renewed enthusiasm. Perhaps my luck had changed.

I made it to the interview stage, but I didn't get the job. For the first time in my life, I became deeply depressed. My family was now in dire financial need, and Jill, who was overworked and underpaid in her hospital job, suggested gently that I give up anthropology and find work outside of academia. I began to read the want ads in the newspaper, looking for positions in which my advanced degrees in anthropology and biology would be an asset. I applied to the Department of Fish and Game. They weren't interested. I investigated Caltrans, the state's transportation department, which employed archeologists to do site surveys, but California was in the midst of an economic recession and there were no positions. I considered becoming a high-school teacher, but having always taught at the college or university level, I didn't have the prerequisite education courses or teaching credential.

My despair grew.

Jill had been monitoring my sinking emotional state with concern, and when I voiced considerable disappointment at not getting the job, she suggested we go to see someone she knew down in the San Francisco Bay area, a Hawaiian *kahuna* named Nelita Anderson who had been raised in the Ka'u district of the island of Hawai'i, where she had been trained by her aunt to work directly with the physical body, among other things.

Initially I felt hesitant about talking with her, because I was aware that many Hawaiians harbor strong resentment toward outsiders trespassing into their mystical traditions. My hesitancy was balanced by my curiosity to hear what this *kahuna* would say about my visionary experiences, however, so we packed the kids into the car and headed down the freeway to Nelita's house in Fremont, where she was living with her husband, a physicist. As we drove, Jill described her first meeting with the *kahuna*.

"I met Nelita at a house on the beach in Oceanside, north of San Diego, back in 1990," she began. "On that day, I arrived at the house to find my friend Carolyn talking with a rather diminutive woman who had short hair and was dressed in Western clothes. She didn't look Hawaiian, so I assumed she was there to be treated. When she introduced herself to me, saying, 'Hi, I'm Nelita,' she saw my look of surprise and burst out laughing, saying, 'What? You were expecting a great big Hawaiian woman wearing a muumuu?' This amused her greatly and she laughed and laughed. I liked her immediately, and we sat and talked for a while about nothing in particular. But I was aware at the time that Nelita was assessing me.

"It was very interesting," Jill continued. "She had me lie down on a massage table. I didn't feel anything in particular when she placed her hands on me, but I gradually became aware of a subtle current of energy moving between her hands and through my body. It was as though one hand was sending and the other receiving. Nelita talked to me in a quiet voice, startling me with her intuitive perceptions. I remember that I felt very good in a dreamy sort of way. When the treatment was over, she placed her hands in a bowl of water. When I came out into the living room, I sat down in a chair and automatically started to cross my legs. Nelita immediately stopped me, saying that would disrupt the treatment. I felt very clear and sat quietly, listening as Nelita continued her conversation with Carolyn. She kept glancing over at me, as though she was continuing to assess me, as if she was checking the results of her work."

On our arrival at Nelita's house in Fremont, we were greeted immediately by our hostess. She invited me to play with the children outside in the yard while she worked on Jill. An hour later, a groggy, smiling Jill emerged, and she asked Nelita, "Are you going to work on Hank now?" The *kahuna* looked me over carefully, then smiled. "I don't need to work on him," she said. "There's nothing wrong with him. He's in great shape. He needs to talk."

I was startled by her intuitive perception. Nelita picked this up and laughed, then gestured gracefully and invited me in. As we sat down in her living room, I was very much aware that I could feel her personal power, her *mana*. This woman radiated energy.

I opened by saying that I had had some strange experiences while I was living in Hawai'i in the late 1980s and that I would be most grateful for any insights she might have that would help me understand them more fully. She watched me with interest and smiled, but said nothing.

Cautiously I began with my initial encounter with the dark guardian spirit almost ten years before, while I was still living in California. Much to my surprise, she knew exactly who I was talking about. I then told her about my visionary experiences in Kona and about my curious relationship with Nainoa. I included details of the inner conflicts generated by these episodes, relating how my scientific side had struggled to accept them as real. When I recounted how I had become the *kahu* of the spirit stone at Kealakekua Bay, she threw back her head with glee and shouted, "I love it!" Encouraged by her response, I opened up.

For the next two hours I gave Nelita an abridged version of the entire story. She said little, but her eyes alternately clouded and cleared as she listened.

Finally, when I finished, she said, "There are some things we cannot fully understand, Hank. You may never fully comprehend why these experiences happened to you. It's possible that your ancestry includes individuals who had the ability to vision in this way. They may have been persons with psychic awareness, or they may have been dreamers, or both. In the old days, most Hawaiian families included at least one person through whom their *aumakua*, their ancestral spirit source, could speak and offer help during times of trouble. The fact that your visionary states happen just before dawn is not unusual, either. Hawaiian *kahunas* often do their main work during this time.

"Visions can occur at any time, to anyone, even to nonpsychic people. Everyone dreams, and it is during our dreaming that important information is often received. It is at this time that the *uhane*, the thinking conscious soul, can drift free of the body and have adventures. Often it is during our dreaming that we make contact with our ancestral *aumakua* spirit most directly. In old Hawai'i, when people were in need, they prayed to their *aumakua*, asking for information to be revealed in their dreaming. Upon awakening, they studied their dreams carefully to find the answer. But I think that what you are experiencing is different.

"Among the Hawaiians, the ability to foresee future events fell within the expertise of the *kaula*, the prophets. Sometimes they had visions, *akaku*; sometimes they heard voices, *ulaleo*. Many *kaula* were recognized at an early age and received special training. Many became *kahuna*. Often such people had a special relationship with specific deities. On the island of Hawai'i, many became dedicated to Pele, the volcano spirit. Today we would call such people psychics. Unfortunately, you grew up in a society that knows very little about psychic awareness." She broke off, shrugging as if to say that such things happen.

"People with psychic awareness who are also *kaula* possess a great gift. Some read tarot cards or throw the I Ching to discern future events, and these are very useful and powerful tools. But others simply know. The information just comes to them. This is not something they learn to do. They are born with the ability.

"Your relationships with your spirits are most important because they are undoubtedly assisting you in many ways. There are very few sources today who have direct experience and knowledge of the spirit world, and among these, few can take the rawness of that dimension and give it form or put it into words." She smiled at me. "The deep prayer is, for most, a silent one.

"But you are highly educated," she went on. "You are a trained scientist, no less, with impressive academic credentials. You are also an accomplished teacher with strong skills of communication. It is tempting to observe that you may have been given these experiences for a reason." Nelita paused and looked at me for several moments, as if to emphasize with her eyes the gravity of her words.

"Your relationship with your spirit stone is most interesting as well. Stones were traditionally of great importance to the Hawaiians, and it is well known even today that spirits can reside within stones. Any stone can be inhabited by an *aumakua* or a deity, and there are many stories of how such spirit-imbued stones often chose the individual who became their *kahu*. Often these stones revealed themselves to that person in their dreaming. It is also known that such stones became quite attached to their caretakers, and that they often revealed special information to them. Even today, there are families in Hawai'i who have sacred relationships with stones."

Suddenly there were a thousand things I wanted to discuss with her, but the afternoon was advancing and when Jill came in with the children in search of something to drink, Nelita's words drifted into silence. The children walked up to me and announced they were hungry, causing Nelita to laugh merrily. I sensed that our discussion was over, but I also knew that a corner had been turned. I had given an account of my mystic experiences to this *kahuna,* and in return she had offered me a great gift—the acceptance and validation of my experiences. Deep within myself, I felt something shift and settle into place.

As we made our preparations to depart, Nelita approached me and put a dark reddish-brown piece of lava into my hands. "This is one of Pele's stones from Ka'u, from the place where I grew up." Her eyes twinkled. "This is for you."

I felt greatly honored as I took the rough chunk of rock from her. It felt warm. As I held the stone reverently and looked at the two women regarding me, I abruptly felt the sensations of power appear in my body at low levels of intensity, a mild vibrational buzz accompanied by a ringing hiss in my ears. Simultaneously I saw a vague but distinct outline of light around the women's forms. Startled, I glanced around the room and perceived that I was seeing everything with remarkable clarity. I realized that I had received *mana* through the stone. Whether it was Nelita's *mana* or Pele's, I could not tell. Unspoken thoughts raced through my mind as Nelita beamed warmly and patted me affectionately on the arm.

As I headed back up the freeway to Sacramento, I thought about my ancestral lineage. My mother was a strikingly beautiful, rather childlike woman who became enamored of mysticism later in life. She found a spiritual teacher, began to practice meditation with great fervor, and became the sole vegetarian in a family of dedicated carnivores.[1] Unfortunately, my parents' marriage was filled with discord, and her spiritual pursuits seemed to separate them even further. Not surprisingly at the time, my reaction to her guru was not a positive one.

I was away at a prep school when they decided to divorce. My father remained in New York and remarried about two years later. My mother took my younger brother and moved to California, where she changed her name, took up painting, and had a series of relationships. She finally married and picked up her spiritual practice where she had left off. The guru became a regular visitor in her house, staying as a guest for weeks or even months at a time.[2]

At forty-eight years of age, while living in Switzerland with her second husband and her guru, she became ill with hepatitis, went into a coma, and died seven days later. I was told by her Swiss doctors that her rigidly vegetarian diet had contributed to her untimely demise. My opinion of gurus and the spiritual life sank to an all-time low.

I learned years later that my father, even though he never came to terms with my mother's spiritualism, had a mystical side that he never fully understood. A boyhood friend, Steve McAllister, told me this during a visit to California many years after my father died. As we filled each other in on all the major steps, and missteps, of our lives over a bottle of champagne in my backyard, Steve turned to me, saying he had something interesting to tell me.

"As you well know," Steve began, "our fathers were the very best of friends." I concurred, mentally excavating a long series of cherished memories of the two men, both dead now for many years.

"Well, one night back in the late 1950s or early 1960s," he continued, "the two of them apparently had a long talk. It was at the end of one of those long summer evenings when everyone had had a lot to drink. It was very late, the time of night when close friends often do a lot of soul sharing, and on that particular evening, your father told my father about a strange visionary experience he had had: a vivid, dream-like memory of being a swordsman in the employ of one of the kings of France during the seventeenth century."

I sat very still as Steve said these words, and abruptly felt a surge of the sensations of power. I glanced at the spirit stone, which was near us, with growing excitement.

"Your father was very explicit about both the nature and the content of this strange experience, even revealing the man's name as well as the name of the town where he was living at that time. I don't remember those details now, of course," Steve finished, "but I do recall that your father talked about being killed in a duel in this town and even described the type of sword his opponent had used to do the deed. My father was very impressed at both the intensity and the obvious sincerity with which your father revealed this strange story to him. He told me of this conversation many years after your father died, when he was reminiscing about him one evening. I've never forgotten it."

I drained my glass with a gulp, my mind racing. The information suggested that there was a genetic predisposition in my lineage toward visionary experience, one that included time traveling. My father had been a lawyer, a very private man who had never shared this part of his life with me. The blood hissed in my ears. I glanced again at the stone, thinking about the connection between my father's experiences and my own. Was I predisposed for these encounters? The question still remained unanswered.

As I drove the family back to Sacramento, feeling charged from my visit with the *kahuna,* I felt as though a rebirth was near, and in fact it was.

Within a couple of weeks, I was teaching a couple of anthropology classes at nearby American River College and was then invited to teach two more for the fall semester. By luck, I also managed to line up an additional two at Sierra College, about half an hour's drive up the freeway. I became a part-time teacher, a life I still lead today. I work with no benefits, no paid vacations, and no guarantees that I will be hired to teach for an additional semester.

Fortunately, the financial and psychological hardships of this rather exploitative dynamic have been balanced by my relationship with my students. Each class has provided me with an ongoing confirmation that teaching is my gift, and every semester I watch my students respond and grow, a most gratifying experience. It was during this time that I found the words credited to Mōshi that preface this book. I photocopied the quote and fastened it to my refrigerator, where I would see it every day—words of comfort and of affirmation.

During the months that followed my visit with the *kahuna*, I continued to feel deep concern about Chief Kaneohe's condition and about Nainoa's reentry into his own society. My personal and professional lives were full, however, and I had no new expanded states. Then in August, almost six months later, I regained the contact, and once again it occurred in response to my being in dynamic association with nature.

Since the middle 1970s I have been in the habit of visiting an old resort called Tassajara Hot Springs, located in the rugged mountains behind the Big Sur coast. The San Francisco Zen Center acquired the property in the 1960s and converted it into a Buddhist mountain monastery closed to the outside world during the fall and spring practice periods. But during the summers, paying guests are invited to visit. Jill and I had not been to Tassajara since our move to Hawai'i in 1985, and so we decided to take the children there for a short holiday. I recalled a visionary experience I had had during a *sesshin*, or Zen Buddhist retreat, at Wood Valley Temple in Hawai'i and was curious to see if I could make contact with Nainoa while at Tassajara.

On the morning of our departure, while Jill and I were packing the car, I made a large mug of tea and walked out into the backyard, where the spirit stone stood under the grape arbor. I sat down in a chair and regarded the *pohaku* thoughtfully. The grapevine was beginning to lose its leaves in response to the change of seasons, but a month before, it had been loaded with clusters of pale green grapes. One day the owner of the property had come over to make minor repairs to the sprinkler system that watered the grass, and upon seeing the grapevine, his mouth had dropped open.

"Well, I'll be," he had said. "I planted that grapevine almost twenty years ago, and it has never borne fruit." Then he turned to me and asked good-naturedly what I had done to it.

I had eyed the stone positioned under the vine and mentioned offhandedly that maybe it was my sculpture, that maybe the vine responded to the presence of fine art. He looked at the craggy chunk of lava doubtfully and we both chuckled appreciatively, and that had been the end of it. But once again, I chose to interpret this event as oblique confirmation of the presence of large amounts of *mana*—generative life force—associated with the *akua* that resided within the stone.

I finished my tea and let my attention rest on the stone for a while. Then I got up and placed my hands on its rough surface. I greeted the spirit within it and related where I was about to go. I asked it to accompany me and to help facilitate a connection with my esteemed descendant. I waited but detected no perceptible answer, no feelings of force. I was preoccupied with the upcoming trip, so I got up, bowed to the stone, and finished loading the car.

We headed south into the mountains east of Big Sur, into wild country inhabited only by animals and the spirits of the paleo-Indians who had once resided there. After we left the paved highway twelve miles inland from the coast, I ascended a steep dirt road for eight miles in first gear, crossing a heavily wooded ridge at the five-thousand-foot level before descending eight more miles down an even steeper grade into a landscape of endless mountains and bottomless ravines. At the end of the road, we parked the car among a cluster of others before the impressive wooden gates of the Zen Mountain Center.

The day was hot and breathless as we checked in at the office and were directed to our cabin, one of the original wood-and-stone buildings built along the stream. There was no electricity, no television, not even a telephone. There were kerosene lamps to provide light at night, and the only sounds were the occasional raucous calls of jays and the omnipresent murmur of the creek chuckling among the stones in its bed. The aromatic scent of the alders and sycamores drifted through the cabin, contributing to the sense of peace and tranquility.

After a sumptuous vegetarian lunch of soup, salad, and homemade bread, we took the children to the large swimming pool beyond the vegetable gardens, where they swam all afternoon. I spent much of the time in reverie, remembering former visits to this place and recalling the people I had met here over the years. In the late afternoon we heard the temple bell, and we withdrew to the open courtyard between the kitchen and the dining hall, joining the Zen students for tea and refreshment.

We took the children to the communal baths before dinner, alternately simmering in the natural hot springs, steaming in the steam room, and cooling off in the stream among the rocks under the sheltering trees before returning to our cabin and dressing for dinner. The children were enchanted by the place, as we had thought they would be.

The communal tables on the wide screened porch were covered with red tablecloths and lit by kerosene lamps in the fading light of the day. Jill and I ate heartily of the gourmet vegetarian food. The children, unfamiliar with many of the delicacies, stuffed themselves on salad, bread, and dessert. As we ate and exchanged pleasantries with the other guests at our table, my eyes drifted out through the screens to the rocky, fern-covered slopes above the stream. I felt a sense of presence, a perceptive watchfulness that caused me to wonder if the leopard man was out there, watching me eat and waiting for me to come out to play.

After dinner we walked through the twilight, inspecting the gardens, before reading stories to the children and tucking them into bed. They were asleep within moments, so Jill and I drifted back to the baths, enjoying an intimate soak in a private tub and cooling off in the stream while bats flitted across the stars. All around us were massive, stony mountains standing in expectant, monumental silence, as if listening for incoming messages from the universe. When we returned to the cabin, we checked on the children, slipped into bed, and blew out the lamp. I was profoundly relaxed by the hot water and dropped down into sleep almost immediately.

About four o'clock in the morning, one of the Zen students ran through the center in the darkness, ringing a bell to announce the first period of *zazen* (sitting meditation). The children woke somewhat alarmed, and we explained to them that guests were free to participate with the students, if they wished. As Jill and the children drifted back into sleep, I remained awake, listening to their soft breathing. Instead of going to the meditation hall, I decided to attempt the luminous emptiness of no-mind right there in bed.

Thoughts appeared. I watched them until they departed, then focused my awareness on my breathing, counting each inflow, each outflow. My mind became still and I succeeded in dropping down into the silence. Our cabin was not far from the *zendo* (the meditation hall), and when I heard the bell sound at the end of the first period, I emerged from meditation and decided to try to induce the expanded state in which I connect with Nainoa.

I accessed my *ku* but did not succeed. Instead, memories of long-forgotten people and events appeared ghostlike in my mind's eye, proceeding in sequence, one after the other. I remembered having similar experiences while on expedition in Africa, nights spent in wakefulness, face-to-face with wraiths of people from my past with whom I carried on long conversations. When the bell sounded at the end of the second period, my awareness shifted and my visitors departed.

The family awoke, emerging slowly while I thought about what had just occurred. I had gone in the opposite direction, into the past instead of the future. The children jumped into bed with us at this point, terminating speculation. They were quite taken with the communal baths, so back we went, soaking together in one of the long sunken tubs and swimming in the stream before returning to dress for breakfast.

There is a place at Tassajara of which I am very fond, a spot called the Narrows, about half an hour's walk downstream from the center. The children preferred to remain at the swimming pool for the day, so Jill volunteered to stay with them, generously allowing me some private time. I made myself a picnic lunch, slipped a towel and some sunscreen into my day pack, and strode past the cabins toward the trees east of the center.

Once out of sight of the buildings, it was as though they no longer existed. The stream snaked back and forth through the trees and boulders, bracketed by the sheer rock walls of the canyon. As I walked through the woods along the rocky trail, I remembered the forest spirit Nainoa had encountered on his long walk. I studied the trees, their greens punctuated by reddening clumps of poison oak and the yellow ocher of grassy swatches dried by the sun. Lizards foraging in the brush resembled small dragons, and occasional turtles, sunning on logs in the stream, watched me as I passed. I caught sight of trout swimming in the pools and felt something shift within me. Once again I sensed the presence of a watchful awareness.

As I crossed and recrossed the stream, following the trail, greeting a familiar meadow and scrambling over a recent rockfall, I was reminded of Nainoa's walk again and again. The bottom of this canyon was much like the one he had climbed to achieve the rim of the barrier, but his was filled with tropical flora and fauna, tree ferns, banyans, and clumps of giant bamboo, while mine was populated by oaks and alders, manzanita and yucca. I passed the spot where Jill and I had seen a rattlesnake years before and mentally replaced it with one of the pale, heavily scaled tropical rattlers of Nainoa's time. As the trail paralleled a long pool, I shivered as a huge anaconda appeared in my mind's eye. I caught myself searching the tree limbs above the stream for iguanas that weren't there, and somewhere inside myself I missed the company of Nainoa's bow and spear.

As my memories continued to shift back and forth between Nainoa's reality and mine, the pervasive sense of presence increased. It was there, just at the edge of my awareness, but my primary focus couldn't quite touch it. By the time I arrived at my destination, however, my *ku* was positively effervescent at being in this wild place once again.

The Narrows derives its name from the narrowed canyon floor with its exposures of smooth, water-scoured rock, providing many comfortable places to sit or lie down. It is a favorite place of both the center's guests and the Zen students, and many local residents from the Monterey-Carmel area sometimes hike in just for the day. The place is remote from any road or settlement, and most visitors simply discard their clothes to swim naked in the stream and sunbathe on the rocks. It was still early in the day, and I found "my spot" unoccupied, a naturally shaped stone bench under an alder tree where I always sat when I was here. I settled in, hung my pack on the tree, took off my clothes, and applied some sunscreen. Then I walked barefoot across the smooth rocks to the stream, bent, and drank deeply from the cool water. I splashed some water on my face, then reclined in a shallow depression in the stone, closed my eyes, and let the sound of the water sink into me.

I remained at the Narrows for much of the day, moving from one spot to another, alternately sunbathing near the stream or sitting in the shade under my tree, writing in my journal or reading from a book. When I got too hot, I swam in the deep pool below the waterfall, watching dragonflies and water ouzels while my mind moved restlessly from one subject to another. I spent a lot of time just listening to the water while I let my eyes unfocus into the foliage of the trees, watching patterns emerge and disappear in the light breeze that came down the canyon, allowing my glance to move up across the towering mosaic of the rock walls into the deep blue of the sky.

In the midafternoon I slipped into a light trance state, and the rushing-water sound suddenly increased as my sense of hearing amplified. Abruptly all of my senses expanded, and I saw everything around me with great clarity. At that moment I connected with the mysterious presence I had been feeling all morning and recognized it as the life force permeating and flowing through this powerful place—a force that resolved itself in strange shapes and forms, humans and birds, water and fish, rocks and trees, and spirits, lots of spirits.

I heard them speak in the whisper of the wind, the gurgling of the water, the rustle of a lizard in the leaf litter. I could feel them watching from the brooding shadow of a rock overhang, the darkness of the pool, the hollow in a tree, and I perceived quite clearly that these entities were benevolent and that the impulse I was perceiving in the natural world was positive. I understood that our human spirits were inexorably woven together with theirs in a complex physical, mental, and spiritual whole—a multileveled, multifaceted collective awareness that was growing, changing, and evolving in a complex cocreative process. And within me arose the certainty that the vast, composite singularity of nature will continue to provide humanity with all the needed essentials as we voyage together toward our destiny within the great pattern of our universe.

In response to these insights, I suddenly felt urges surfacing within me, needs that demanded to be expressed. I felt an incredibly strong impulse to reveal my awareness to the spirits whose watchfulness I felt fastened upon me. I felt the need to honor them and offer my respect and gratitude. I understood in those sun-drenched moments the true nature of ritual and ceremony as well as the veracity of the Eightfold path in Buddhism. I also looked into the darkness that pervades our society and perceived its opposite.

I thought about the rationalized avarice of industrialized humanity and understood quite clearly that if "civilized" man continues to regard nature as a resource to be dominated, subjugated, and modified to suit our purposes, then the compact with these powerful natural forces will be broken. And then there will be no escaping their retribution.

The handwriting is on the wall. If humankind continues to behave like a virus, indiscriminately overreproducing, devouring and destroying the environment that provides us with food to eat, water to drink, and air to breathe, we're done for. And I perceived in those moments that a test of unbelievable magnitude is almost upon us. If we fail this test, neither the sanctified misunderstanding of our mainstream religions nor the misguided ideology of our political and economic systems will save us. If we fail the test, our place within the great pattern will have to wait for the evolution of another sentient species, perhaps millions or hundreds of millions of years down the road.

At this moment a Steller's jay landed in the manzanita bush next to me and called raucously, drawing my awareness back into the now. I reached into my lunch bag, extracted a plum, and gave him half. The bird bore it away with shrieks of triumph, attracting other jays.

I recalled William's animist worldview, his profound understanding that everything has a spirit aspect, even nonliving things such as rocks and hills. The Ennu believe that because everything has a spirit, everything has a certain capacity for action as well. They consider each person, animal, tree, and plant, each cliff face, mountain, boulder, and pebble to be holy, intelligent, and filled with mystical power and vitality. The Ennu feel that each creature or thing has tasks unique to its being, and the correct performance of these tasks is what keeps the universe functioning in life-enhancing ways. In this manner, order and balance are maintained, and disorder, including illness, is kept within bounds.

The Ennu believe strongly that if any among the multitudinous forms fails to meet its obligations, all will suffer. Human beings in particular are required to live in ways that will foster this universal order and balance. They feel that a person's every action, thought, intention, and feeling contributes either to the greater good of the universe or to its suffering. And so, within every aspect of a person's life, one's proper activity lies in maintaining and furthering this order and balance.

My ruminations were disrupted when I spied a snake in the pool. I got down from my rocky perch and approached the brown serpent, which was about two feet long. I have always been very fond of reptiles and recognized it as a water snake. It dived and proceeded to glide among the rocks on the bottom, hunting for small fish.

Cautiously I waded into the pool to see it better. The snake continued toward me, flushing small minnows and striking at them as I stood knee-deep in the pool. It surfaced about a foot away and regarded me with its glassy, expressionless stare. I remained motionless. After several minutes the snake swam gracefully forward and wound a coil around my right leg just below the knee. I didn't move. After staring up at me for several long moments, it turned its head to look around the pool's edge. The forest was silent, broken only by the sound of the water. Then the snake gave my leg a slight squeeze and released me, swimming away toward the reeds at the end of the pool.

I stood in the pool lost in thought. I chose to interpret this strange interaction as contact, and considering my ruminations of the past half hour, such contact with a wild creature filled me with a sense of wonder. "The serpent of wisdom," I thought, remembering another snake and another pool. Silently I expressed my gratitude to the spirits of the place and was rewarded by catching a last glimpse of the snake as it turned and regarded me once more before disappearing downstream. At times like this, it was difficult to deny that magic is real.

The changing light and lengthening shadows revealed the passing of the day, and after a last swim in the pool, I dressed and returned up the trail feeling blessed by the day's events. I walked through the breathless hush of late summer, recrossed the stream twice, and returned to the center. When I found my family at the pool, Jill smiled at me warmly and asked, "Have an interesting day?" Our daughters called, "Come for a swim!"

On the third morning of our stay, the air temperature was decidedly cool when the four o'clock bell passed our cabin. I let my mind drift into watchful, meditative calm and again attempted *zazen* in a prostrate position. I let my awareness follow my breathing, and was just achieving the state of inner emptiness when a memory suddenly appeared—a recollection of something that happened in an expedition field camp out in the deserts of southwestern Ethiopia many years before, the time that I had the flying dreams.

These experiences began one night when the air was unexpectedly cool, and I recalled having the same rush of heightened feeling that I now experience during my expanded states. As the intense somatic sensations emerged within me, I felt like I was levitating in my tent. I remembered slowly drifting upward to bump along the ridgepole until I looked down and saw my motionless body below me.

The first time this happened, I experienced quite a shock and immediately zipped back into my body. The dreams occurred frequently thereafter, becoming more and more intense. One evening I drifted through the tent's walls by accident and somehow found myself soaring up and over the camp, flying high in the night sky with great speed. This was an extraordinarily real experience and involved roller-coaster-like flight that produced feelings of extreme euphoria. As I learned by trial and error that I could control my movements, I roared through the starry darkness over the torn trees, impulsively "strafing" the tents of some of my colleagues with joyous abandon.

In retrospect, these experiences resembled what tribal shamans describe as spirit flight, and curiously, there was almost always a feeling of someone or something else being there with me while they were happening, but I was never sure who or what until I discovered by chance that a fellow graduate student was also having these dreams. We had become close friends the previous year, and one morning, as we were covertly discussing the nature of our midnight journeys while brushing our teeth at the water tank, one of the Africans, a Wakamba tribesman named Kaumbulu, walked up to us and said, "Hey, what were you doing flying over my tent last night?"

As I thought about this in my bed at Tassajara, I could still feel the shock produced by the African's words across the intervening years. At that time I was deeply immersed in science, and now I realized I had missed an important opportunity. At that time the inner doorway was beginning to open, but I had not yet been ready to believe in such things as inner doorways, let alone the experiencing of spirits and other levels of reality and time. Yet below these experiences, or perhaps within them, was something else, and now I suddenly remembered what it was and could put it into words—a deep, spiritual connection with that empty, arid land.

One night toward the end of my time in Ethiopia, I drove alone out into the open savanna. About five miles north of camp, I turned off the engine and the lights, got up on the roof of the Land Rover, and just sat there, watching the wind come rushing toward me as long, billowing waves through the pale moonlit ocean of grass. And that night I sensed with a definite certainty that the whole vast, ancient African landscape around me was alive—that it possessed its own form of collective awareness, and like Nainoa in the forest, I became cognizant that night that "it" was aware of me.

I thought about the possible existence of a genetic program enabling visionary experience on the "main menu" of the human species, an old program encoded into our DNA millions of years ago that many humans may still possess as part of their biological heritage. Perhaps this was what was reactivated within me in response to millions of square miles of savanna inhabited by wild animals and traditional people. This was the ancient motherland, the original ecosystem that formed and molded the human species through the initial millions of years of our evolutionary history. This was where humankind's story had begun.

As these memories and thoughts traveled vividly through my conscious awareness in my bed at Tassajara, I realized I was drifting into the past once more. This was not where I wished to go. Cool air flowed through the cabin as I drew the covers closely around me and reversed the directional focus. I accessed my *ku*, requesting the most recent memories of Nainoa's settlement somewhere to the north. He was there now, less than two hundred miles away. As the thoughtform began to take shape, the image of the spirit stone appeared in my mind's eye unexpectedly, and I wondered if Nainoa had seen it since his return.

With that thought, the power sensations appeared within me. They were incredibly strong, causing my body to become rigid as a stick in an instant. As I gasped for breath, the phosphenes began to stream toward me, coalescing into the grid in the distance. It was very fast, and I wondered if I was somehow drawing on the power of this place. The hot spring was less than a hundred yards from the cabin. The water that bubbled from it was heated deep within the earth. A memory of the volcano spirit Pele flitted through my mind.

The shimmering crescent of light appeared and started to open, extending into a fiery ring with a dark center as the points of the arc touched. The sense of movement began, and as I rushed toward the brilliant circle, my last thought was of the spirit stone.

Then thinking stopped as I passed through the doorway in a flash of light and traversed the darkness of the zone of silence in a long instant. A sense of coolness again swept over my body, and the power sensations began to release me from the invisible fist. Disappointed, I thought my mission had failed. It was then that I smelled the wood smoke and opened my eyes.

CHAPTER 8

Fourth Journey: The Healing Ritual

I T WAS THE evening of the day of his return, and Nainoa was seated on a stool along the edge of the large meeting room in the administrative center of the Kaneohe land division. William and Zaki were sitting beside him. The older man's eyes were closed. His hands held his medicine bundle made of tiger skin, within which he kept various objects of power.

The doors were open, allowing the cool night air to enter. Small fires burned in stone bowls around the room's perimeter and aromatic incense smoked from several carefully placed braziers. He watched the assemblage of people taking their places as memories of the day's events moved through his mind.

At the close of their audience with the chief that afternoon, he had taken his companions to his cottage, where they deposited their gear and tied the dogs, providing them with food and water. Servants had arrived with bedding, watching the dogs warily as they arranged sleeping mats, pillows, and woven blankets for the three men. He had then taken William and Zaki to the communal baths, where his increased status was manifested for the first time. As he automatically headed for the servants' quarters, he was gently steered toward the chiefs' bathhouse by Koma and his attendants.

Nainoa and his companions had stripped off their meager clothing in the outer room and washed with heated water before slipping into the room-sized hot pool lined with closely fitted planks of wood. The Ennu had been delighted with this new experience, laughing and luxuriating in the steamy water. Nainoa had showed them how the water temperature was controlled by water fed into the pool through a series of wooden troughs from a heated metal cauldron outside. Flowering gardenia bushes were planted along the pool's outer periphery to provide fragrance. In the midst of examining the construction of the roof, William's mood had suddenly turned serious. "That man, the one you call your chief, is seriously ill. We should do a healing for him immediately."

"What do you think is wrong with him, William?" Nainoa had asked. The older man looked thoughtful before responding, "I don't know. We must do the trance dance to find out. Then we have to decide on a course of action on his behalf. We must do it tonight or he may die."

At that moment a shadow fell across the door, and Chief Wilipaki looked in. The *kahuna* greeted the trio cheerfully. Then he slipped out of his pants and cloak, hung them on a hook, scrubbed and rinsed, and joined them in the steamy water. "You have made quite an impression, Chief Nainoa, returning with your guests from the east. I can't wait to hear of your travels. And who are your new companions, if I may ask?"

Nainoa introduced William and Zaki, revealing to the Ennu that Wilipaki was a renowned *kahuna* healer. He gave Wilipaki a rough outline of his journey and his discovery of the Ennu, describing their nomadic life and egalitarian ways in the vast grasslands to the east of the mountains. Wilipaki's eyes gleamed when Nainoa told him about the horses.

"That is a discovery of great merit. The presence of horses could affect the transport system of the settlements in a most positive manner. But from what you have said of the terrain, getting them here may pose some challenges."

Nainoa nodded. Then he ventured, "We were discussing the director's health as you entered, sir. William is an acknowledged medicinemaker among his people and has suggested that a healing ritual be performed immediately. Do you think the director might agree to this evening?"

Wilipaki looked at William as he replied, "My wife and I have just arrived from the capital. We too feel grave concern. Your companion's suggestion is a good one." He smiled at William with warmth, then turned. "You have heard the rumors, I suppose."

"About sorcery? Yes, sir."

"Call me Wilipaki, Nainoa. I remember you as a boy when you came to the governor's court with your father, Kiwini. You certainly have grown into an interesting individual." He smiled again, his blue eyes sparkling. "But to return to our common concern, the director's health. This sorcery business can be messy. One must find the sorcerer and prove his or her complicity in the illness. The whole thing can be very tricky politically." He looked again at William, who was regarding him with interest. "Would you be so kind as to ask William what he thinks should be done?"

Nainoa translated, though he had difficulty finding an appropriate word for *sorcerer* in the Ennu language. "You mean an *ungagok* who has negative intentions?" asked the hunter. "Hmmm . . . that's not so good. Negative thoughtforms can indeed be a source of illness. If a spiritwalker thinks bad things about you, it can affect you at all levels of your being. When such a person gathers power and then couples it with a strongly focused negative intention, it can do damage to a person's soul—damage that, in turn, will be manifested in the body.

Your chief's illness appears serious. If someone has been wishing him ill, this may have been going on for quite a while."

"In our society, the sorcerer usually uses more than just bad intentions," Nainoa said to the older man. "An enemy or rival of the chief may have accumulated a large supply of *mana* and directed it toward him in a negative way. Usually sorcerers utilize material things to help them send the negative force toward their target." An unformed thought moved through his mind, but as he turned toward it, it eluded him. Instead he turned and gave Wilipaki a rough summary of the conversation.

"You have fallen in with good company, Nainoa," said the *kahuna*. "Please inform Chief William that the mystics among us also conceive of illness in the same way. Negative thoughtforms cause a diminishment of our sense of well-being, our protective mantle. This in turn affects the *ku*, which is, among many things, the aspect of our self that sustains and repairs the body. Sometimes the negative force is so powerful that it causes death, but more often it progressively diminishes our life force. This allows illness to gain entry to the body, where it feeds on the person's remaining energy, diminishing their essence still further. As its effects get stronger and stronger, the body wastes away, and unless the effects are counteracted and the cause reversed, the person may die.

"Illness gains much of its meaning and power from its spiritual aspect. Many of the healers among us are skilled at dealing with disease on that level. How wonderful that you have returned with one of the Ennu mystics." Wilipaki beamed at William, who grinned in return. "I feel it would be most beneficial if William would perform a healing for Chief Kaneohe this evening," he concluded.

William, at hearing the translation, responded with enthusiasm. "Let's work together. Among the Ennu, our medicinemakers gather in groups to pool their power in facilitating healing." Then he looked thoughtfully at Nainoa and said, "You also have powerful spiritual helpers, Nainoapak. They will provide strong assistance in our endeavors. You will work with us. Are there others among you who can provide help?"

"There are," replied Wilipaki after Nainoa conveyed William's request. He promptly summoned a servant and dispatched him with messages to the director and to several *kahuna* mystics known to him in the community. "Let us go now and confer with Chief Kaneohe without the fanfare of ceremony. Let us see what we can do to help him."

Nainoa and his Ennu companions dressed in new clothes presented to them at the baths—wide woven cotton pants and cloaks dyed with an interesting pattern. Among the Hawaiians, only those of chiefly rank wore pants, so this was the first time Nainoa had ever put them on. He combed out his hair and tied it back in the Hawaiian fashion and helped the Ennu do the same, then took his friends and Chief Wilipaki directly to Chief Kaneohe's inner rooms, where they were admitted after a short delay. The director looked semicomatose. He smiled weakly at Nainoa and Wilipaki, then beckoned to them to sit beside his bed.

"Chief Kaneohe," the young man began, "I have a most interesting story to tell you, but first I must reveal to you that I have returned in the company of an accomplished healer. This older man with me serves his people as a medicinemaker. He has suggested that we do a healing ritual for you this evening. Allow us to work together with Chief Wilipaki and Chiefess Lowena to determine the cause of your illness and reverse its course."

The ailing chief's eyes looked dim as he listened to Nainoa's words. Nainoa saw this and realized the man needed to sleep. But before he rested, the sick man's will needed to be engaged. Nainoa leaned close to his ear and said, "You must rest, sir, but before we leave, let me say that I found the horses—uncountable numbers of horses. I found the horses, sir." The director's eyes suddenly refocused. He looked directly at Nainoa and said, "I thought you would."

There was a long pause, after which he whispered, "I know something interesting about your ancestry, my boy. But first I would be most grateful for anything you and your companions might be able to accomplish on my behalf. Let it be as you suggest." The older man turned to Wilipaki and said, "Assist him in any way needed. He is now part of my lineage." Then the chief's eyes closed and he slept.

They left the chief and went to the men's house to eat a light meal. The Ennu passed up the sticky *taro*, sweet potatoes, breadfruit, and steamed greens, preferring only the roast pork. Nainoa was delighted to eat familiar food again and had to restrain himself from gorging on delicacies long missed.

Later that evening, Nainoa refocused his attention in the community center as the last chiefs and senior servants took their places. When all were present, Chief Kaneohe was brought in on a litter and laid on a padded platform at the end of the room. His supine form, heavily propped with pillows, conveyed his physical weakness. The gathering was hushed.

Chief Wilipaki spoke first, briefly describing his meeting with Nainoa that afternoon. Nainoa then addressed the assembly, promising accounts of his journey rich with detail in the sessions to follow. He then spoke of the chief's illness and of William's abilities as a medicine man. He described an instance when he had seen William cure a sick kinsman. When he declared that his guest had offered to perform a healing ceremony for the chief, Nainoa saw expressions of relief among the assembled people. The director was well liked by his community.

Nainoa turned then and nodded at Zaki, who assumed a place on the floor near the chief. The Ennu youth took up a wooden slit drum borrowed from one of the priests and began to strike it with a beater, producing a sharp, monotonous sound.

William then opened his medicine bundle and extracted his small antler headdress. He rose to his feet beside Nainoa, and all eyes turned in his direction. The older man discarded his cloak, revealing that he had painted his upper body and face with geometric designs. His bone whistle was suspended around his neck on a thong and his rattle hung from his wrist. He walked to the doorway and faced outward into the night. Then he tied the headdress onto his head, and when he turned around to face the room once more, his eyes looked vacant. He looked at the ill man for long moments, then began to dance, stamping his feet and moving sideways, following the rhythm of the slit drum.

His head was thrown back, his eyes were raised to the ceiling, and his hands were extended upward, fingers quivering as though beckoning to something. After circling the chief a dozen or so times, his hands dropped and his eyes closed, and his lips began to articulate a wordless song, his voice rising in volume to produce a shrill, quavering melody. He continued to dance sideways with his eyes almost closed, and he began to shake his rattle, matching Zaki's cadence. Periodically he raised the whistle to his mouth and blew into it, looking up into the vast distances that only he could see. The company sat in silence and watched.

At a sudden gesture from William, Nainoa took a place on the floor near the chief, whose eyes were closed and whose breathing was shallow. He wasn't sure what else to do, so he watched the chief and listened to the rhythm. Soon he felt a dreamy state creeping over him, and the sharp, dry sounds of the drum and rattle seemed to resonate deeply within him. His mind began to drift, to shift, and quite suddenly he felt the arrival of the sensations of power. Simultaneously a voice appeared within him—a voice he knew well.

"Greetings, descendant. It is indeed fortunate that I have been able to visit at this moment. With the assistance of my spirit helpers, I have gathered and sent a large supply of *mana*. Reach inward and receive it. You can then transfer it to the chief to enhance his personal power. It is the first stage of his healing."

As Nainoa's surprise subsided, he responded to the suggestion and gasped involuntarily as the *mana* swept into him. The exquisite paralysis was overwhelming, and he slowly slumped to the floor. Swirling spots of light appeared behind his tightly closed eyes, and his ears filled with a roaring rush of sound. He could still hear the cadence, but it seemed far away. He lay on the floor, completely rigid as the power surged within him, his mind marveling.

"Try to get up," came the words in Old English. "You must go over to the chief and place your hands on him. We must augment his life force, and quickly." As Nainoa tried to rise he wondered what the word *augment* signified, but the force within him was too great, and he could not move. "Ask for assistance," commanded the voice.

Nainoa mobilized his will, whereupon the spots and lines of light dancing in the darkness began to shift position, assuming density and form to coalesce into the luminous, distinctive feline shape of a spotted tiger. He opened his eyes and saw that the creature was there, silhouetted against the night sky in the open doorway to the large meeting room. He watched, amazed, as the spirit looked around the room speculatively and then fastened its attention on him. Nainoa glanced at the people nearest him, but they didn't appear to notice the spirit.

The spotted cat abruptly stood up on its hind legs and shape-shifted, assuming a humanoid form and stance before walking slowly, gracefully, toward him. The proportions of its muscular body suggested great physical strength. Nainoa gazed into its pale eyes as his request for assistance took final shape within his mind. The beast man paused, looking at him curiously. Then, unexpectedly, it leaped at him *and into him,* merging with him in some impossible way. Nainoa's startled amazement was offset by a tremendous surge in the sensations of power permeating his body.

At this moment his ability to move returned. He rose to his hands and knees, his blood sparkling with light as his pulse hissed in his ears. He felt absolutely marvelous. He looked around at the assembled throng, and each person seemed luminous, surrounded with an outline of colored light. "Go to the chief," came the voice.

He stood up then, and never in his life had he felt as powerful. He walked over to the ailing man. He heard William's rattle behind him assume a faster, stronger rhythm, which Zaki followed with the drum. He looked down at the chief's body and saw it had assumed a curious transparency. It was as if he could see into it, as if he could perceive the bones and organs, the arteries and veins, the entirety permeated and surrounded by a field of light of varying degrees of density and color. Lines of brilliance were apparent, congealing into glowing centers that seemed to run up and down the chief's body. His gaze was drawn to the middle of the chief's abdomen, where a large, dark stain loomed within the man's organs below the bright wings of his lungs and the pulsing fist of his heart.

"Place your hands on him and transfer the *mana*," came the voice. He formed the intention within his mind, then asked his spirit helper for blessing and assistance. A rattling growl formed in his throat, emerging spontaneously from his lips in a deep, resonant purr. Then the power surged, radiating outward through his arms and hands as he placed them upon the chief's torso, the fingers of one hand resting lightly above the dark stain. The man's body stiffened visibly, and Nainoa saw the field of light within and around the chief assume greater density and brighten perceptibly.

As the power shook his body, he concentrated fiercely on the dark stain within the chief's abdomen and imagined it infused with the force he felt flowing through him. To his surprise, the stain seemed to become dimmer. As the chief's radiant field continued to grow brighter, the dark smudge became ever more indistinct, until it virtually disappeared. The large organic mass it inhabited began to sparkle with light, as though hundreds of tiny bubbles were percolating through the stain. He recognized the mass as the man's liver.

As he gazed, fascinated, into the chief's body, he was surprised to see something within the stain—it looked like a tiny arrow with black feathers, only different. Then he saw another, and another. From somewhere he heard the voice say, "Take them out. Reach in and take them out." As Nainoa wondered how to accomplish such a task, he recalled the presence of his spirit helper and stretched his fingers experimentally. He was astonished to see a set of formidable claws extend from his hands as curved lines of brilliance. He glanced up to see William's eyes locked with his. There were others clustered around him, shadowy shapes and flowing forms made of light. He realized that he was seeing William's spirit helpers. "Just do it," said the older man with a smile. "Take them out."

Without hesitation, he reached into the radiance of the chief's field with his claws of light and extracted the tiny feathered barbs, one after the other, tossing them to the floor until there seemed to be none left. The man's field brightened still further, and his breathing deepened with a drawn-out sigh of relief. As Nainoa wondered at the nature and source of the tiny projectiles, his head swiveled involuntarily and his eyes swept the assembled company, coming to rest upon the shape of a man standing in a doorway, just beyond the light. Much to his surprise, the darkness brightened and he locked eyes with the man. It was the priest, Chief Paleko, and he was looking at Nainoa with undisguised hatred.

Nainoa's intense distaste for the man surfaced, and once again the rattling purr emerged from his lips, this time rising in volume into a deep, grating snarl. Paleko's face changed as the accompanying emotional charge hit him with full force. Nainoa held the man's eyes as the growl rumbled in his chest once more. A recent memory surfaced—an image of this same man disappearing into the night with the chief's shirt concealed beneath his cloak. He realized with some amazement that he had found the sorcerer. Abruptly Paleko turned and disappeared into the darkness of the night.

"I'm beginning to feel much better—much stronger," came a familiar voice. The rattling and drumming suddenly ceased, and the night became silent. As Nainoa's awareness shifted, he felt the departure of his feline ally and found himself kneeling on all fours, looking down at the chief, who was regarding him fondly. "Whatever you did was quite remarkable, my boy. I feel better than I have for many, many days."

Nainoa smiled down at the director. The man's body had reassumed its normal solidity. He glanced at the floor where he had tossed the tiny arrows, but he saw nothing. He looked up. William was smiling at him, his big teeth gleaming in the firelight. "Well," the old hunter began in Ennu, "it seems we have a new medicinemaker in our midst. You did that very well, Nainoapak, you and your ally."

"I have just had a most interesting experience," he said to the Ennu shaman.

"I know," replied William. "You were able to perform a healing on behalf of another person. With your ally's help, you were able to perceive the illness-causing agent in its symbolic form and extract it from your chief's body. The effect of the illness on the chief has been diminished, and the illness will now leave the body, driven out by his own stronger sense of well-being. And where did you gather all that power, Nainoapak?" The older man grinned with delight.

Nainoa glanced up at the assemblage and saw expressions of amazement and interest. Impressed despite himself and tremendously relieved, he reached out and clasped the chief's hands impulsively. The director smiled and sat up. "I believe I would like something to eat," he said. Everyone smiled.

Chief Wilipaki stood and addressed the company. "It seems that the director is on the mend." Everyone smiled again, and the silence cracked as people began to converse in low tones. Wilipaki turned to Chief Kaneohe and raised his voice so that all could hear his words.

"I'm delighted to have been present tonight, Chief Kaneohe. It appears that Chief Nainoa has been working with a truly accomplished teacher during his year away." Wilipaki's eyes came to rest on William for long moments. The Ennu grinned at the man, his lined face and dark eyes radiating goodwill. Then Wilipaki turned to the gathering and said, "As regards the degree of Nainoa's chiefly status, I suggest that the rank of *kahuna* would fit him well."

Chief Kaneohe smiled as exclamations of affirmation filled the crowded space. The director turned and looked at his advisory board of chiefs and senior servants. They beamed their approval. The chief's elder brother nodded with a broad smile. None spoke in opposition. Chief Kaneohe looked at Nainoa, and his lips curved. "You realize that this will mean enduring a lot of painful tattoos," he said. Everyone laughed.

Nainoa bowed, acknowledging the honor. He spotted a servant he knew and summoned him with a look, then asked him to get the director some food. "Only meat boiled in water. Soup with no fat," said William. Nainoa looked at the Ennu and wondered how he had known what was being discussed. William saw his look of puzzlement and grinned. Suddenly the room was filled with conversation. Wilipaki was talking animatedly with his wife as Nainoa caught his glance. The *kahuna* beamed at him in response, then rose to his feet once again.

"We have witnessed something of great merit tonight, Chief Nainoa," he boomed. The room momentarily quieted to hear his words. "This community now possesses a new *kahuna* healer, one of obvious accomplishment. The prestige, balance, and harmony of the community will be enhanced by his presence. It is my suggestion that we openly celebrate this great event this evening and that we postpone until tomorrow the beginning of Chief Nainoa's chronicle of exploration. I have heard a few details and can assure you that you will find his story of great interest. No other Hawaiian has accomplished what he has." He left the idea hanging in the silence, then announced, "The director needs rest—as much rest as possible. With your permission, we will resume tomorrow."

The roar of voices began to rise, whereupon Wilipaki raised his arm and the room quieted once more. "At the completion of Chief Nainoa's narrative, we will perform the ceremony formally inducting him into the Kaneohe lineage and establishing him as chief in the Order of Kahuna. Let the singers be present so that they can compose a chant worthy of the occasion. Let the dancers listen well so they can create a hula depicting his accomplishments."

A great stillness descended as all eyes watched Nainoa. He was still crouched beside the chief, who was clasping his hands. He looked into the director's eyes and saw the man's happiness. The smoky room erupted into applause.

CHAPTER 9

Elemental
Encounters

THE BELL THAT signaled the end of the second period of meditation sounded, drawing me back across the threshold to my bed at Tassajara. My mind worked furiously as the paralysis diminished in surges and finally disappeared. Once again, Nainoa had entered an altered state while I was merged with him, enabling us to communicate directly.

I thought about the healing ritual that we had just done and felt my amazement increase. In response to my suggestion, Nainoa had been able to receive the *mana* that I had sent off six months before, while at Esalen. I noted the time lag and realized that I had no idea if time even had meaning in the levels of reality in which we were operating.

In transferring the energy to the ailing chief, Nainoa had augmented the man's life force, after which he had then performed a classic example of shamanic illness extraction with the assistance of his spirit helper. The leopard man (the spotted tiger man, as Nainoa thought of him) had merged with him, allowing him to acquire the spirit's strength, power, and abilities. Needless to say, this had been an extraordinary experience for me as well, for I had been there, or rather my conscious awareness had, contributing what I could while witnessing what transpired.

Among many traditional peoples, shamans often use their mouths to literally suck illness intrusions from their client's body. Often they place a piece of meat, a bloody chicken gizzard, crystal, or other object in their mouth to trap the intrusion as it is extracted, because the last thing they want to do is suck an illness into their own body. This has often confused Western investigators, most of whom are in ignorance of the object's true purpose; when they see a healer spit an object out and proclaim it to be the offending source, they see it as a sort of sleight of hand and so declare the healing ritual to be a hoax. In the West, we are not used to people extracting illness in this way, nor do we expect doctors to suck on our bodies, and so other, more socially acceptable methods are utilized by contemporary shamans, such as the use of the hands to accomplish the extraction.

A year would pass before I had another connection with Nainoa—a year filled with classes and students, family concerns and responsibilities. During this time several interesting events occurred, circumstances that led me to the inescapable conclusion that the spirit stone had catalyzed some sort of sweeping shift of balance within me. And once accomplished, the stone had somehow stabilized the shift, or the shift had stabilized itself—it was hard to say which.

I began to observe the stone in the backyard from time to time, brief visits during which odd thoughts often appeared in my mind. These thoughts often took the form of ideas, but just as often they were more like memories, but memories of the future, if such a thing is possible.[1] It was as though the essence of the future event was contained within the stone, a pattern that I could sometimes perceive, at least to some degree. The translation of the percept into concept took place when the memory moved from the stone into the energetic field of my own body. In this way, a whole parcel of information could be received in a split second—a package that could be excavated from my subconscious *ku* immediately afterward or at a later time.

I began to suspect that the reverse could also be true, that my own experiences and memories were somehow being programmed into the stone when I was in proximity to it. I couldn't prove this, of course, using the methods of objective scientific investigation. Nevertheless, I found the possibility intriguing and came to wonder if the stone was in the process of becoming a repository of my own experience and knowledge.

One day in November I went out in the backyard to sit with the stone. The sky was a deep blue, and that curious, somewhat melancholic stillness of late autumn was broken only by the whisper of the occasional falling leaf. I placed my hands on the stone, greeting it with my focused attention, then sat down in a chair facing it. I formed an intention with my ego and felt myself settle into the light trance state. There is no mistaking this state because my mind suddenly becomes extraordinarily clear, my thoughts assuming a razor-sharp edge. I had a notebook on my lap and decided to attempt a dialogue with the stone, or more accurately with the spirit within it, using mental questions that would produce yes-or-no answers. I do not know whether this is something practiced by traditional shamans, but I suspect that it is.

I focused on the stone and asked the first thought question: Was the stone's awareness expanding through its experience of me? A thought response appeared in my consciousness immediately, a clear sense or impression that the stone's awareness was already fully formed. This wasn't the answer I was expecting, but as I thought about it, the response was reassuring. It suggested that I was not creating the answer myself, producing some self-fulfilling prophecy to satisfy my ego needs.

I refocused my attention on the stone and asked the second question: Was the impression that I had just perceived an answer? Another clear feeling appeared within my awareness—it was more of a pulse, really, one that carried a definite sense of meaning. The response seemed positive, one that implied agreement.

I then asked if the stone was receiving my thoughts and experiences. Another positive pulse appeared in my mind—a sense of agreement. Pressing on, I asked, "Are you an intermediary between Nainoa and myself?" I felt a definite affirmative.

As I thought this over, I was aware that I was doing something quite unorthodox, even "crazy" in some people's minds: I was interviewing a stone. Was I in dialogue with what William had called an earth spirit? A sense of the positive appeared once again, a pulse of thought-feeling my own mind translated as definite agreement.

As I stared at the stone, I wondered if it represented what northern European mythology calls a gnome or what the Australian Aborigines call the friendly *mimi* spirits. A response appeared immediately: definite agreement.

I recalled William's statement about the earth spirits—that they were the repositories of the knowledge of the universe. I didn't even form this as a question before the answer arrived: definite agreement. My *ku* then coughed up something else William had said—that the earth spirits didn't have to think about anything, that they simply "knew." This implied that the earth spirits were all *ku*. I perceived a sense of strong agreement.

As I continued to stare at the stone, I reflected that it was a piece of the volcano Mauna Loa, and an image of that immense mountain immediately appeared in my mind's eye. Without warning, I suddenly felt a huge presence, and goose bumps formed all over my body. I wondered if I was in connection with the mountain's spiritual aspect, the form of awareness that the Hawaiians call Pele. Instantly I felt definite agreement.

I was stunned as the stone's answer sank in. I hadn't expected this at all. I recalled an encounter I'd had with Pele while we were still living in Kona, and her powerful image took form within my mind, a massive humanoid form that had a curious layered effect, as though her shape was interrupted by surfaces of red and orange, like leis of flowers or flows of molten lava. Then the image shifted to become a set of eyes looking straight into mine, accompanied by an enormous surge of the power sensations within me. As I gasped for breath the eyes boring into mine never changed expression.

My feelings of awe were transformed into deep feelings of bliss edged with a line of tension that was infused with a sense of enormous weight. As the expanded state deepened and the blood started to hiss in my ears, this weight surrounded me with an extraordinary sense of constraining pressure. I could feel my boundaries, the edges of my self dissolving. Somewhere my mind was still aware and clicking. I was certain I was in some sort of connection with the mountain.

As this insight moved through my mind, the eyes became luminous and I heard a soft sigh of sound: *"Vaaayyy-leeee-naaaah . . ."* It sounded like the wind, but as I glanced around my woodsy backyard, the trees and shrubbery appeared absolutely still. Once again I heard the soft dry whisper in my mind's ear: *"Vaaayyy-leeee-naaaaaaaah . . ."*

The end of the word, if that was what it was, was drawn out into a breathy tone that evaporated into the stillness of the yellow autumn light. I had no idea what it meant.

At that moment the family cat rubbed against my legs and my awareness shifted, reorienting on my immediate surroundings. I looked around quickly, but aside from the cat, I was alone. The year's jack-o'-lanterns were collapsing on the compost pile, their eyes dark and filled with fruit flies. I glanced back at the spirit stone surrounded by the dusty, curled leaves from the grapevine above and considered what had just occurred.

I had come to perceive the inner levels of reality as ever-changing places of experience and awareness in a supernatural sense, and as symbolic sources of information and knowledge in an ideological sense. Within these inner worlds, I was able to journey through some sort of subjective spiritual subway system across time and space to connect with Nainoa.

I was startled as a confirmation from the stone, a sense of definite agreement, appeared in my mind. I had momentarily forgotten that I was still in connection with it. Had it offered this expression of affirmation on its own, without my asking? If so, it had provided an oblique fragment of confirmation that it indeed had its own awareness and agenda. I refocused on it and posited several more questions.

I formed a mental image of the vast grid I saw at the onset of my altered states and wondered if it could be some sort of psychic-energetic map within the subjective levels of experience and awareness through which everything everywhere was connected. I felt definite agreement.

And the zone of silence, I thought. Could it be the stage in which my conscious awareness was disconnected from my own physical nervous system, and thus theoretically devoid of a physical body's sensory systems through which perception was accomplished, until it reestablished connection with Nainoa's? Again I felt definite agreement.

And what about the awesome grip of pressure that seized me in those moments? This was not a yes-or-no question, but an answer came immediately—a realization that this power was the energy associated with my spiritual aspect, my *aumakua*, and that I experienced it while I was going through this aspect to connect with my future self. As I wondered about this chunk of knowledge and where it had come from, another answer appeared in my mind—that the information was a direct communiqué from my spirit aspect, functioning as teacher, and that only about 20 to 25 percent of my life force energy was associated with my current physical embodiment.

I was stunned. This implied that 75 to 80 percent of my personal energy was in the spirit world in association with my *aumakua*. Was this why I experienced the ecstatic paralysis while connecting with Nainoa? The stone conveyed definite agreement.

I sat and just stared at the stone for some time, digesting this knowledge. A few minutes later the telephone rang inside the house, shifting my awareness back into the ordinary and terminating the "interview." On impulse later I got down my Hawaiian dictionary and looked up the word I had heard. In Old Hawaiian, *welina* (the *w* was pronounced as a *v*) is a greeting of affection similar to *aloha*. I couldn't recall ever having heard the word before this moment.

This episode led me to try to find out more about the "elementals"—earth spirits, fire spirits, water spirits, and the like—but most of what I found written on them struck me as fanciful and fictional. Why is it, I wondered, that when we humans look deeply into the universe, we expect it to look back at us with a human face? If we make a connection with a tree spirit, why do we expect it to speak in the king's English? I realized that what the scientific empiricist within me really wanted was direct experience.

Shortly after my interview with the stone, I had one such opportunity during a spontaneous altered state one morning at dawn. On the morning in question, I had just emerged from a dream and was drifting between sleep and wakefulness when I felt the sensations of power appear within me, accompanied by a sense of presence. My conscious awareness emerged into full wakefulness as the power surged. I waited, wondering if it was Nainoa, but as soon as this thought took form, I knew it was not. This presence felt utterly alien and it seemed to be below me. As the power feelings grew stronger, I could feel the presence growing larger, as if spreading out from under the floor of the house.

Suddenly a thin column of fire appeared at the foot of the bed. I felt immediate alarm and sat up. I blinked. There was no fire. The movement had shifted my awareness back into the ordinary state of consciousness. I got out of bed and examined the rug. No scorch marks. Not even warm. As my emotions calmed and my heart slowed, I realized that the image I had perceived had been a visionary one, and that the house was not on fire.

I lay down again and tried to relax my body. Perhaps ten minutes passed before I reachieved the dreamy state. I reached for the sensations and felt them reappear within me. They were at low levels, and once again I felt the presence below me. As before, it seemed to be spread out under the house. I wondered if I had perceived a fire elemental, and with the thought, the thin column of fire reappeared. As I looked at it with incredulous wonder, my memories contributed a paradoxical description, perhaps a biblical one, of "a fire that burned yet did not burn." This seemed to fit the vertical shaft of flowing light before me. It was about as tall as myself and flickered constantly. I wondered if I could detach my awareness from my physical body and move closer to it without getting up, and as I had the thought, I did. The experience was much like being a zoom lens, except that as I got closer to the fiery pillar, I could feel its warmth.

As my conscious awareness moved around it, observing it from all sides, little sparks seemed to fly off its edges and apex. Its source was definitely spread out under the house. It felt huge. Another column appeared and then another, until I was observing a group of them. The fire entities seemed to exist as separate individuals clustered around me, yet I knew somehow that all were connected to their single unseen source below.

Their subtle vibrating movement made them appear as if they were dancing—flowing, flickering pillars of moving energy that reminded me a little of Giacometti's elongated sculptures, but these lacked any semblance of human form. As my mind marveled and sought terms with which to define them, the concept "angels of fire" seemed most fitting.

How long I stood among them I do not know, but all at once I emerged from the altered state and found myself back in bed, staring at the place where the fire spirits had been. The sensations and the presence had simply ceased, much like switching channels on a television set.

My inner store of anthropological knowledge immediately disgorged an association—a chunk of information about the Huichol Indians of Mexico and their great regard for the spirit they call Tatewari, or Grandfather Fire. This spirit is their oldest god, and it is a special deity of shamans, to whom it gives the power to heal. I recalled that the Huichols believe Grandfather Fire to be the mediator between gods and humanity and thus the special protector of human beings. Could this be what I had just seen? As the first birds began to call outside in the growing light of dawn, my scientist's mind filled with questions.

Another event of note occurred in the late spring of 1992 when I was in the Sierra Nevada on a weekend camping trip with my older daughter's second-grade class. There must have been more than sixty parents and children in our camp, the tents spread out among the tall pines and cedars along the shore of a mountain lake in which we had spent most of the day swimming and playing. The class teacher was skilled at organizing such trips, and as dinnertime approached, the mood among our merry crew was definitely up.

On impulse, I decided to make for a small island nearby that was attached to the beach by a narrow spit of gravel. At the island's far end were some willow thickets whose shoots would provide excellent wands for roasting marshmallows. As I took my pocket knife and headed through the trees, I encountered one of the mothers, a woman named Nancy with whom I enjoyed talking, so I invited her to come along. She agreed, but indicated that she had to attend to her son before following me through the forest toward the beach.

I went on ahead, and as I walked through the trees parallel to the lake's shore, I kept glancing at the water. There was no wind, and the sun hung above the western horizon, producing a blindingly bright sheet of light that reflected off the lake's glassy surface directly into the trees. I squinted and looked into the brilliant glare, perceiving it as the energy from our star lying in a luminous plane upon the water, dazzling my eyes and brain.

Just before I left the forest and headed down to the beach, I stopped by chance on a spot behind two tall, straight-trunked trees. Between their black silhouettes, the sheet of light was sliced into a single vertical shaft of brilliance. As I looked into the light, an inner shift occurred and my breath caught in my chest as my awareness spontaneously expanded. Before me, the blazing bar of light had been subtly but definitely transformed into the bright obelisk of the *dorajuadiok*, the towering spirit Nainoa and I had met at the spirit hills.

I was momentarily stunned. I looked carefully at the spirit. There was no mistake—the luminous monolith was there before me. I extended cautious greeting combined with good intentions. The response was immediate, reflected back at me in a pulse of thought-feeling: "Friendly greetings—good intentions."

The outline of the spirit seemed to flicker or waver, giving it the appearance of motion, but it was quite unlike the fire spirit I had seen in my bedroom. It looked somewhat like an immense candle flame, but without quite the same proportions. It was wider at its base somehow and the apex was blunt or truncated. It resembled the Washington Monument, but its edges were slightly curved and it was thicker. I wondered if it was the same entity I had seen in Nainoa's company years earlier, and in response, a pulse appeared in my mind. I couldn't tell if the answer was positive or negative, but one thing was certain: The bright spirit was in connection with me.

At this point Nancy came up behind me through the trees, and as she approached she asked me a question. My awareness shifted in response, and before me once again was the sheet of light reflected off the water. Then, just as quickly, something flickered around and within the light, and there again stood the shimmering prism of the huge spirit. I was in my ordinary state of waking consciousness now, but I could still see it.

I turned and looked at Nancy, breaking the connection, then took several steps backward. I pointed to the exact spot on which I had been standing, the trees framing the light precisely, and asked her to stop right there. She did so, looking somewhat puzzled. Then I slowly pointed at the lake and said, "Take a look at that."

As the slim, dark-haired woman in sweater, jeans, and hiking shoes turned and looked into the vertical shaft of light between the two trees, her arms shot up reflexively as though to shield her eyes and face, and she was propelled backward a step. She caught herself in the act of falling, recovered, and looked at me with a startled expression, breaking the contact. "Whoa, what was that?" were her first words. Then she looked back at the lake's surface and observed practically,

"Boy, that sunlight sure is bright." Inwardly I exulted. I was certain that she had seen it too, although briefly.

The moment passed, the sheet of light became ordinary once again, and we descended to the beach, traversing the island to the willow thickets, where I cut a good supply of sticks for the children. I looked at the shrubby trees with respect and mentally apologized for cutting their branches, thanking them for the joy their sticks would provide the children. As if in response, a hummingbird appeared, buzzed a series of tight arcs around my head and shoulders, and alighted on a branch just out of reach. It sang its raspy song—*scree, scree, scree*—right in my face, then hovered over my head once again before rocketing off into the trees. Nancy smiled and said, "That hummingbird seems to like you."

Several months later I headed into the mountains once again. For more than two decades I have been in the habit of camping with the same group of friends each year over Labor Day weekend in early September. On this particular holiday, Jill had acquired theater tickets for a performance of *The Secret Garden*, which she knew would be of interest to the children, and so I went into the mountains alone.

I drove south from Sacramento in my aging Volkswagen van, then turned east an hour later, cruising through orchards and farmlands shimmering with heat. I felt relief as I left the lowlands behind and ascended into the cooler pine forests of the foothills, heading for Sonora Pass. As my eyes drank in the familiar Sierra vistas, I recalled imagery from Nainoa's walk and reflected on how different these same mountains appeared in his time. I was also aware that somewhere buried below me was the fault system that would respond to tectonic movements of the earth's crust, producing the formidable cliff that Nainoa called the barrier. I had often thought about that huge wall, wondering if five thousand years were really sufficient to produce the topographic relief I had observed.

I recalled an episode from Charles Darwin's famous voyage around the world on the *Beagle*—a day the famous scientist was investigating the geology of a steep mountainside on the western flank of the

Andes when a strong earthquake struck. He threw himself down and held on to the substrate with his fingers and toes to keep from being flung down the slope until the tremor subsided. When he returned to his camp, he discovered it was twenty feet higher than when he had left it that morning, providing him with a dramatic explanation for the presence of marine fossils embedded in the rocks high in the mountains.

If a large fault system existed somewhere below me on the western face of the Sierra Nevada and if it were elevated twenty feet at a time by similar tectonic events that occurred, say, roughly once every hundred years, then five thousand years could theoretically produce an elevation of a thousand feet.

Interestingly, a series of earthquakes in southern California earlier in 1992 may have provided oblique evidence that such a fault system does indeed exist and that it may be becoming active. The first jolt occurred on April 22, under a region east of Los Angeles known as Joshua Tree. It was a comparatively modest trembler, registered at a magnitude of 6.1. On June 28 a second earthquake with a magnitude of 7.5 emanated from the same fault, but slightly further to the north. Called the Landers Quake, after a nearby town, the second shock was the largest to strike the state of California in thirty years. When a magnitude 6.6 aftershock occurred several hours later along a different but nearby fault beneath the Big Bear region of the San Bernardino mountains, something of interest was revealed.

The strongest seismic waves from these tectonic events raced northward into the Mojave Desert instead of westward into the densely populated basins of Los Angeles and San Bernardino. Starting on a previously unknown fault, the Landers Quake ruptured the surface of the earth's crust in a line that extended almost due north for twenty kilometers; then the fault turned northwest for another fifty kilometers, confirming the suspicions of many geologists that a major new fault is becoming active in the Mojave Desert—one oriented directly up the western face of the Sierra Nevada.

Several other quakes occurred along this same northward-pointing transect earlier in the century, in 1908 and 1947, suggesting that this hundred-kilometer-long line does indeed represent a newly active fault that could eventually take the place of the famous San Andreas Fault, shearing off most of what is now California along the western edge of the Sierra Nevada and sending it inching toward Alaska.[2] As if in support of these ruminations, another aftershock of the Landers Quake, only 3.2 in magnitude, would rumble through Sequoia National Forest's southern edge northeast of Lake Isabella in January of 1993, north of the earlier geoforces.[3]

As I scanned the roadcuts along the highway for evidence of such a fault, memories of the past appeared in my mind. I had first experienced these beautiful mountains in the late 1950s, when my mother took me and my little brother to live on a ranch in western Nevada. While there, I had developed a close father-son relationship with the ranch's owner, a painter and photographer named Gus Bundy, who served as a strong male model for me during my adolescence. As I thought about Gus, I was very much aware that I had become who and what I was largely in response to him.

It was Gus who taught me to paint, encouraged my first efforts at sculpture, gave me permission to write poetry, and directed me to study philosophy and Eastern thought. His wife, Jeanne, taught me to cook, encouraged me to laugh at myself, exposed me to the music of Aaron Copland and Jack Teagarden, and told me stories about her childhood growing up in the Orient. Their daughters, Tina and Molly, became the sisters I never had, and in the company of this family I experienced my very first camping trips, sleeping under the stars with the smell of sagebrush in my nostrils and coyotes singing in the distance.

In the mid-1970s, almost twenty years later, Gus and his family had acquired a marvelous piece of land at the eight-thousand-foot level high on the eastern slope of the Sierras, and every year since then, an ongoing group of friends has made a point of camping with them on their land at least once or twice every summer. These are always marvelous reunions filled with laughter and dialogue, sumptuous feasts, and lengthy hikes into the surrounding high country. It always seems that each year, conversations begun the year before continue where they left off. Every trip has been unique, and as I climbed higher and higher into the mountains, my mind roved back through time, savoring the nourishment that good friendship and good company provide the soul.

In 1984, Gus died of cancer, and the dynamic suddenly changed. We scattered his ashes beneath the ancient, gnarled junipers that grow on their land and mourned his passing with food and wine, stories and folk songs, tears and laughter. Now his widow, Jeanne, had Parkinson's disease, shifting the dynamic further. Despite these transitions, the group was gathering once again—to feast and hike and celebrate life.

It was late afternoon when I turned off the highway, followed an unpaved gravel road through several miles of high desert, then climbed a rocky track through the mountain forest to arrive at their land holding at the foot of a long valley filled with willows and surrounded by peaks that soared to almost twelve thousand feet. As I carefully wound through the boulders and sage, I saw a scatter of cars among the trees, revealing that the company had gathered. On my final approach, several dogs of varying breeds and sizes came toward me, barking and wagging their tails, informing all that the last of the tribe had arrived. I alighted from the car, greeted the dogs, exchanged warm hugs with all, set up my sleeping arrangements in my van, and poured myself a large glass of wine, and the weekend began.

It was the second night there that it happened. I was highly stimulated by a long day spent hiking with my friends among spectacular mountain scenery followed by an evening of food, wine, and dialogue. The cold, crisp air of the high altitude also had its effect, and I found myself wide awake at midnight, wandering in the dark among the ancient trees and rocks, listening for coyotes and watching the starry universe for incoming meteors from the rest of the galaxy.

As always, I missed my old friend Gus intensely. I remembered Nainoa invoking the spirit of his mentor Nagai during his long walk, and I tried to access Gus's spirit. My eyes searched the darkness, trying in vain to see his broad-shouldered silhouette. I recalled the death poem of a celebrated Zen worthy named Ikkyu that Gus had once quoted to me. It was one of my favorites.

I won't die.
I won't go anywhere.
I'll be here.
But don't ask me anything.
I won't answer.

I walked over and sat on Gus's stone, a slab of Sierra granite carried from a nearby glacial moraine and placed over his ashes. I felt his presence all around me in the cold dark. "Gus . . . are you there?" I asked in a soft voice. But as he had predicted, there was only silence.

Sometime before dawn I retired to my van, climbed into my freezing sleeping bag, waited for it to warm up before taking off my parka, then settled down, preparing to slip into sleep. For a long time I tossed and turned. Sleep was elusive, but I finally entered that state in between consciousness and unconsciousness. Vague, unformed imagery moved spontaneously through my mind, attracting my attention but eluding comprehension.

Toward dawn, I still had not slept when I heard coyotes calling from the ridge to the east, and, looking up through the rear window of my van, I saw a meteor streak in from the zenith, tracing a bold line across the sky. Provoked by that spectacular release of energy, perhaps, the sensations of power roared into my body, and the stars shifted into the now-familiar phosphenic patterns—the brilliant dots and lines that ultimately resolved themselves into the grid. Almost immediately the mysterious crescent appeared and slowly opened, drawing my conscious awareness toward it as my body stiffened in paralysis.

My last impressions were of my sleeping bag snug around me in the cold, accompanied by the comforting thought that I was safe in my van. There was an enormous surge of the sensations, then the transition was achieved through the zone of silence.

My first perceptions were of being cold. As my thinking mind clicked on, I wondered if I had made it. Then I heard the sounds of roosters crowing and knew that I had.

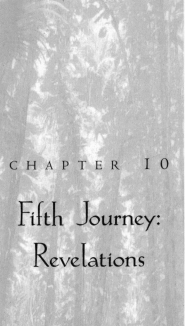

CHAPTER 10

Fifth Journey: Revelations

NAINOA WAS SEATED cross-legged on his bed, his cloak wrapped around him to ward off the chill of the cool air flowing through the thatched structure of his cottage. Roosters were crowing all over the settlement, heralding the start of a new day. He immediately sensed the presence when it appeared within him. When memories of the recent past began to spontaneously move through his mind a moment later, he sat and watched, well aware of what was happening.

For the past twelve days he had held the community's leadership and their invited guests gripped with the story of his long walk. There had also been moments in private when he had discussed some of the more personal aspects of his story with Chief Kaneohe—his connection with the spirit stone and the nature of his relationship with William's daughter, for example. The director had smiled warmly in response to his mention of the stone.

"When the *pohaku* came into my dreaming expressing the wish to meet with you, I knew that you would become its next *kahu*. When your report is complete, we will meet for a game of *gocheka* in my *heiau*. There we can talk freely about such issues that concern us alone. As I have mentioned, there is also an interesting story concerning your ancestry."

In response to Nainoa's revelation of his relationship with Kenoje-lak, the chief's eyes had narrowed thoughtfully. "The fact that you have established a familial bond with the Ennu people beyond the mountains is highly desirable. It will create strong political connections between our two peoples and allow you to come and go freely. We must bring horses back to our settlements, and your relations with the Ennu will prove critical in the success of such a project.

"We must also consider your future connections here within the settlements most carefully. Your accomplishments on this long walk will bring you great prestige and extend your connections far beyond the boundaries of this land division. I have already sent a communication to the governor revealing that a person of exceptional merit has accomplished a truly great deed." He smiled. "I included a rough sketch of your story, so I am sure that an invitation to visit the governor's mansion in the capital will arrive shortly. This will provide you with an opportunity to establish strong political connections with those of the highest chiefly rank." He smiled again. "The ruling class is going to look you over, Nainoa. Marriage to a high-ranking chiefess would be very desirable."

When Nainoa described his mystic experiences to the director, the chief replied: "Your visionary connections with your ancestor reveal that you are one of those rare people who can access the mystic states of awareness to travel across time as well as distance. This will provide you with much, not the least of which is the experience itself. It will also allow you to recover lost knowledge of the past—wisdom that may be of great use to us all." The director looked at him closely and continued, "In addition, it seems you are becoming a medicine *kahuna*, and so your life will be different from that of the more ordinary people. You will see what I mean."

The director had been right. As each day passed and the community saw the chief recover from his illness and regain more and more of his strength and personal power, Nainoa perceived a new level of formality invade his everyday relationships, one that created deferential spaces in his formerly more intimate connections to members of the community. In their minds, he was responsible for the chief's cure.

He felt a little uneasy with his new role of medicinemaker. He wasn't sure what he had actually done. William had tried to explain it to him that same evening as they sat on the edge of the wall outside his cottage and looked out across the settlement in the starlight.

"You entered an expanded state of awareness and perceived the negative intentions directed toward your chief as spiritual arrows embedded in his body," the hunter had said. "These negative thoughtforms diminished his life force, allowing the illness to invade his body and gain the upper hand. When you removed them with the assistance of your spirit helper, their effect was neutralized and he began to recover. In addition, I saw your chief's body become infused with energy. How did you know how to do that, and where did you get that concentrated supply of power?"

As Nainoa explained, William's eyes gleamed. "It means your ancestor, in addition to being a spiritwalker, was also a medicinemaker. You are most fortunate to have such a teacher, Nainoapak. From what you have said, he served his community in other ways as well."

"It is true," said Nainoa. "He seems to have been a historian like myself, although he was concerned with the far, far distant past. At times he functioned as a teacher for his people."

"I also observed your new *dordok*, your spirit helper," William continued. "It seems that the spotted tiger spirit has decided to assist and protect you in your work. And from the look of that man you call Paleko, I would say that this is a very timely thing."

Nainoa thought about Chief Paleko and had to admit that what William had said was true. Paleko had dropped in to hear portions of his account from time to time, never staying until the conclusion of the session, as if to show disdain. Nainoa detected a dark, brooding enmity from him. He knew that the man had always been this way, but now Nainoa felt his hostility most definitely focused upon Nainoa himself.

In one of his private moments with the director, he mentioned having seen Paleko making off with an article of his personal clothing the night of his visionary reconnaissance. The director had become very still in response. "Eleven days before your return, you say? It was about then that I became ill." He thought awhile, then said, "That man's spirit has always had a dark shape. He is also highly intelligent and very shrewd. He will have destroyed any evidence of his misdeeds by now, so to accuse him of sorcery would only provoke open enmity with the group that supports him, and as a priest, he is very strongly connected. But we know now who and what he is. I have an interesting story to tell you about Paleko. It will wait until we meet in the *heiau*."

Nainoa had finished his formal account of his adventure to the assembled community during the afternoon of the previous day. It was then that he had opened the woven basketry sack in front of the assembly and taken out the horse skeleton, arranging the bleached bones on the floor until the creature was revealed, from its high-crowned teeth to its hoofed feet. He had discussed what he had learned about horses—about their social and reproductive behavior, their dietary and habitat preferences, and so forth, providing a dramatic close to his narrative. Faced with this evidence as well as the presence of William and his son, nobody could doubt the veracity of his story. The applause that had followed his conclusion was tumultuous.

The celebratory feast that followed was extravagant. Due to the significance of the occasion, it was deemed appropriate for the community to gather and for the *kapu* to be lifted so that men and women could eat together, enjoying each other's company as they discussed details of his adventure. Many speeches were made, declaring Nainoa's walk a major accomplishment—an auspicious event both for him and for the settlement at large. Many women cast lingering looks in his direction, but he felt strangely detached, separate from his younger self, who would gladly have gone to their beds. He also realized that he felt strong sentiments of attachment to Kenojelak. He sighed. His feelings for William's daughter nourished him, but at a deep level they accentuated his loneliness.

A servant arrived, interrupting his reveries. The director was awaiting his presence at his personal *heiau*. Nainoa rose from his bed and quickly arranged his clothing as the servant combed out his hair, gathering it into a thick knot, which he tied with yellow cord at the base of Nainoa's skull.

He was alone in his cottage and had been for several days. William and Zaki, unable to understand his words during his long account and unused to being inside buildings for long periods, had become increasingly restless, so he had arranged for them to visit with the hunters they had encountered near the cove. He smiled and wondered if his friends, driven by the need to communicate with their hosts, would finally learn some of his language. He glanced around his quarters, momentarily missing their presence intensely. He had become quite fond of their dogs as well, especially the white female they called Ziku. He put these thoughts aside as he turned and headed out the door for his meeting with the director.

High Chief John Kaneohe and a small number of servants were awaiting him when he arrived, smiling in welcome. "I have long looked forward to this day, Chief Nainoa," the director proclaimed. Nainoa said nothing but bowed deeply, taking the older man's hand in his and placing the man's fingers against his forehead in deference. The chief lifted him to his feet with a smile. Next to the temple platform, an area bordered by *ti* plants had been covered with newly woven pandanus mats. In their center was an area covered with several freshly cut banana leaves, with two large piles of cloth cushions placed at either side. With a sweep of his arm, the older man invited Nainoa to sit.

Servants arrived from the kitchens bearing wooden trays of fruit, roast pork, smoked fish, and cold sliced sweet potatoes. There was also a large bowl of breadfruit *poi* mixed with coconut cream, a metal pot of hot coffee mixed with milk and sweetened with cane extract, and two finger bowls half filled with water. A servant bearing a tray with two metal cups approached, bowed, then poured coffee for them.

The chief said a brief blessing, then reached down, took a choice piece of meat, and popped it into Nainoa's mouth. The honor of personally being fed by the director still took the younger man some-what aback. Chief Kaneohe seemed to be aware of this and said, "You are now a member of my family, Chief Nainoa." He let the phrase hang, aware that the retinue of servants were listening as well as watching. After a few moments he added, "Have some of this fish. It's delicious."

As they ate, the chief fondly regarded the servants in attendance, calling each by name and inquiring after the well-being of their families, asking for news of this person or that. In this way he kept abreast of what was transpiring within his estate, giving each person a chance to share bits of information and gossip. Nainoa ate in silence, studying the chief's style. The director had the ability to value others, no matter how lowly their status or menial their job, and because of this, his people would do anything for him. His open-ended way of conducting interviews gave all a chance to comment on what they themselves thought was important, adding considerably to his store of knowledge.

When they had finished eating, they rinsed their hands in the finger bowls, drying them on cotton napkins. As the servants cleared away the remains of the meal, the *kahu* of the *heiau* approached, bowing deeply and touching his forehead to the closely placed stones of the courtyard pavement.

"Come, get up, Kaniela," the chief scolded jovially, reaching down to him. The elderly man rose and took the director's hand between his own, bowing again to touch his forehead to the chief's fingers. Then he took Nainoa's hand and surprised him by repeating the gesture before standing to face them both. Nainoa had known the old priest since his boyhood and still felt very much the servant in the presence of the director's head priest and ceremonialist. Kaniela was also the custodian of the ruling family's temple and the relics it contained. The *kahu* was very old, his chest sunken and his hair and beard completely white. Long rows of tattoos ran from his scalp line across his face and down the entire right side of his body to his foot, sets of tiny triangles, lines, and other geometric designs tightly arranged into precise patterns. The old man's face cracked in a friendly smile as he looked Nainoa over approvingly. Then he glanced at the director and raised his eyebrows questioningly. "Speak, Kaniela, speak," said the chief in mock exasperation, acknowledging the man's deference with a chuckle.

"We are most fortunate to have this new chief return to our community," began the old priest formally, his head and hands trembling slightly as he talked. Nainoa discerned the man was almost blind now. Kaniela cocked his head at the younger man and continued, "I have heard your report, Chief Nainoa. You have strong powers of memory and excellent skills of recall. As a storyteller, you are quite a spellbinder as well. How I wish I were young enough to go adventuring with you, but I fear my aging knees would not fare well in the forest. Fortunately, however, as the body grows weaker, the spirit grows stronger." He broke off with a comical gesture and all three laughed in appreciation. The director summoned a servant with a gesture and gave him instructions to prepare some *awa*. Then the man left, leaving the three of them alone.

"Kaniela is a repository of great knowledge," began the director, praising the old man to Nainoa. "This historian knows things that no one else knows. He is the keeper of information about the sacred objects in this *heiau*, for example, knowledge he will transfer into your keeping, Nainoa. He is also a master *kahuna* mystic. You and he will have much to discuss in the days and years ahead."

"It is the director who is the master," protested the old man with a smile. "I am still *haumana*, a wonder-struck apprentice." Kaneohe gestured at the old man in mock exasperation. They were old friends.

Kaniela then fastened his cloudy eyes on Nainoa and said to him, "There is a body of knowledge that is not generally known—knowledge that is shared among the mystics of our people. This collective wisdom is not written, but is passed down in the oral tradition from generation to generation, in keeping with our clear understanding that the shape of truth changes as it travels through time.

"When spiritual teachings and revelations are compiled into books, the resulting sacred texts tend to bind the mind rather than open it. The different sects of our own formalized priesthood provide us with constant evidence of this, each lineage bickering with the others about which is the possessor of the real truth.

"The *kahuna* mystics learned long ago that conformity to a rigid set of recorded beliefs rarely encourages inquiry, and inquiry is essential if one is to encounter the realms of the spirits directly as you have. As each individual seeker rediscovers the ancient mystic method and reexperiences it directly, the process remains vital, providing us with a continually refreshed body of knowledge that enriches our lives and provides direct connection to the great mystery in all its forms. Each seeker perceives this wondrous adventure in his or her own way, and each way is valid."

The old *kahu* became silent then, as if waiting to see the effect of his words on the younger man. Then he bowed once more and said, "The director has shared with me the news of your relationship with the *pohaku kupua*. The *akua* that resides within this stone has chosen you to be its next *kahu*, and in my opinion, it has chosen well." He smiled and bowed again, backing away deferentially. "I will go now and leave the two of you to talk. I will see the *awa* is prepared correctly.

"Oh, one more thing," Kaniela shot back over his shoulder with a cheery grin as he headed for the kitchens. "Chief William killed an elephant in the forest yesterday. We will eat well tonight."

The director stood then and, taking Nainoa by the elbow, ascended the steps of the *heiau*, stopping short of the thatched *hale mana*, where he bowed and uttered a short prayer, requesting permission to enter. Then he unlatched the low wooden door. Stooping to clear the low doorway, Nainoa stepped over the carved wooden threshold and followed the older man into the house of power.

The inside was dim until the chief used a long pole to open a pair of windows high in the walls at each end near the roof peak. The room's center was cleared, the floor covered by woven mats, providing a soft, resilient surface on which two cushions were placed in the room's center. Nainoa looked at the interior with awe. All around the perimeter were tiers of raised benches on which were arranged objects that contained the chiefly *mana* of the director's ancestors. From the walls were hung woven and decorated sennit bags containing his ancestor's bones. There were many tightly woven cloaks and crested helmets edged or covered with feathers. One end of the room was occupied with chiefly standards propped against the walls, long poles with clusters of brilliant feathers and gay streamers attached to their upright ends. In a corner were stacked many long elephant tusks, trophies of former hunts.

A number of carved images occupied a long table along the wall of the opposite side of the room. Some were done in ivory and represented the major *akuas*. Others were *aumakua* images in which the collective *mana* of deceased ancestors resided. Some of these were beautifully sculpted, with shell eyes and human hair affixed to their heads; others were cruder. Among them Nainoa recognized several images of great antiquity, including a small, eroded statue of the white master Iesu standing beside an equally eroded seated image of Kotama, the two positioned as though engaged in silent conversation. Near them was a ceramic figure of a standing female sage with long eyes. There was also a metal sculpture of a horse that seemed frozen in the act of running; the sculpture was placed among a cluster of oily-looking stones partially wrapped in dry *ti* leaves.

But it was the dark shape of the spirit stone that drew his full attention. It was unwrapped and stood alone, propped upright on a low altar next to the two cushions. A fresh *lei* of red flowers encircled its pointed end. To one side squatted a stone lamp filled with candlenut oil, which the director lit. To the other was a square flat tray filled with clean sand for burning incense. The director got some going, then broke the silence. "You may place your hands on the stone and ask for its blessing."

As Nainoa knelt and did so, the stone's rugged surface seemed warm. The heat penetrated into his hands and arms, invading his chest, where it activated the sensations of power within him. Startled, he sat back on his heels and rubbed his hands together. The director laughed merrily, saying, "The *akua* in the stone is glad to see you; it has enhanced your personal supply of *mana*."

It seemed to be true. The sensations of power were perceptible, but at low levels of expression, allowing his sensory systems to operate in a more expanded way. As he turned and looked at the chief, the tall man's body seemed surrounded by a dim radiance, an outline of bluish green light. Then Nainoa's focus shifted and expanded, and he felt the watchful presence of the American within himself. He recalled the thoughtline that had emerged in his mind earlier and wasn't surprised.

"A warm welcome to you, ancestor," Nainoa thought in Old English.

"And my warm greetings to you, descendant," came the reply. "What an interesting time to have established connection."

At this moment Chief Kaneohe knelt and placed his own hands on the stone, closing his eyes as his lips whispered a brief greeting. Nainoa watched the man's body stiffen slightly as his face assumed a tight grimace. Then he too sat back on his heels and laughed with delight. "You see," the older man addressed the stone, "your new companion has returned, as I knew he would."

Then the director turned to Nainoa and confessed, "I did have many uneasy nights when you didn't come back before the rainy season began. I sensed correctly that something had happened to you." He gestured toward a cushion. "Sit, Chief Nainoa, and let us begin the next stage of our relationship."

Chief Kaneohe's arm swept the room's interior, taking in its contents. "Kaniela will tell you the histories connected with each of these objects. To know these stories is to possess their *mana*. Knowledge and power are intimately connected, as you have discovered. Today our focus rests on one particular object, the stone that travels, Kapohaku'ki'ihele." He glanced affectionately at the dark rock beside them, then patted it and said, "How extraordinary that it was in the care of your ancestor, the one you call the American. You have actually seen it during your visionary visits?"

"I have, sir," replied the younger man. "And from this man's memories I have seen the place that the stone was first found, a wide bay on the western side of the home island of Hawai'i. The American appears to have been the stone's first *kahu*. I have learned that it was in his care that the stone first traveled to America. Perhaps this man, or one of his descendants, took it back to Hawai'i at a later time. I do not know this for sure, but it found its way into your lineage on that island."

"It's your lineage, too, Nainoa," replied the chief. "Let me now share something about your past." He paused dramatically, then reached over and briefly gripped Nainoa's shoulders affectionately.

"You were raised as the adopted son of my clerk, Kiwini. As you may know, your true mother and father were both commoners who met an untimely demise. Your father was killed in an accident, and your mother succumbed during childbirth shortly thereafter. They were fine citizens from among the ordinary people, but it is your grandparents who concern us here—your maternal grandfather, to be exact. He is of interest because he was a chief." There was a long moment of silence. "We don't speak about him or say his name in my family because of, let us say, a great error in judgment he committed.

The memory of his misdeed will die with my generation, as none of us will speak of it nor commit it to written record. Nor will I discuss it with you. I will tell you some interesting things about him, however.

"He was a *kahuna* mystic of great natural ability, for which he was revered, but his character lacked a certain balance. He was overly focused on his dark side, and he became a powerful sorcerer who was greatly feared. Eventually the darkness he espoused destroyed him. But during his short, colorful, and sometimes sinister life, he had a great many love affairs with women from every level of society. Your maternal grandmother was one of them.

"As you are well aware, the chiefly families keep track of how the *mauli*, the life force, in their lineages travels through time, and when your grandmother, who was a commoner, became pregnant by this chief, my family was aware of it and watched to see how the child would turn out. That child was your mother. As she matured, she didn't seem to have your grandfather's spiritual power, his *ike*, but it is known that the gift, the *makana*, sometimes skips a generation. She married, and you were the son of that union. The question was, how would you turn out?

"Now here is something interesting. Political and spiritual considerations ensure that chiefs always marry within the chiefly class, but it is also known that the most vigorous and successful lineages throughout history have been those that outbreed." The chief paused and smiled. "It seems strange to say it that way, but it's true. We observe the same phenomenon with our livestock.

"When your natural parents died, my family had no way of knowing what you were like. You were only a newborn. We decided to take you in and assigned you to Kiwini's family. His wife, Koana, was unable to bear children, so you brought great joy to her and she became your heart mother. Kiwini and Koana did not know the details of your ancestry and thought you an ordinary commoner. But as you matured, your *makalapua*, your flowering, revealed that you possessed abilities and qualities of character that distinguished you from the more ordinary people. It became clear that you carry your grandfather's *ike*. Since this man was also my uncle, it means that you and I are actually cousins."

There was a long moment of silence as Nainoa digested this information. "Sir, does the fact that I carry his *ike* mean that at some level I am him?" he asked.

"We are talking about his spiritual power, not his personality," replied the older man. "A person's *ike* is incorporated into their *kino'aka*, into their energy body, around which the physical body is formed. Both the energy body and the physical body are quite distinct from one's personality or character, which, in turn, is a part of the *ku* that is redeveloped in each lifetime, providing the experiential field through which continual personal growth is achieved.

"Through your life experiences you have developed your own distinctive character, and in this sense, you are an individual who is very much your own person. Speaking at the level of energy, however, a slightly different insight is possible.

"The mystical power or force that pervades the universe is called *mana*, and it is a form of pure energy that is impersonal. But when *mana* is manifested as the life force that carries your spiritual aspect, it becomes personalized as *mauli*. At the time of your birth, your energy body was infused with your *mauli*, your life force, which is actually a blend of the *mana* from many lineages—that of your parents, grandparents, great-grandparents, and so forth, stretching back into time.

"Your *ike*, your spiritual power, is distinct from your life force, and yet it is ultimately an aspect of it. It is obvious to me that a large portion of your *mauli* is derived from your maternal grandfather, because you have his *ike*, his mystic ability. Your *ike*, like your *mana*, is impersonal. It simply exists, so in this sense, you are most definitely not your grandfather, despite that fact that you inherited it through him. Do you understand?"

Nainoa nodded. The chief stopped talking and looked thoughtful for long moments, then he continued. "Now here is something else of interest. As I said, your grandfather had a great many love affairs, and one of these was with a low-ranking chiefess who subsequently gave birth to a child. The child grew to maturity, married, and produced a child of her own. Accordingly, there is one other descendant of your grandfather who is still living. He is Chief Paleko. That makes him your cousin, too. Very mythic, don't you think?" he asked with a smile.

The director broke off and reached for a polished wooden bowl filled with small, round lenses of stone used in playing *gocheka*. Half were white, half black. He picked up a black one and said, "In Paleko, it's almost as if your grandfather's *ike* has manifested a strongly negative shape once more, much like him. But in you"—he picked up a white one—"the opposite seems to be true. This may reveal something of interest about the nature of *ike*.

"With the demise of our physical bodies, our energy body does not die. It exists in a free state at that point, carrying many of our feelings and memories within it. During the interval between our ongoing successive lives, our *ike* as well as our *mana* is closely bonded with our *aumakua*, our spiritual aspect. Indeed, our *aumakua* is actually carried by this body of energy. When this *ike-mana-aumakua* composite becomes associated with a new physical body, it provides the energetic-spiritual core around which the new individual is formed. Part of our life force energy is also derived from that of our birth parents, of course, which means that the *mana* that enlivens our *aka* body is ultimately derived from two sources, one from our birth lineage, the other from our personal, immortal spirit source.

"So in this sense, you do indeed carry your grandfather's essence, but an impersonal essence diluted and transformed by the essences of your parents and grandparents, and that of your own personal *aumakua* as well. We tend to think of ourselves as individuals, as singularities, but we are really composites of many energetic and spiritual lineages that stretch back across time to all of our ancestors.

"Sometimes I perceive a great, brilliant net in my own moments of vision. You have seen it, too, I know." As he spoke, the chief reached over and started to draw a diagram with his finger in the sand tray. "In my own case, I perceive each of us as a bright, energetic knot within this great *aka* field with our personal connections branching endlessly, in contact with everyone and everything else around us." His finger created randomly spaced dots across the grid he had created. "This living, energetic net is in a constant state of change as new connections are formed and old ones are lost. Sometimes new connections produce new knots, which, in turn, become new individuals who will form their own connections as they grow and mature."

"Does this mean that part of the *mana* within my energy body is derived from that of my ancestor, the American?" Nainoa asked.

"Very likely," the chief answered, "and from the energy body of his wife as well, because she was the mother of his immediate descendants. The connection between his awareness and yours probably occurs through this shared *mana,* which, in turn, is ultimately a part of both the *aumakua* aspect that you share as well as the greater human spirit and the great *aka* field of which everything everywhere is a part."

The chief broke off and regathered the threads of his thought. "As each immortal *aumakua* travels through time, continually remanifesting as successive, descendant selves through *ola'hou,* through the process of reincarnation, it either grows or is diminished in response to what we do and become here on the physical plane of existence. Because of this, I think of the energy body as our *kino'wa,* our time body or personal piece of time. And because each *aumakua* is part of the greater whole of the human spirit, *kapo'e'aumakua,* this, too, either grows or is diminished in response to our personal evolution. It follows that the great net of which everything, everywhere, and everywhen is a part, in turn, is affected by what we do and become.

"This is our *kuleana,* our responsibility." The chief smiled wistfully. "During each lifetime, each of us contributes not only to the evolution of our own personal spiritual aspect, but to the evolution of the great universe itself. Our minds are destined to become its mind; our spirits, its spirit.

"But let's bring this back to the level of what is personally meaningful right now. Let's consider Cousin Paleko. This man is aware of his relationship to your grandfather and has used this knowledge to become a powerful chief. Paleko does not yet know who you are. When your ancestry becomes generally known, and it will very shortly, he will not take it well.

"Your spirit helpers will provide you with protection, of course, especially the one who growled at Paleko that first night—the one who merged with you during the healing ritual you did on my behalf. You have a most powerful ally in that one, Nainoa." The chief fixed the younger man with a level stare and said, "You must be very careful with your intentions from this time onward. A strongly negative thought backed by an intense emotion such as anger or rage could activate your spirit helper to actually kill a man or do him serious damage.

"This is always part of our test," the chief concluded, "both as human beings and as *kahunas*. If we use our *ike*, our spiritual power, in a negative way, the negative force usually comes back to us and eventually destroys us, much as it did to your grandfather. This reveals why you cannot go after Paleko. He, on the other hand, may try to go after you."

The chief got up and rummaged around among the dusty baskets nestled among the poles of the chiefly standards. He found the one he wanted and returned with it to sit across from Nainoa once again.

"It always helps to have a little extra *mana*," he chuckled. He opened the basket and took out a black *tapa*-wrapped bundle tied with faded yellow cord. Inside was an old chief's necklace: a piece of whale ivory as long as a finger and carved to resemble a flat, projecting hook or tongue, suspended by many cords of tightly braided human hair. Some of the cords were black, others gray or white, providing a pleasing pattern. The creamy yellow surface of the pendant exhibited the glassy luster of age.

"This power object, *kamea'mana*, belonged to a *kahuna* mystic in my mother's lineage, a woman named Helena Kuamangu. She wore it for much of her life, and so it is infused with her *mana*. As you know, she came from the home islands on the great voyage that brought our ancestors to the shores of America one hundred and thirty-one years ago. She was the *kahuna* who communicated with the huge shark that ultimately guided the flotilla to landfall during those last stormy days and nights. She outlived all her children, and so her necklace has resided in this *heiau* since her death more than one hundred years ago. I pass it now into your keeping. I know you will use the *mana* associated with it wisely."

As he reached over and fastened its cool weight around Nainoa's neck, he added, "The white cords of hair are hers. Woven cords of your own hair will be added at the death of your physical body to further enhance its power for the benefit of your own descendants."

Nainoa closed his hands over the chiefly power object and felt overwhelmed by the feelings coursing through him. The chief understood and embraced him warmly, then rose and said, "I am going to visit the *lua* and check on the *awa*. Remain silent and meditate on what has passed. I will return shortly."

As the door closed behind him and Nainoa began to digest all he had heard, he remembered the American and listened, but detected no voice or presence within.

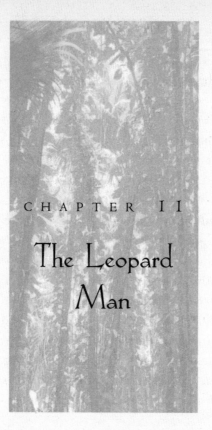

CHAPTER II

The Leopard Man

BACK IN THE high mountain camp, I lay in my sleeping bag feeling my own emotional shock waves in response to what I had perceived through Nainoa. I was particularly struck by the information about the nature of the self, for it offered an additional perspective from which to understand my ongoing connections with this man. I had often wondered, for example, why Nainoa's *ku* didn't perceive my presence and my requests for information as foreign right from the start. If a part of his life force was derived from mine, a partial explanation was provided. It also threw the concept of reincarnation into a whole new light. As the laws of thermodynamics state, energy can be neither created nor destroyed.

I felt feelings of conflict as I reached for a yellow pad and made hastily scribbled notes. I was very much aware that orthodox science and Western psychology don't yet regard the energy body as real, although parapsychologists speak of it using terms such as *psi plasma*, *bioplasm*, or *ectoplasm*.

The *kahunas* of old Hawai'i believed the *aumakua*, the immortal spiritual aspect of the self, to be the source of the *aka* body, which in turn provides an energetic blueprint or pattern around which the physical body is formed.[1] They understood that the subconscious mind aspect, the *ku* (or *unihipili*), follows this pattern in restoring the physical body. The *ku* is not creative, and without the existence of the *aka* pattern, there would be no plan or design for it to follow in making repairs. The relationship between the physical body, the energy body, and the spiritual aspect of the self was thus felt to be critical in maintaining health, and it was believed that the subconscious *ku* continually sought to keep the physical body matched as closely as possible with the *aumakua* using the *aka* body as a guide.

The *kahunas* were also aware of the tremendous influence that thought can exert on the energy body. It was understood that distorted thoughts originating within the conscious mind intellect, the *lono* or *uhane*, can distort the *aka* pattern, especially if held for any length of time, as this sustained attention charges them with *mana*, thus increasing their overall effect. It was also understood that the distortions within the energy body could be transcribed into the physical body and manifested as illness and disease. To accomplish the healing of the physical body, medical *kahunas* worked on returning the *aka* pattern to its former undistorted state, utilizing *mana* to accomplish the repair. As the distortion was removed, the *ku* was once again able to effect the repair of the physical.

Several years ago I read about an interesting medical case that occurred in the 1950s involving a Hawaiian boy who was brought to Queen's Hospital in Honolulu with a broken back. X rays revealed his spinal cord had been severed, and the boy's family was informed that he would be permanently paralyzed. The boy's mother insisted on bringing in a traditional medical *kahuna la'au lapa'au*, and the doctors, wishing to be as helpful as possible under the circumstances, acquiesced. They were astonished when further X rays revealed that this traditional healer had been able to induce the boy's spinal cord to knit back together, a medical miracle documented in the hospital records.[2]

I was infused with enthusiasm following my return from the mountains. During the weeks that followed, Chief Kaneohe's comment about "mythic qualities" stuck in my mind, and by chance I found some notes I had made over a decade before while listening to the mythologist Joseph Campbell give an all-day presentation about the hero's journey at San Francisco's Museum of Modern Art.

"As the hero ventures beyond his or her mundane world into the realms of the unknown," Campbell had said, "the values and distinctions that seem so important in ordinary everyday life seem to disappear. This loss, which includes the loss of one's personal individuation, is unbearable for those who are unready, but the hero-adventurer goes boldly in, rediscovering once more the eternal truths concerning the great mystery of existence."

As I thought about my own mystical encounters with spirits in the nonordinary levels of reality, Campbell's words leaped at me off the pages of my notebook.

"The great key to understanding myth and symbol is that the two realities, ordinary and nonordinary, are actually one. The deed of the hero is to explore both dimensions and then return, to teach again what has been correctly taught and incorrectly learned a thousand times throughout human history.

"The great quandary for the returning hero," Campbell had continued, "is how to translate, into terms of yes and no, revelations that shatter into meaninglessness every attempt to define the pairs of opposites. How can the hero communicate the message of the all-generating void to people who insist on the sole evidence of their own senses?" As I considered this paradoxical question, I recalled my own excursions into the endless darkness of the void and shivered.

"Another problem for the hero," Campbell had proclaimed, "is how to reenter a world filled with all that was once meaningful but which no longer is. How does one make plausible the bliss of tran-

scendant experience to people preoccupied with passion and material-
ism? The easy way out is to withdraw, to keep the message to oneself
and forget about the world and its limited concerns."

I thought about my fellow academics as I considered his words.
How would they react to my visionary journeys? As I continued to
apply and be rejected for jobs for which I was qualified, I realized I
could no longer worry about my colleagues' comfort level.

In December 1992 I was grading my students' final exams one
afternoon when I felt a strong sense of presence. It was that old
feeling of something or someone watching me. I wondered if Nainoa's
conscious awareness was in connection with mine. It was the end of
the semester, Christmas was only days away, and I was too busy to
drop everything and go into trance. But as I turned in my grades,
shopped for gifts, played with the children, and cooked meals for my
family, the feeling of presence continued to reappear at odd moments
for almost two days. Was Nainoa here, tapping into my mind, acquiring knowledge and information as he watched what life was like
before the fall of our civilization?

I tried to pay particular attention to everything that occurred
during those two days. As I drove across town, for example, I deliberately created a mental review of our public transportation systems,
beginning with the recovery of fossil fuels and their conversion into
gasoline and tracing the lines of connection to the car I was driving.
While shopping for food, I reviewed what I knew about our system of
intensive agriculture as well as the industries associated with food
processing, packaging, and distribution. Afterward I wondered with
some amusement if my intentionality had really been the activator of
my mental review. Perhaps it had been his.

It was also about this time that I received a phone call from one of
my colleagues inviting me to attend a scientific conference and present
a paper based on some research I had done in Africa several years
before. I looked at the prospectus, which was accompanied by a list of
more than thirty world-class scientists from Africa, Australia, En-

gland, Europe, and North America. My name was on the list. Flattered, I agreed to come, and the following May I found myself at an old Virginia country estate called Airlie whose manor house had been converted into a luxurious conference center surrounded by hundreds of acres of hardwood forests and beautifully manicured grounds.

During the week that followed, the impressive gathering of oceanographers, geologists, paleontologists, and anthropologists discussed what is known about the paleoclimates of the past and attempted to discern the effects of climatic change on the evolution of the paleofauna and paleoflora of various regions of the world.[3] Particular attention was paid to paleoclimatic shifts associated with the earlier stages of human evolution, a classic example being the emergence of the genus *Homo* and the first appearance of stone tool technology during a major climatic change between 3.0 and 2.5 million years ago.

I was also delighted to reencounter several old friends with whom I had worked in Africa many years before. Among them was Dr. Tim White, who now held a professorship in my old department at the University of California at Berkeley. In the late 1970s Tim had worked with Dr. Mary Leakey, excavating the famous 3.6-million-year-old bipedal human footprints at the site called Laetoli in Tanzania. He had also done the descriptions of the hominid (human) fossils found at that site and had collaborated with Dr. Don Johanson in naming and describing *Australopithecus afarensis*, the oldest human species then known. It is with this species that the famous partial skeleton called "Lucy," dated at 3.2 million years, belongs. Now it seemed Tim was pushing the frontiers of knowledge back still further. During a break, he approached me with an interesting proposal.

"Hey, Hank," he opened with a smile, "we've been checking out some deposits in the Middle Awash region of Ethiopia, south of Hadar. We're not sure exactly how old they are yet, but they're probably older than four million years, based on the fossil fauna. We've also seen some indication of micromammal remains. That's your specialty. Once we've nailed down the stratigraphy and the geologic dating, how'd you like to go out there with us and have a look?"

I felt a surge of excitement in response to his invitation. I hadn't been back into the African bush for some time. I also knew that fossil-bearing sediments of this age were extremely rare. With the exception of a few sites in Kenya that had begrudgingly yielded a few fossilized bits and pieces—a chunk of arm bone, a couple of jaw fragments, and a few teeth—virtually nothing was known about human evolution in this range of time. The same held true for micromammals—insectivores, rodents, bats, small carnivores, and the like. These creatures tend to be very habitat-specific, and if they can be found, they are extremely useful in the reconstruction of the environment immediately around the site at the time it was laid down.

"When the time is right, give me a call," I responded with a cheery grin.

There is a curious intimacy that develops between those who have done fieldwork together, creating friendship bonds that can last a lifetime. Encouraged by being with members of my "tribe" again, I came to a decision and shared some of my mystic experiences with several of my colleagues. Their response was mixed, to say the least. But among them was one who responded with interest.

Dr. C. K. "Bob" Brain has been director of the Transvaal Museum in Pretoria, South Africa, for much of his life. In his scientific research, he has been one of the primary investigators of the earlier stages of human evolution. Much of his fieldwork has been done at a southern African cave site called Swartkrans, an underground catchment that contains the fossilized bones of animals that lived on the high veld during the Pleistocene epoch, beginning about 1.8 million years ago. This site is of particular interest because it preserves stone tools and the fossilized bones of two different types of early humans, a more primitive kind, called *Australopithecus robustus,* and a larger-brained form, called *Homo habilis,* regarded by many paleoanthropologists as the ancestor of all later species of *Homo.*

More than a decade ago, Dr. Brain discovered something interesting in the collections from Swartkrans: a partial juvenile *Australopithecus* cranium, found in 1949, with two holes about 6 millimeters in diameter and about 33 millimeters apart piercing the vault. Brain, an accomplished field biologist, had noted similar holes in the skulls of contemporary baboons killed by leopards. By chance, he found a fossilized leopard jaw in the deposits at Swartkrans, one whose lower canine teeth fitted neatly into the holes in the cranium, suggesting that these early humans (about 1.5 million years old) were being attacked and eaten by this efficient predator.[4]

I had first met Dr. Brain while I was doing research on African micromammals at the Transvaal Museum back in the early 1970s. When I learned he was going to be at the conference, I wondered how he would react to my relationship with the leopard man.

Our initial encounter took place during the very first day of the conference. After I checked in at the hotel, several hours remained before our first formal gathering, so I set off on foot to explore the wooded environs. I was standing immobile, silently observing some water snakes searching for fish in the shallows of a small pond, when I detected movement coming through the trees. It was Bob Brain, in a khaki windbreaker. He was also alone, his eyes scanning the trees with alert interest as he walked.

I waited until he saw me, then silently indicated the pond's edge before me with a glance. He drifted forward soundlessly until he too could see the handsome mahogany-banded serpents foraging among the pond weeds. For long moments the two of us stood in stillness, watching the ancient drama unfold before us. Then I reintroduced myself, and we talked of the upcoming conference in low tones while our eyes drifted across the surface of the water into the trees beyond. I hadn't seen Bob in twenty years and kept the conversation on safe ground as we got to know each other once again.

Several days later I again found myself alone with him and decided to share portions of my strange story. As I broached the topic of my visionary experiences and correlated them with the curious abilities of traditional shamans, he volunteered that he had read an interesting book on shamanism written by an American anthropologist named Michael Harner. That was all I needed. His scientist's eyes regarded me levelly as I told him about my spirit helper's first spontaneous appearance in my life as a childhood imaginary friend, then went on to describe how it had reentered my life from the mythic Lower World at Harner's workshop. I followed with a brief description of the role the leopard man had played since that time. Bob's response betrayed immediate understanding tempered by the scientist's habitual caution.

"I must say, I don't know what to make of the rather stereotyped monster- and dragonlike creatures that travelers experience in the Lower World," he offered. "They seem to be archetypes from Jung's collective unconscious, common to us all. I suspect that leopards are also built into our unconscious imagery, as you experienced from childhood. It could be that, prior to our use of fire and other technology, we humans were continually subjected to the tyranny of leopard predation, with the result that a leopard image is genetically programmed into our cortical makeup."

Bob went on to discuss a writer he had known, an Englishman named Bruce Chatwin, who had visited him at Swartkrans back in 1983. "Bruce was immensely excited by my suggestion that some of the big cats may have been specialized killers of primates, including the Swartkrans hominids [an informal term derived from the formal scientific name for the human family—*Hominidae*]. He was very taken up with the idea that hominid-killing cats had been part of our evolutionary scene for so long that their images were now built into our subconscious minds. He actually equated the predator with Coleridge's "Prince of Darkness" in one of his books. It is possible that we freed ourselves from its sinister presence when we domesticated fire, and since then, the memory of it has grown dimmer and dimmer." Bob fell silent for a minute, then added thoughtfully, "Bruce expressed a certain nostalgia for the beast we lost. Did you know that he died a few years ago?"

I had read Chatwin's book *Songlines,* and was aware of his untimely demise.[5] As I watched Bob Brain's eyes, I could feel his sadness at the loss of his friend. "He knew a lot about tribal peoples, didn't he?" I said. The scientist nodded, then added, "He was especially interested in nomads. In fact, he himself was never happy unless he was on the move."

"A tribal person with a stronger sense of our mystical connection with the animal world might say that the leopard spirit, having been with us for so long, feels nostalgia, too," I offered. "Perhaps, for some of us, he returns to visit in our dreaming."

"Perhaps so," he chuckled appreciatively. Then his eyes softened as he looked inward. "Bruce said something else that I've never forgotten—that we should be grateful to the Prince, who bowed out gracefully."

This made immediate sense to me. "Throughout the years of our early evolutionary history, we became who and what we are in response to him," I murmured. Bob smiled and gave me a long steady look as the feeling of mutual understanding grew between us. I then had one of those flashes of insight that boggle the mind—one that emerged fully formed within my conscious awareness.

One of the great unresolved questions in human evolution is why we became bipedal, for this was the first definitive morphological feature that evolved within our lineage, separating us forever from our cousins, the African apes. Those bipedal footprints at Laetoli revealed that humans had achieved habitual upright standing and walking more than a million years before the appearance of stone tools or the beginnings of an expanded brain. The shift from walking on all fours typical of other primates into the habitual bipedalism utilized by humans required profound changes in the anatomy of the legs and feet, pelvis and back. Various theories about why this characteristic mode of locomotion developed have been put forward over the years. Early investigators felt bipedalism opened the way for later tool making, but in the early 1960s anthropologist Gordon Hewes proposed that bipedalism freed the hands to carry things, allowing individuals to gather food in one locale and carry it to places of safety for later consumption.

I had always felt that drastic climatic change was the causative factor. It is known that the worldwide tropical climate of the latter part of the Miocene epoch (from roughly 25 to 5.5 million years ago) came to an end about 7 million years ago as the global climate changed and became progressively cooler and drier. For the next 2 million years, glaciation produced ice ages in the polar and temperate regions, while in the tropics, the rainy seasons became shorter and the dry seasons grew longer, causing the great tropical forests to shrink and the great savanna grasslands to expand. The forest-living African apes and monkeys survived in refuges where their primary habitat persisted, primarily in the great drainage basins of the rivers of West and Central Africa. I had always felt that the ape populations trapped in shrinking forest blocks along the rivers and lakes within eastern Africa's rift valley could have been forced into a new way of life, one that forever changed them, producing a speciation event that gave rise to the earliest protohominids. But what was the nature of the new lifeway? Many have offered opinions, but as in all other areas of science, no consensus of opinion exists among the experts.[6]

Some, such as Drs. Henry McHenry and Peter Rodman at the University of California at Davis, believe that bipedality offered an effective way of covering a large amount of territory in the foraging for more widely dispersed plant foods. Others feel that erect posture provided an elevated vantage point for spotting predators or distant food sources across tall grasses. An English physiologist, Dr. Peter Wheeler, has suggested that bipedalism reduced the overall exposure of the body surface to solar radiation while foraging in the newly opened environments, providing a temperature-regulating function that was followed by the later reduction of body hair and the development of sweat glands all over the body surface. Others, such as Dr. Nina Jablonski at the California Academy of Sciences in San Francisco, have concentrated on the context of social control, stressing the use of bipedal displays in resolving conflicts.

Dr. Owen Lovejoy, an anatomist at Kent State University in Ohio, has proposed a theory stressing the reproductive benefits of walking upright. He feels that bipedalism began in the relative safety of the forest floor, where protohominids spent most of their time gathering fruit and vegetable foods, much like contemporary chimpanzees. As the forests declined at the end of the Miocene, the diversity and availability of food sources probably declined as well, reducing both the quality and the quantity of the resource base. Increasingly poor nutrition may have accounted for an increasingly slower maturation rate in the young, prolonging their time of dependency upon the mother. As long as females were nursing, ovulation would have been suppressed and females would have been unavailable for copulation, creating a low reproductive rate of one infant every five years or so.

Dr. Lovejoy believes that the low number of sexually active females might have created an incentive for males to provision them, enabling females to spend less time foraging and more time caring for their young, thus increasing their infant's chances of survival and possibly speeding up its maturation rate, allowing females to become sexually receptive once again. In this scenario, the males would gather food on their daily walks and carry it back to exchange for sex, much like bonobos (pygmy chimps) do today, with those males most effective at gathering and food-sharing appearing most favored as potential mates in the eyes of the females. In this line of reasoning, the males who were the most competent bipeds could carry the most food, making them the most proficient providers, which in turn would help them achieve greater mating success, thus allowing them to pass on genes favoring physical modification for upright walking to their descendants.

All this passed through my mind in an instant as I looked at Bob Brain and thought about the spontaneous statement that had just issued from my lips: "We became who and what we are in response to him." What if Brain was right and there had been a predator in the system, a carnivore who was specialized in killing and eating primates? I knew that leopards were equally at home on the ground or in trees, so tree-climbing or sleeping in trees would have provided no defense for our earliest ancestors, who probably looked much like chimpanzees. Was it possible that bipedalism provided some protection from carnivore predation at its inception, increasing the survival rate of the protohominids by making them appear different and thus confusing the primate hunter?

It was an interesting thought. In such a case, the initial use of bipedal displays would have less to do with social control or provisioning and more to do with defense. In becoming taller, these early hominids may have appeared to be considerably larger to the leopard (or the leopard's ancestor). In an evolutionary sense, upright posture would be especially effective if practiced by the young because any physical or behavioral trait that conferred a selective advantage to them would increase their survival rate and thus their chances of passing their genes on to the next generation. Selective success is determined by reproductive success, and if leopards preyed more effectively on more familiar-looking (and thus preferred) quadrupedal primates and tended to avoid the strange new bipedal forms with which they were unfamiliar, an anatomical-behavioral shift could have occurred quite rapidly.[7]

All of this rose to the surface, and I opened my mouth to speak. Then, ironically, Brain and I were joined by several other colleagues, and our conversation came to an end. My inner thoughtline continued, however, and a memory emerged, a composite recollection of my many visionary contacts with the leopard man. He usually appeared first as a feline, looking much like a real leopard. But as the connection between my conscious awareness and his became active, he almost always shape-shifted to become bipedal, a stance that mimics the way humans habitually stand and walk.

Real leopards would be incapable of achieving such a posture, but the leopard man is not an ordinary reality creature. A traditional Western psychologist might be inclined to say that the leopard man is an aspect of myself, a metaphor for something that has its source within my own mind that I utilize from time to time to augment myself. Because of my own direct experiences with this entity, I had rejected this theory and had come to think of the leopard man much the way a tribal person might—as the group soul or spirit of all leopards with which I had entered into relationship and alliance. I had come to believe it to be a separate entity with its own persona and its own agenda.

Could it be that this spirit remembered the earlier stages of both its own evolution and ours? It was likely that bipedalism had not protected us for long (as the pierced hominid cranium from Swartkrans revealed). But maybe it had conferred an advantage just long enough to produce the speciation event that propelled us away from our traditional foe—until he figured it out and the ancient predator-prey relationship was resumed. Was that what the leopard man was communicating to me by assuming a manlike posture? Was that the hidden irony embodied in his alien smile?

I thought about the rarity of both hominid and carnivore fossils in the Pliocene sediments with which I was familiar and admitted to myself that it was highly unlikely that we would ever find evidence to support such speculations using the scientific method. These ideas would most likely remain speculations. But intuitively I suspected that what I had just perceived was true, and that I had uncovered another piece of the ongoing puzzle of human origins—an ancient cocreative relationship in which both leopard and human became who and what we are in response to each other. My feelings of respect for my spirit familiar took on new depth.

I spent part of that evening with a dozen or so colleagues in the bar located in one of the retreat center's outbuildings, where the discussions of the day were continued in a more lubricated and less cautious format. Toward ten o'clock I left the bar and walked back alone through the night to the building where my bedroom was located. I was almost there when I sensed a presence. There was no mistaking it. I stopped walking and looked carefully across the dark grounds. I could see nothing unusual, but given the day's insights, there was little doubt in my mind who it was. I continued to walk, watching the trees with my peripheral vision, but whatever was out there remained beyond the range of my ordinary perception.

I retreated to my room and climbed into bed, but sleep was elusive. I tossed and turned as the knowledge I had gained during the intensive week of science ran through my mind in an ongoing stream. Toward midnight I was still awake. My attention kept being drawn to the window, so I got out of bed and pulled up a comfortable chair that allowed me to semirecline with my feet propped up on the sill. I stared out into the darkness of the trees and recalled the Zen retreat in Hawai'i when the leopard man had come for me out of the forest. I wondered again if he was out there now. Eight months had passed since my last connection with Nainoa. Perhaps I could utilize my spirit helper to facilitate a journey to the future.

About forty-five minutes passed before I let the intention go and got back into bed. I relaxed at last, surrendering into a dreamy mind state in preparation for sleep, and had almost slipped off when I felt the first approach of the sensations of power. They were there, just at the edge of my awareness. My dissolving consciousness reformed and turned toward them excitedly, and *wham!* They slammed into me, rendering my physical body rigid in an instant.

As the ecstatic rush of feeling filled me and the familiar phosphenic hallucinations appeared, I recalled how I had left my body at the Zen retreat, and with that thought, I felt a curious pulling sensation high up between my shoulder blades and the base of my neck. Then there was a pop, and I rose effortlessly from the bed. The dark room seemed to brighten as I looked down. There I was, lying under the covers, my face immobile and my body fully extended. As I marveled, I heard a sound I remembered well.

Tok!

It came from the trees beyond the window. Without making the decision to do so, I drifted toward the door and opened it, then walked down the hall and descended the stairs. At the bottom, I glanced across the large room that served as a foyer. One of my colleagues was seated on a couch with the attractive, dark-haired barmaid, who was now obviously off duty. The two seemed involved in an intense discussion. Curiously, I could feel their emotional states as I observed them. Perhaps a romance was in bloom.

Tok!

The sound summoned me. I left them and drifted out through the door. The trees that had been concealed by darkness only moments before were now illuminated by the golden light of an early summer dawn. I felt absolutely marvelous. I looked around for the leopard man. I didn't see him, and was about to head for the pond where I had seen the snakes when—

Tok!

It came from the opposite direction, down toward the lake. As I turned and headed that way, I saw my spotted friend. He was near a stream, half concealed by the trees, and was humanoid in shape. I raised my arm in greeting and saw him close his eyes, then open them again in that distinct catlike squint. The trees had a curious vibratory quality to them, their outlines flickering slightly in my peripheral vision. I was aware that I could see in all directions at once, although as I refocused on my spirit helper, that location became primary.

I joined the leopard man, noting that the spots on top of his head had shifted somehow to become a pattern of broad stripes, creating a vague symbolic resemblance to my hair that didn't quite work. I murmured a phrase of greeting and got a deep, throaty rattle in response. Then I ran my fingers through his coat as I always do— along the jaws and up behind the ears. The rattle deepened as his green eyes closed with pleasure. I scratched his head, and the sound rose in volume, producing a soft, rhythmic roar. I wondered why he didn't purr, then reflected that I had never heard a real leopard purr. Maybe they don't.

The leopard man opened his eyes, then abruptly turned and walked downhill through the trees. I followed. As we approached the lake, swans appeared from under the bridge, and the therianthrope immediately dropped down onto all fours, becoming entirely feline as his attention fastened on the waterfowl. I saw the manor house on the hill overlooking the lake below. It looked different somehow. I wasn't sure why.

A rushing sound began to manifest itself in my ears. It appeared to come from the stream flowing into the lake. I glanced at the leopard and saw he was now watching me curiously. He still appeared entirely catlike, and as I locked eyes with him, I reflected that this was probably the last thing seen by many an australopithecine.

I glanced at the manor again and recalled something from my last vision, a memory of Chief Kaneohe saying that he had sent a message to the governor. Seeing the opulent mansion may have provided some inner connection, because I suddenly felt myself being drawn outward. As the rushing, roaring sound increased, I remembered Dorothy in *The Wizard of Oz* clicking her heels together and saying, "There's no place like home . . . there's no place like home." I wasn't sure if I had heels at that moment, and I had no time to think about it as a gust of wind hit me and a sense of movement began.

The scene before me darkened as the sensations of power increased enormously. The last thing I saw was the leopard's coat as it shifted into color negative, its black spots becoming light as the tawny background of its coat went dark. Then only the spots remained until they too flattened out and stretched into lines of light that streamed into the infinite distance of the grid. One line distinguished itself from the others, curving and opening into the brilliant crescent that looked like the sliver of a new moon. As it opened still further, its points seemed to meet, and I was drawn into it with a roaring rush of fiery sensation. Then the lights were gone. The darkness was total and all sound ceased as I passed through the zone of silence.

In the next moment I wondered if I had fallen into the lake. I clearly felt my body cleave the surface and heard the rush of water as I rose to the surface, the phosphenes reforming as light-filled bubbles rising with me. In the next moment, I found myself blinking water out of my eyes and looking up at one of the most striking women I had ever seen.

CHAPTER 12

Sixth Journey: Kahalopuna

NAINOA FLUNG WATER from his hair and face with a single sweep of his head as he surfaced. It was late in the day, and he was swimming with his Ennu friends in the lagoon below Chief Wilipaki's private residence at the outskirts of the capital. They had arrived that afternoon on Chief Kaneohe's double-hulled state canoe, a sixty-foot-long craft that was moored beside the dock jutting out from the shore. The three of them were due to be presented at the governor's mansion within the next few days.

As he glanced toward the dock, his attention was caught by a human figure backlit by the setting sun. A tall young woman was standing near the canoe holding a large bundle in her arms. Her long dark hair was worn loose, and she was dressed in a plain cotton garment that covered her from her shoulders to her ankles. A *lei* of yellow flowers wrapped around her head matched another encircling her neck. Her height and bearing revealed her as a chief, but unlike most of the ruling class, her build was slight and she had dark eyes. And right now, those eyes were regarding him with interest.

"So this is the new Chief Nainoa Kaneohe," she said. "Ali'i Nainoa . . . ," she repeated, using the classic term for "chief" in Old Hawaiian, as if testing the sound of it.[1] Then her serious look was replaced by the hint of a smile. "I've heard you have become a *kahuna* of some ability, Ali'Noa."

Nainoa looked her over carefully. He had no idea who she was and wondered at her familiarity in giving him a nickname combining the first syllable of the word for "chief" with the last half of his name. William swam up beside him. "Nice-looking young woman," he whispered in Ennu. "Who is she?"

"I must confess that you have the advantage of me, chiefess," Nainoa began formally. "My friends and I are visitors to the capital and are staying in Chief Wilipaki's guesthouse. Have we met before?" He swam closer to see her more clearly, then stopped and treaded water as he remembered he was naked.

"We have, but you obviously don't remember. And I had heard so much about your skills of memory," she teased good-naturedly. Nainoa studied her high cheekbones and finely chiseled features but couldn't recall ever meeting her before. He had to admit to himself that William was right. She was very attractive. Unlike most chiefesses, whose beauty tended to be judged by their size, her body was long and slender, producing a rather flat-chested figure not unlike Kenojelak's.

The woman stooped and placed her bundle on the dock at her feet, revealing long, slim legs and strong feet as her dress parted. She glanced at the Ennu dogs tied to a dock post, then bent with a graceful gesture and slowly extended her hand to the nearest, the white female, Ziku. As Nainoa opened his mouth to warn her, William placed a hand on his shoulder, stopping him. They watched as the dog sniffed her hand at length, then allowed her to scratch its head. It was the first time that anyone besides Nainoa or the Ennu had done so. The woman's full smile revealed a flash of white teeth.

181

"Ziku likes her," William chortled in Ennu. "Good sign." The woman straightened at his comment and looked down once again at the three men in the water. "Chief Wilipaki has sent these clothes for you from his personal stores." She indicated the bundle with a rather imperious glance. "The cloak and pants with the spotted pattern are for you, Ali'Noa. Wilipaki said you would understand why. You will appreciate the softness of the cotton grown in this land division. Those tattoos still look rather fresh."

Nainoa glanced down at the right side of his body. Long rows of zigzags, lines, dots, and triangles descended from his hairline, across his face, and down the length of his frame to his foot. Another series of designs encircled his right biceps. He had received the tattoos as part of the ceremony inducting him into the chiefly Order of Kahuna. Chief Kaneohe's personal tattooist had done the honors using the traditional comblike needles and ink freshly prepared from the soot of burned *kukui* nut shells. The scars were almost healed now. He looked over at his Ennu companions. They too had received a set of tattoos in honor of the occasion and were quite taken with them.

All this passed through his mind in an instant as the woman spoke once more. "Chiefess Lowena and Chief Wilipaki are preparing a feast in your honor and invite you and your companions to dine with them and their family at their residence this evening." She paused, as if undecided about what to say next, then concluded, "You certainly have grown into a chiefly-looking individual since I last saw you, Ali'Noa." Abruptly she pivoted and climbed the wooden steps up the steep riverbank. At the top of the levee she turned and looked back at him for one long moment, then she disappeared into the chief's compound.

"Heeeee . . ." William let out a breathy laugh. "That one has plans for you, Nainoapak. And what a beauty! Did you see her eyes? And those legs? I'll bet she could dance for half the night and still hold a man captive until dawn with those legs."

Nainoa looked at the older man with amusement. "And how much sleep have you had recently, William? Are there any women left in the

Kaneohe land division who have not taken it upon themselves to comfort you?" In addition to performing hundreds of healings during the past month, William's physical strength and personal charm had made quite an impression on the women of the community. Despite his age and minimal knowledge of the language, he had taken at least a dozen lovers, from chiefesses to commoners. Such ribaldry was customary during the dry season following the harvest.

Delighted at the question, the older man threw back his head and laughed. "When you get to be my age, Nainoapak, you don't need sleep." His eyes grew wistful. "There are all these affectionate women who want me to visit with them. I can't understand it myself." He tugged at his long hair with a strong hand. "My hair is turning gray, yet still they invite me. And how can I refuse? They are all so lovely."

He paused again, then observed stoically, "Your Hawaiian women are very strong, and they have wonderful hearts. They are filled with this thing you call *aloha*. This is an interesting word to me. It has many meanings according to context. I am not sure how we Ennu would express it, but 'heart-spirit' comes close. Even though I cannot talk your language well, your women express a strong sense of heart-spirit, and this has a language of its own."

Nainoa looked at the older man with affection. To William, it made no difference if a woman was beautiful or homely, young or old. He loved them all with a friendly, humorous fervor, to which they responded with equal warmth, generosity, and depth of spirit. William was one of the kindest people he had ever met. In the year he had known him, he had never seen the old hunter lose his temper or express anger or irritation in word or deed.

Nainoa recalled incidents from his younger days when he too had established strong alliances among the women of the settlement. This year he had not taken part in such enjoyments, to the disappointment of many. As he watched others indulge in affairs of the body and heart, his spirit had yearned for Kenojelak, creating an emptiness within him that was not yet ready to be filled by another.

William had observed him with concern as he gently deflected one potential lover after another, including many of the highest-ranking young women of his settlement. "It is not in our nature to sleep alone, Nainoapak," the older man had said to him one morning as he returned bleary-eyed from an all-night tryst. "These women can feel the loneliness within you, and they yearn to comfort you. My daughter will be your Ennu wife whenever you come to live in our camp. The heart connection between the two of you will last all of your lives. But you must take another wife here among your own people. In this way, balance and harmony will return to you. Your emptiness will be refilled with affection, and you will feel complete once again. This is necessary for your well-being."

All this passed through his mind as he swam toward the ladder of the dock. From behind him, William said, "That's the one, Nainoapak. I could see your children looking at the two of you." Nainoa stopped dead in the water and turned to the older man. "What do you mean, William? What did you see?"

"Sometimes I see things, or rather, sometimes things are shown to me," he said vaguely. "When the two of you looked each other over, I saw several others—I assume they are your children-to-be. They appeared within the woman's mind, and I saw them look out through her eyes. They have chosen you to be their father, Nainoapak, and so has she." He grinned hugely and clapped him on the back, letting out a laugh of pure joy. "Get ready!"

Nainoa treaded water while he considered the implications of the older man's words. After a long silence, he asked, "Will Kenojelak accept my taking another woman as wife, William?"

The Ennu looked at him with amusement and answered, "Of course, Nainoapak. She knew before you left our camp that you would do this. The river spirit told her that this was destined to happen and that it was part of your path through this lifetime to meet a woman among your own people and have children by her. The water spirit said that there is an old connection between you and this woman, and that this union had been decided on long ago."

Nainoa felt puzzled. He was quite sure he had never met her

before. He didn't even know her name. He refocused his attention on the older man and said, "Kenojelak didn't tell me about this, William."

"Of course she didn't, Nainoapak," William answered gently. "My daughter is wise. She also understands the nature of men and women and how they must find each other to establish a balanced whole.

"We men are hunters of game and hunters of wives; we are also gatherers of medicinal plants and stone suitable for tools. Some men are hunters of spiritual power and knowledge as well, and many of these men serve as *ungagok* for our people. Our women also hunt, but small game like monkeys and fish, turtles and birds, and they also gather—plant foods and plant medicines and grasses for baskets. But most important, women are the gatherers of family. It is through our women and their ability to bear children that our lineages continue and our survival is ensured.

"Some women also acquire great spiritual power and knowledge. Kenojelak is such a woman. The spirits have revealed that her path is to function as *ungagok* for her people. She takes after her father." He beamed with joy, then his eyes became misty.

"There was a great dreamer in my wife Kalvak's lineage whose name was also Kenojelak. Our daughter is named for her." He grinned and continued. "This dreamer was Kalvak's grandmother. I knew her as a boy, so I remember her quite clearly." His words trailed off as his mind moved down well-known trails.

"The old Kenojelak told me once that when she was first approached by the spirits, she didn't want the power, nor did she want to be *ungagok*. The spirits expressed their displeasure with her rejection by inflicting misfortune and suffering on her. And when she continued to resist, they extended these afflictions to her family. And when she still resisted, the whole camp came down with a serious illness. In the end, everyone begged her to take up her responsibility and cure them of their afflictions, and when she saw how much suffering her refusal had caused, she agreed.

"The spirits were pleased by her change of heart, and with their help, she was able to cure the whole group. She then served her people as a healer and a spiritwalker and became a dreamer of great power until she passed into the spirit world and did not return."

William was silent for a time, then he said, "There were also *ungagok* who were accomplished healers in my father's lineage, but the old Kenojelak was really something. I suspect that the old Kenojelak's spirit has returned with her *odiok*, her name soul, that was given to my daughter at her birth. My daughter is much like her great-grandmother."

"What do you mean, William?" Nainoa probed. "Is Kenojelak in fact her great-grandmother, who has returned for another life on the physical plane of existence?" He recalled the conversation he had had with Chief Kaneohe about the nature of reincarnation and the transmission of *ike* and added, "Does your daughter possess the old Kenojelak's spiritual power?"

"But of course, Nainoapak. Why do you think I sometimes call her 'grandmother'?" The older man looked amused, then his demeanor turned serious. "Nainoapak, that beautiful woman who just addressed you also possesses spiritual power. She is still young, but I could see the spirits gathered around her. I could see her light and sense her abilities to some extent. She could become a powerful *ungagok*, or as you say, *kahuna*. Perhaps she is a spiritwalker, a visionary like you, who is able to visit the inner worlds. You have an interesting ability to ally yourself with such people, Nainoapak, and this is very good."

"I wish to seek closer connection with the inner worlds, and with the spirits that reside there," Nainoa proclaimed. "You have told me that mature spiritwalkers can summon and see spirits at will, eventually achieving the ability to see them all the time, even in their ordinary state of consciousness."

"It is true, Nainoapak. Your intentions will activate the process that will deepen with practice. Seeking connection with the spirits is like shooting an arrow with two points, one that is actually flying in both directions at once. When you reach out to the spirits and they see that the way is open to them, they will enter into relationship with you. Then you will acquire their abilities and their power. You will feel as they feel, see as they see. You will speak with their voice and think with their thoughts, gaining the benefit of the enormous wisdom that they possess. When you become one with the spirits, you will be able to do many things. You will have access to all the many levels of the inner worlds, both those below this one and those above. And you will be able to accomplish certain things here in this level of reality. Your body and mind will be like a flute through which the breath blows without hindrance, both your breath and theirs."

"But what if I encounter a malevolent spirit, William? Surely there are some less-than-positive forces in those levels of awareness and experience."

"There are indeed, but here is something truly wonderful, Nainoapak. Once you have spirit helpers, the negative forces cannot touch you. If you find yourself in difficulty, simply summon your *dordok*, and they will deal with the problem. Spirit helpers are the providers of power and protection, guidance and direction, teaching and information, and as I have said, sometimes they allow you to merge with them, enabling you to access their abilities and their capacities for action.

"The realm where the spirits reside is largely a level of information. This everyday world here is a level of action, a level on which many things are possible. It is here that we hunt and find mates and have families. You see, it is through propitious pairings and having children that men and women have the opportunity to further the growth and the balance and harmony of the universe. This is our true work as human beings. It is a big responsibility, when you think of it. We are actually involved in creating the mind-spirit of the universe." His voice drifted off as he considered the magnitude of the endeavor.

At this point, several servants appeared on the levee above and descended to the dock, bringing refreshments to the travelers. Nainoa's thoughts were preoccupied with everything William had said as he climbed the ladder and was handed a towel. He thanked the servant as he dried himself, then combed and tied back his hair. Then he dressed in the pants and cloak with the spotted pattern and put on his chief's necklace before turning to the servant in charge and asking his name. The man bowed in deference and said, "My name is Milo, Chief Nainoa."

"Tell me, Milo, who is the tall woman with the dark eyes who just brought us these clothes, if I may ask?"

"That is High Chiefess Maraea Kahalopuna, second daughter of High Chief Pita Wilipaki and High Chiefess Lowena Kahalopuna. She is also the granddaughter of Governor Ruth Kahalopuna and great-granddaughter to the old governor, High Chiefess Mary Kahalopuna." As the servant began to recount the woman's genealogy of esteemed ancestors, Nainoa stopped him with a gesture, thanked him for the information, and withdrew into thought.

The image of a gawky little girl emerged from his memories, and with it, a long-forgotten episode that had occurred during his first visit to the capital almost twenty years ago. His adoptive father, Kiwini, had been chosen to accompany Chief Kaneohe on a state visit, and he had come along, a nine-year-old servant's son who had gazed wide-eyed at the wonders of the court. One day, while his father was engaged in business, he was wandering near the river looking for turtles when some older boys of the chiefly class decided to bully him.

"Who is this low-born boy walking uninvited in our territory?" the ringleader had opened in a nasal voice thick with condescension. Before he could answer, four others grabbed him by the arms and legs and pinned him facedown on the muddy riverbank. A blow had landed on his back, knocking the wind out of him. As he struggled to breathe, the older boy continued speaking in a flat tone. "He certainly lacks manners. I believe he needs a lesson. What do the rest of you think?"

"Indeed, Kulo," said another. "Cut a switch from the thickets and give him a dozen or two to teach him." And so it had happened, Nainoa gasping with pain as the measured, stinging blows landed on his buttocks and the backs of his thighs. Suddenly a high voice rang out. "Enough! Stop that at once, Kulo, or I'll see you receive twice as many across your own tender backside!" With those words the hands holding him down had vanished and the blows had stopped.

"Well, if it isn't skinny Maraea," said the nasal voice mockingly. "Since when do you take on the defense of insolent servants, Your Highness?"

"I saw the whole thing, Kulo. The boy did nothing to merit your insufferable behavior. I intend to have a word with your mother about this. I suggest you and the rest of your low-ranking vermin crawl back to the manure piles where you usually play."

A shocked silence had followed this statement, and Nainoa had taken this opportunity to rise, blood oozing from his welts. To his amazement, a thin little girl with long legs and big feet was standing between him and his tormentors, her fierce poise in direct contrast with her diminutive size. She couldn't have been more than five years old, maybe six. The older boy had glowered at her in response and made a crude gesture. Then he had turned and slouched off, followed by his henchmen. The girl was obviously of higher rank.

The girl's blazing eyes had softened as she turned to him and examined his backside and legs. "Who are you, boy? Do you have a name?"

"My name is Nainoa, Chiefess Maraea," he had answered politely. "My father, Kiwini, is senior clerk to High Chief John Kaneohe, who is visiting the governor on business." He had glanced down deferentially, his eyes coming to rest on a bracelet encircling her wrist. It had an ivory turtle fastened to its center. She raised her hand toward him and he took it, pressing her fingertips to his forehead as he bowed in acknowledgment of her rank.

"And what are you doing here by the river?" she had asked.

"Looking for turtles," he replied.

"Come with me, Nainoa. My mother is a skilled *kahuna,* and I know where she keeps a medicine that will help your wounds to heal. Afterward I'll show you a place where some baby turtles have recently hatched. If we're lucky, we'll see them sunning on driftwood. If we are skilled, maybe we can catch one. You certainly are tall for a servant."

Little Maraea had become his friend and ally during the next few days, showing him all her secret places in the forest and introducing him to her pets. Her parents had been away, so he had been unaware until now that she was Lowena and Wilipaki's daughter. He had missed her when he and his father returned with the high chief to their own community.

All this passed through his mind as he stood on the dock. He couldn't believe the skinny little girl with big feet was the same beautiful and commanding person who had just stood before him.

When the night sky darkened and the first stars appeared, Milo arrived at the large guest house where the travelers were resting and summoned them to dinner. "I am to serve you and your friends personally during your stay at the capital, Chief Nainoa," said the servant, bowing his head. "Please request anything of which you might have need, day or night."

As they walked across the stone-paved courtyard of Chief Wilipaki's compound, Nainoa glanced at his friends in the torchlight. William and his son had put on weight during their stay with the Hawaiians. Their hair was tied back in the current style, which, combined with their tattoos and chiefly attire, had completely transformed them. They were now ready to be presented to the governor. He hoped they would remember to bow when the moment came. William caught his eye and grinned at him.

Chief Wilipaki and Chiefess Lowena were awaiting them on the broad *lanai* of their personal residence. *"E komo'mai . . . e komo'mai."* The ancient words of welcome were offered with warm smiles and strong embraces. "In honor of the occasion of your visit," began Chiefess Lowena, "we have lifted the *kapu* and prepared a *lu'au* in which all of our family will eat together, both men and women, so that all may share in the *mana* generated by our collective presence. You are welcome in our household for as long as you wish to stay and are under our protection. If there is anything of which you have need, it is yours."

As Nainoa translated for his Ennu companions, the rustle of clothing revealed the approach of a tall woman coming through the growing darkness. It was Chiefess Maraea. She was wearing a long white
dress of woven cotton with a high collar and long sleeves that empha-
sized her height. A chief's necklace rested on her chest above her
flower *lei.* He could smell its fragrance as he bowed and said, "Good
evening, Chiefess. Do you still watch for turtle hatchlings near the
bend of the river?"

"I do." Maraea's dark eyes glowed under her strong eyebrows and
her teeth flashed with a merry peal of laughter. "So Chief Nainoa has
found his memory after all." As she tossed back her dark mane of hair
with a flourish, her back was straight and her poise regal. She raised
her hand to him, and he saw her slim brown wrist encircled by the
bracelet with a carved ivory turtle fastened in its center. He took her
hand and pressed her fingers to his forehead, bowing his head in
acknowledgment of her higher rank. Her hand squeezed his before
letting go.

"I remember," he replied with a smile, "but I must confess that I
had to ask Milo who you were. It has been a long time, and you have
bloomed so beautifully." Maraea accepted his compliment with a level
gaze, then said, "Milo told me you asked." Her eyes narrowed speculatively. "So you are still a person of integrity. I remember that quality
in you as a boy. That you still possess it reflects your honor, Chief
Nainoa."

As the other guests arrived, Nainoa and his friends were introduced
to Wilipaki and Lowena's older daughter and her husband; Wilipaki's
mother, who was quite old; various uncles and aunts and their mates
as well as selected older nephews and nieces, and several close friends
of the family. All were dressed for the occasion, the women sheathed
in long gowns and bedecked with flower *leis* and personal ornaments,
the men wrapped in patterned cloaks and loose pants cut long. The
broad *lanai* filled with talking, gesticulating people, exchanging news
and trading bits of gossip.

Nainoa thought about William's perceptions as he watched Maraea

191

interact with members of her family, her eyes and teeth catching the torchlight as she laughed in response to humorous comments. She seemed at ease with them, and they with her. For the first time since his parting from Kenojelak, he felt himself responding to another woman and realized that she reminded him of his Ennu wife. They were similar in physique, but more to the point, Maraea had the same directness of manner. As these thoughts passed through his mind, she caught him looking at her and held his eyes for a long moment. He felt a hollow place appear in his chest. Aware that he was staring, he glanced away politely and saw Milo directing the servants who were setting up the dinner party. He walked over to him.

"Tell me, Milo, I haven't met Chiefess Maraea's husband. Is she married?"

"No, Chief Nainoa," the servant replied with a smile. "The chiefess has proven most difficult to her parents, refusing many politically desirable matches for reasons that are obscure. Her grandmother, the governor, has indulged her in these matters, proclaiming that High Chiefess Maraea will marry whom she chooses. They are much alike, she and her grandmother—very intelligent and very strong-willed."

A commotion drew their attention toward the entrance of the compound as torch-bearers appeared, heralding the arrival of yet another guest. Wilipaki and Lowena excused themselves from their family and headed for the open courtyard. Wilipaki caught Nainoa's eye and beckoned to him, saying, "There is someone who wishes to meet you, Chief Nainoa."

Behind the torches appeared an ornate open litter borne on the shoulders of half a dozen husky servants. Upon the litter's carved seat sat a tall, elderly woman in a long white dress, her gray hair drawn back from her dark face and held in place by a thick yellow flower *lei* that matched another around her neck. As the bearers approached, Wilipaki and Lowena bowed, going down on one knee. Conversation ceased as the assembled gathering followed suit.

Nainoa's heart pounded with excitement as he stared down at the paving stones and saw the bearers' sandaled feet come to a halt before him. As the litter was lowered to the ground, he glanced up and found himself looking straight into the commanding dark eyes of Governor Ruth Kahalopuna. "She has eyes like her granddaughter," was his first thought.

For long moments the older woman looked into his soul, then her formal expression softened into a smile and she extended her hand to him. He took it, touching her fingertips to his forehead in deference, then rose to his feet and met her gaze. She did not relinquish his hand. Silence filled the courtyard.

In one fluid movement the governor stood and gracefully descended from the litter, using Nainoa to steady herself. She squeezed his hand, then beamed at him and said, "Greetings, Chief Nainoa Kaneohe, and welcome to the Kahalopuna land division. My daughter"—she directed a warm glance at Chiefess Lowena—"has told me so much about you that I couldn't wait to meet you at court."

"I am greatly honored, Ali'i Nui," Nainoa replied, using the ancient title. He gestured to William and Zaki and said, "May I present Chief William and his son Zaki, visitors from the east." To his great relief, both took the governor's proffered hand and bowed, touching her fingertips to their foreheads, as he had done before, straightening to gaze directly into her eyes.

"Welcome to our visitors. I am told that they are the descendants of the American people and that they speak a language unknown to us," the governor remarked, looking them over. She was a head taller than both. "I have also heard you have discovered vast numbers of horses in the country east of the mountains."

"That is true, Ali'i Nui. I have an interesting account to relate," Nainoa responded.

The governor smiled. "I have issued invitations to the ruling chiefs of all the land divisions to come to Kahalopuna. Many have arrived already. When all are here, we will gather at court. I wish to hear a full account of your extraordinary adventure. I also wish to consult with you and Chief William about a matter of personal concern. Come to my residence soon." She thought for a few seconds, then added, "Perhaps the day after tomorrow, in the midafternoon."

Then the older woman cast her glance across the assembled chiefly families and smiled warmly at them, giving a collective greeting to which all responded with raised hands and broad smiles. She beckoned to Maraea, who approached and bowed gracefully. The governor took her hand affectionately, then turned to Nainoa and said, "I remember the time you came to Kahalopuna with your father, Chief Nainoa. I have been told that you used to play with my granddaughter. She has turned out rather well, don't you think?"

The feast that followed was lavish, with every effort made to produce a memorable event. The governor sat on a pile of cushions behind a low table in the center of the raised platform at the end of the reception hall with Nainoa on her right and Maraea on her left. To Nainoa's right sat William, Zaki, and Wilipaki. To Maraea's left sat her mother and sister. About fifty of the governor's immediate family members and friends sat or reclined on large cushions around several long tables below them. The men sat together on the south side of the hall, the women on the north. The floor was spread with newly woven mats and the low tables were covered with fragrant flowers and freshly cut banana leaves on which seasonal delicacies and fresh fruit were placed. Around the room's perimeter, small fires burned in stone bowls filled with *kukui* oil.

At the beginning of the meal, the governor complimented her hosts, using ancient words in Old Hawaiian to proclaim the gathering to be one of great import.

"This *aha'aina ho'okipa*, this feast of welcome for Chief Nainoa Kaneohe and his guests, brings merit to all," she announced in a ringing voice:

E aumakua
Mai ka la hiki a ka la kau

E ho'omaikai keia hale
E ho'omaikai keia ai
E ho'omaikai keia po'e ohana
E na aumakua
Mai ka po makana olakino a me lawa pono
Ho'ike a mai ike ola
Amama . . . ua noa.

Ancestral spirits
From the sun's rising to the sun's setting
Blessings on this house
Blessings on this food
Blessings on this family gathering
Ancestral immortals
Bring forth from the spirit world the gifts of good health and
    abundance
And manifest these blessings
The prayer has flown . . . the restrictions are lifted.

Servants then appeared in an endless stream bearing wooden plat-ters of food. There were roasted and steamed meats, including pork, beef, goat, and, most prized of all, roasted dog. There was game from the forest and several kinds of fish, octopus, and squid, as well as shrimp sieved from the lagoons and served in great pink piles on platters of steamed greens with bowls of spicy sauce for dipping. Sweet potatoes, taro, and breadfruit were served in a number of different ways along with chickens and wild birds, rubbed with herbs and salt and roasted whole. There were mounds of sweet fried plan-tains and wooden bowls of cooked beans. Several different puddings of coconut cream mixed with mashed bananas, sweet potatoes, or breadfruit were served wrapped in the *ti*-leaf bundles in which they had been steamed.

The chiefly families talked and laughed and ate with their fingers, often leaning across the table to pop some delicacy into the mouth of a close family member or friend. Behind them stood their personal attendants, serving the food, emptying scrap and finger bowls, and replenishing the cups of drinking water. When *oki*, made from fermented *ti* root, was served, the celebration grew in volume.

Ruth Kahalopuna accepted a small cup of *oki*, then poured some for Nainoa and said, "I have seated you next to my good ear so that we may talk, Chief Nainoa. Tell me more about our esteemed guests. I am curious about what happened to the once-great Americans and their civilization."

As Nainoa began to speak, he saw Maraea and her mother listening intently. Slowly the rest of the guests took note and the room quieted. All listened as Nainoa the voyager related a tale from his long year's reconnaissance into the unknown interior of the continent beyond the mountains.

When he finished, all called upon Maraea to rise and perform a *hula* to a chant composed in Nainoa's honor. As he watched her dance, the hollow place in his chest returned. She concluded her performance with the traditional low bow offered to him, and all, including Nainoa, applauded her mightily. William shot him a conspiratorial look and grinned.

It was late when the governor and the guests departed, their minds filled with the stories that Nainoa had told them. When he finally bid Chief Wilipaki and his family good night, Nainoa asked, "Might I have your permission to use the bathhouse, sir? I feel the need to steam off the *oki*."

Wilipaki smiled and dispatched a servant to ensure that the water in the large soaking pool was still hot. "My compound is yours, Chief Nainoa. Please consider this your home at the capital."

William had caught the fancy of a handsome middle-aged widow and gave Nainoa a cheery wave as he discreetly slipped off with her into the night. Zaki returned to the guest house to feed the dogs and go to bed. Maraea was the last to approach him before leaving for her quarters. The remaining guests had departed, and aside from passing servants, they found themselves alone, so she spoke informally.

"I enjoyed hearing of your adventures tonight, Ali'Noa, and look forward to the detailed accounts at the governor's court." She smiled warmly. "Who would have guessed that the boy interested in turtles would have become such a famous explorer? But then, you are descended from esteemed ancestors. My father has told me about your grandfather, the great sorcerer whose name is never mentioned. I have heard that you have inherited his *mauli* and his *ike*, his life force and mystic ability. I have also been told that unlike him, you possess a bright spirit. I remember you as a child and I have watched you all evening, and I know that this is so."

In the silence that followed, her dark eyes took on a luminous quality. "Only the Kaneohes, my immediate family, the governor, and a few others know of your ancestry at present, but word will get out. There are few secrets of this magnitude that remain secret for long, and as the account of your great voyage of discovery spreads throughout the land divisions, your genealogy will become known. You are going to become a person of power, Chief Nainoa." Her eyes narrowed mischievously under her dark eyebrows in an expression he remembered from long ago. "You are going to enjoy your stay at the capital, Ali'Noa. I bid you good night."

A few minutes later Nainoa entered the darkened inner room of the bathhouse and slipped into the large stone-lined pool, luxuriating in the steamy, chest-deep water. He had missed hot water more than anything else during his year away. He floated on his back in the dark and looked out at the night sky through the open section of the wall that faced the lagoon below the thatched roof. The stars were indistinguishable in the hazy dry season sky.

He now knew where the haze came from. It was carried by the northeast wind from the vast, dusty plains of the continent's dry interior. He suspected that much of the haze was also caused by the Ennu custom of burning the grasses and shrubs to clear the grassy woodlands of undergrowth before the season of hot winds arrived. They always did this at a certain time of the year, when the ground still contained enough moisture, so that the burn would not penetrate deeply or kill the trees. When the rains returned, the scorched wood-lands came back to life, erupting with prolific greenery, attracting the game animals and making it easy to find them.

Images of the Ennu lands moved through his mind, and as always, a sense of emptiness appeared within him as he imagined Kenojelak in the camp below the scarred mountain where he had left her. She was probably sharing a hut with her mother. He wondered if she was sleeping, or if she too was awake, staring into the night sky and thinking of him.

His thoughts turned to Chiefess Maraea, and William's insights about her surfaced in his mind. Was this the woman that destiny intended for him, the governor's granddaughter? Chief Kaneohe had ruminated about the advantages of a political marriage. Maraea was certainly politically well connected. Among the chiefly class, it was the women who chose their husbands. Children were members of their mother's descent group, and the men who were politically powerful rulers achieved their position by virtue of their relationship to high-ranking women. As Maraea's husband, he would have very high rank indeed, and so would their children. But would she choose him?

Nainoa thought of a recent connection that he had had with his ancestor. It had happened spontaneously one morning while he was lying in bed just before dawn. His body had been invaded by the overwhelming feelings of power or force, whereupon his conscious awareness had detached and journeyed across time to merge with that of the American once again. As always, he had listened to the Ameri-can's thoughts, able to perceive his recollections and feel his emotions, receiving the entirety of the man's mind-shape as a multileveled expe-rience within his own mind. How simply amazing this phenomenon was.

He thought about the American's wife, Jill, and his dreamy state sobered with a jolt. As he recalled her physical beauty, her quick sense of humor, and her direct, incisive intelligence, he realized that Maraea was much like her—so much so, in fact, that it was almost uncanny. What an extraordinary insight! He had come to accept the fact that he and the American could very well be differently manifested incarnations of a single spiritual source self. Could it be that Maraea was the descendant self of the American's wife? Could it be that the two of them had found each other once again across space and time? Intuitively he sensed it was possible. He had spent time with Jill and had even been "there" once when the American had made love with her. Yes, he knew her very well indeed.

His ruminations were interrupted by a strong sense of presence. He wondered automatically if it was the American, but then the bathwater rippled and he looked up in surprise. Someone had gotten into the other end of the pool with him, but it was too dark to see who it was. "Good evening," he said tentatively, then stopped awkwardly when he saw the person slip completely under the water. It must be some member of the Wilipaki-Kahalopuna family, but who? His speculations were abruptly terminated when the person surfaced directly in front of him and sprayed water in his face.

"Good evening yourself, Ali'Noa," Maraea said with a giggle. "I could not sleep, and so I came to talk to you without my entire family listening in."

As he blinked the water from his eyes, a memory of her doing the same thing to him as a child appeared in his mind. They had been swimming in the river, and she had emerged from underwater and squirted a mouthful of water full in his face. He had impulsively ducked her under before remembering her status and freezing with uncertainty. She had not rebuked him, but had seized his legs instead, pulling him under as well.

Without thinking, he reached out now and ducked her under, then stiffened as her body collided with his and he realized she was naked. In the next moment she knocked his legs out from under him. They surfaced together, sputtering and laughing. The darkness created a sense of safety—and intimacy. Nainoa was the first to speak.

"It is wonderful to see you again, Chiefess Maraea," he began formally.

"Ali'Noa," she replied, "when we are alone, never call me chiefess.

199

And furthermore, you cannot see me, nor I you." She briskly climbed the stone steps at the pool's edge and walked into the outer room. A moment later she returned with a flat stone oil lamp whose several wicks were alight. As she carefully placed it on a low table in the corner, his breath caught in his throat.

The lamplight gleamed off her long, wet body, accentuating her hollows and curves dramatically. She straightened and looked down at him, raising her slender arms to pull back her long mane of hair and revealing her small, high breasts with their dark, prominent nipples. He saw the dark hair in her underarms matched by the thick bush sparkling with drops of water below her flat belly. Her torso and legs seemed impossibly long. In that instant he knew with certainty that she was without doubt the most beautiful woman he had ever seen. The moment passed as she gracefully slipped back into the water beside him and whispered, "Now we can see each other, Ali'Noa."

She came close to him, then slowly reached out and took his face between her hands. Long moments passed in silence as they looked into each other's eyes, whereupon he slowly reached out and took her face between his. She did not stop him as his fingers traced the contours of her prominent cheekbones and the convolutions of her small ears. Then, very slowly, he took her into his arms.

"Maraea," he murmured, then gasped with delight as he felt her nipples make light and momentary contact with his chest. She rubbed herself against him again and exhaled with a sigh of pleasure as his growing erection brushed against her belly. Her legs closed, trapping him between them. Then, with infinite slowness, her full mouth found his.

As the kiss between them grew and deepened, she reached down and grasped him firmly, investigating his manhood curiously before wrapping herself around him and guiding him deeply into her body. The warm water supported them as they flowed together in the ancient ritual of union and affirmation. Laughing and whispering, their hands explored each other ceaselessly, her fingers as bold as his own. As he responded to the eroticism of making love with this beautiful woman in the dark pool, Nainoa felt the bond between them deepening.

Their lovemaking was protracted as the tension within them grew. And when her moment approached, she held him deeply inside her and thrashed her hips against him feverishly, sobbing with pleasure as she reached for the release that would carry her beyond the edge. As it arrived, she fastened her mouth to his, stifling her groans with his lips as her fingers wove themselves into his long hair. He held her tightly in his arms, his fingers guiding her into and through the deep ecstasy until he felt her rigid body relax. Then her mouth slowly disengaged from his and her body released him. Her words drifted in the steam off the water.

"What a thoroughly wonderful man you have become, Ali'Noa. You are indeed a treasure. Let us dry off and lie together on the sleeping platform in the outer room."

Their passionate investigations of each other lasted for much of the night. Toward the end, Maraea lay in his arms like a contented child, her long legs entwined with his as whispered endearments were offered, drawing them still closer together. She ran her fingertips across his lips and offered him her mouth to kiss again and again. It was close to dawn when she sat up, and her face became serious once more.

"Ali'Noa, the thread of mystic ability runs within my family too. My mother is a famed *kahuna* healer, skilled at working with the body and the soul, but it is my father who is the visionary. There is much that the two of you have to offer each other. He is very fond of you, and I know that a deep relationship will grow between you in the days and years to come.

"Interestingly, I have inherited my father's ability. I am a dreamer, and in my dreams, I travel into the worlds beyond this one, into the realms of *milu* below and *lanikeha* above, to the Lower Worlds of the spirits of nature and to the Upper Worlds of the *akuas* and the *aumakua* spirits. I have always been able to do this, even as a child.

"But there is something else. My perceptive abilities are strong enough for me to have discovered something about you during this night we have spent together." She paused and looked at him, reminding him briefly of her grandmother. "There is a woman in your life, Ali'Noa, and you care for her very deeply. I know this as surely as I know myself." For the first time, Nainoa saw Maraea look uncertain. "I would be honored if you would tell me about her."

And so he told her about his deep affection for William's daughter and of his acceptance that she would always stay with her own people. He described their meeting and the relationship that had grown between them during the year he had been with the Ennu. The eastern sky was lightening and the first birds beginning to sing as he finished his tale.

"So you see, Maraea, in the sacred place within my heart, a fire will always burn for her. There is a heart connection between us, and this will always exist. But I too have discovered something interesting during our night together—something I never expected to find here in the capital. I feel the same deep affection growing within me for you. The connection between us was established long ago, when we were children. The seed was planted then. Tonight it came to life, and it has begun to grow. What I feel for you is considerably more than physical attraction. Yet in the same breath, I must confess that you are the most beautiful woman I have ever met, and from the moment I saw you this afternoon, I felt great desire for you."

His fingers played absently in her hair as he gazed into her eyes in the torchlight. "I feel greatly blessed to have found you once again, Maraea." He smiled slowly with the wonder of it. "Now there are two fires burning within my heart."

Maraea lay back and looked at him for a long time before she spoke. "There have been other men in my life, too, but these affairs were exploratory and lacked the depth of the affection that I feel for you. There is no one in my life now, no one like you."

She sat up suddenly and her eyes narrowed in thought. "There is something else I must tell you, Ali'Noa—something important. When I saw you swimming in the lagoon this afternoon, I felt the presence of others. It was almost as though they were inside me, looking out through my eyes. They were looking at you, and I clearly heard one of them say, 'So he has finally come.' Another said, 'Yes, he is here at last. That is good. Now we can be born.' It startled me greatly. I did not expect this."

"William saw them, too," Nainoa said. "He believes they are the spirits of our unborn children." He lapsed into silence as Maraea slowly reached out and took his hand, weaving her fingers through his and kissing his wrist as her smile returned.

"I believe it, too."

As she released his hand, his fingertips trailed lightly across her breasts, and her nipples stiffened in response. She giggled with delight and kissed him warmly, thrusting her tongue deeply into his mouth. Then she rolled over on top of him, straddling him with her long legs as her tongue continued to dance within his mouth and her mane of black hair covered them both. His fingers trailed languidly down her back to find the cleavage of her soft bottom. She in turn reached down, discovered his growing response, and laughed throatily as she took him deeply into her body once more.

A sense of unrestrained wildness swept through them as their dance began again, taking on a new level of frenzied intensity. She drew back suddenly and gazed down at him with an amazed look, then she buried her face in his neck and whispered, "I have never met anyone like you . . . never before." There was a long silence as both were engulfed by the passion of their bodies. As her moment of ecstasy approached once again, she managed to breathe into his ear the words that emerged from her heart.

"I am fully aware of what has come to pass between us . . . and I too feel the deep affection growing between us at the heart level, Ali'Noa. I perceive the goodness in you . . . and the brightness of your spirit . . . and I feel great honor to ask you, Chief Nainoa

Kaneohe . . . will you take me for your wife? Will you be my lover . . . and my partner in life? Will you be my husband . . . and father to our children?"

A great stillness appeared within the storm of feelings swirling within him, and his response rose from deep within it. "I feel great honor to answer you, Chiefess Maraea Kahalopuna," he breathed into her mouth, "that I most certainly will."

Curiously, with these words, the memory of the American's wife appeared briefly in his mind, and then Maraea gasped and the world as he knew it shattered as he joined her in the deep ecstasy. It was at this moment that he felt the future lock into place and his loneliness depart.

CHAPTER 13

The Scientist and the Mystic

THE DAWN WAS just appearing through the window at the Airlie conference center at the termination of this event. Was it possible? I wondered. Was it really possible that Jill and I would find each other once again across the many millennia? I was completely wonder-struck by this amazing thought and by the fact that Nainoa had intuited it before I had. But then I recalled that it had been he, not I, who had come up with the theory that I was his ancestor. As my mind perused the extraordinary series of experiences to which I had been privy over the past eight years, I had to admit to myself that anything was possible.

I felt incredibly heightened as I rose from my bed and headed for the bathroom. As I stood under the steaming water of the shower, vivid memories from the recent vision streamed through my mind. In addition to everything else, I had discovered something of great interest: Nainoa's people are matrilineal. They trace their descent through the female line, and the rank of the men is determined by their relationship to high-ranking women. Chief Kaneohe, for example, is director of his settlement by virtue of his mother's rank, not his father's. In the same manner, Maraea's children will be members of her lineage, not Nainoa's (providing that all goes well and they do in fact have children). In addition, Maraea is of higher rank than her father, Chief Wilipaki, because her mother, Chiefess Lowena, being the governor's daughter, is of higher status. She is also obviously of higher rank than Nainoa, and so their children will hold a higher rank than their father.

I felt chagrined with myself for taking so long to discover this. Coming from a patrilineal society myself, I had simply assumed that Nainoa's culture was the same. As an anthropologist, I should have asked this question early on, but I had been so distracted by the fantastic nature of this bizarre experience that I had neglected to do so. This knowledge also seemed to provide yet one more oblique confirmation that I was not making all this up and that the information was coming *through* my mind rather than being a product *of* it.

As I headed down the hill for breakfast, I checked the ground where the leopard man and I had walked, but I saw no footprints, no animal tracks, no sign at all that we had passed that way. I looked through the trees and wondered if he was out there, watching me. If so, I did not see him.

As the week-long conference progressed, I felt myself continually shifting back and forth between the mystic's perspective and that of the highly trained scientist. Since I was surrounded by other scientists, the latter aspect of myself prevailed. For instance, I began to ask my fellow scientists about greenhouse warming and was not surprised to learn that there was no consensus on this controversial issue. My probes provoked strong opinions, though, often in contradiction to each other, and little by little I began to pick up information.

Like many in the scientific community, I was aware of the greenhouse warming controversy early on, but I had not been particularly concerned with it until my visionary experiences, in which I saw the California of the future covered with tropical forest and its central valley filled with water. When I began to read the scientific literature focused upon this issue, I found the growing body of evidence most persuasive. In fact, the majority of the scientific community has now begun to accept the hypothesis that a shift toward warmer climatic conditions has started.

A feature that has shown up in many scientists' general-circulation model simulations, for example, involves the effect of greenhouse-gas-induced climate change in warming the polar regions, a phenomenon that could give rise to a substantial retreat of the polar ice caps, releasing the water trapped in the ice and causing the oceans to rise. The supporting evidence for this is impressive.

In the northern polar regions, microwave remote sensing data revealed a significant diminishment in the extent of Arctic sea ice between 1978 and 1987, and an acceleration in the rate of decrease during the period from 1987 to 1994.[1] In the southern part of the world, a vast area of the ice covering the Weddell Sea, east of the Antarctic peninsula, disappeared during the winters of 1974 and 1976. Then, for three years, ending in 1992, the thick ice sheet covering Antartica's Bellingshausen Sea, once thought to be permanent, vanished almost entirely.

In April 1995 the potentially catastrophic consequences of greenhouse warming on the west and east Antarctic ice sheets were debated at the Woods Hole Oceanographic Institute in Massachusetts by specialists from many parts of the world.[2] Antarctica is divided by the Transantarctic Mountains into two icy regions. To the west, the smaller of the two ice caps rests on a submerged archipelago roughly the size of the Philippines. Since great "ice streams" currently flow relatively rapidly through the west Antarctic ice sheet and into the sea, the theory that greenhouse warming might cause the whole sheet to run off into the southern ocean is widely regarded as a distinct possibility. The first warning sign, the experts agreed, would be a retreat of the ice shelves that extend from the Antarctic continental margins into the ocean.

That sign has appeared. Glaciologists with the British Antarctic Survey have revealed that atmospheric warming has caused five of the floating ice shelves to shrink dramatically over the past fifty years. The most recent ice retreat came early in 1995, when a five-hundred-square-mile section of the Larsen ice shelf disintegrated in only fifty days, releasing a large number of icebergs into the Weddell Sea. The British scientists have expressed concern that if the warming continues, the frontier of collapsing ice will move farther south, melting the Ross and Filcher-Ronne ice shelves, each as large as Spain and closer to the South Pole. This will allow West Antarctica's glaciers to flow more easily into the ocean, raising the planet's sea level. Should the West Antarctic ice sheet collapse, it has been calculated that worldwide sea levels will rise by as much as sixty-five feet.

But even more disturbing is the fact that the much greater east Antarctic ice sheet, three miles thick in places, rests on a continent with few inland basins to hold the ice mass in place. Specialists are concerned that greenhouse warming could cause the contact between the ice and the substrate on which it rests to become unstable, causing the entire sheet to detach and slide into the southern ocean.

Those who believe slippage will happen cite evidence for several partial sheddings of the Antarctic ice that occurred repeatedly during the "greenhouse" tropical conditions of the Pliocene, three to four million years ago, when summer temperatures in the Antarctic were ten to twenty degrees Fahrenheit warmer than they are today. At no time since the Pliocene has the earth been as warm as some predict it soon will be. It has been estimated that a shedding of only one third of the east Antarctic ice sheet could raise global seas by 150 feet. A total melting of both the Antarctic and Arctic ice will produce sea levels more than 300 feet higher than those of today.

In support of this dire prediction, the May 9, 1997, issue of *Science* contains a report from a team of glaciologists working in Greenland, utilizing measurements obtained from two European ERS satellites.

The report reveals that Greenland's glaciers are losing more ice by melting from beneath than by iceberg calving. Taken with other data, these results suggest that the ice sheet of northern Greenland is thinning and contributing to the rising global sea level in the process. If the same phenomenon is happening in Antarctica, there is reason for great concern.

And is the ocean level rising in response? Extremely precise measurements made by the TOPEX/Poseidon satellite, launched in 1992, have revealed that global sea levels rose faster during 1993–95 than in any of the previous decades of this century. Data from the joint U.S.-French imaging study initially suggested that the average ocean height of the Pacific has been rising three millimeters per year in 1993 and 1994, a rate that more than doubled in 1995.[3] This calculation has recently (1996) been revised by NASA, citing a programming error. Yet the fact remains that a rise in the ocean levels has been detected, which, when considered in relation to the geographic extent of the oceanic mass, is quite unsettling.

In April 1995 representatives from 120 countries met in Berlin to begin talks concerning cutting back emissions of heat-trapping industrial waste gases such as carbon dioxide, which industrialized countries are obligated to do under a treaty signed at the Earth Summit held in Rio de Janeiro in 1992. At these talks, two recent studies got wide attention.

The German government reported that a computer modeling study done by the Max Planck Institute for Meteorology in Hamburg has found a 95 percent probability that the current warming reported in the scientific press is being caused by greenhouse gases. The second study, done by the British Meteorological Office, which tracks land and sea temperatures, confirms this, revealing that the earth's average temperature in 1994 climbed 0.31 degree Celsius above the mean from 1951 to 1980, making that year the third warmest since the late 1800s, as far back as global records reach. First and second place belong to 1990 and 1991, which followed on the heels of a marked temperature rise that began in the mid-1970s.

Hank Wesselman

It is also generally known that the tropical oceans are warming, particularly the Pacific, where the equatorial water thermometer seems to be stuck on warm. This has knocked normal weather patterns askew and produced the tremendous increase in precipitation in California in 1994–95, as well as other weather oddities across North America. Interestingly, the Pacific warming occurred at the same time as a major jump in global temperatures. The work of oceanographer Nicholas Graham of the Scripps Institute of Oceanography in California has shown why.

As oceanic temperatures climbed in the 1970s, they stimulated evaporation and subsequent storm formation, substantially increasing the amount of precipitation in the equatorial ocean regions after 1975. When the moisture condensed into rain, it gave off heat to the atmosphere, warming the entire globe. According to Graham's modeling work, the most recent portion of the global temperature record (1970–1992) can be closely reproduced by atmospheric models forced only with observed oceanic surface temperatures. Graham's research reveals a disquieting similarity between the modeling results and the observed climatic trends over the recent decades.[4]

The warming of the oceans is most important, because when it comes to storing heat, it is known that the upper three meters of the ocean can hold as much heat as the entire atmosphere. It makes sense, therefore, that the atmosphere is following the ocean's lead. And what is warming the oceans? Most scientists are reluctant to say the fearsome words "greenhouse warming," but most will agree off the record that this phenomenon is being created by increased atmospheric concentrations of carbon dioxide and other heat-trapping gases—the result of the activities of industrialized man.

The earth's average surface temperature climbed 0.4 degree Celsius in 1995 (compared to an average 0.2 degree C increase *per decade* since 1975), jumping to a new high for the 140-year period in which reliable global temperatures have been recorded. This increase makes 1995 the warmest year yet, a clear sign that the ongoing accumulation of greenhouse gases is altering the climate of the planet.

As if in response, the northern Pacific Ocean from Alaska to Mexico was uncommonly warm between the fall of 1995 and the spring of 1996. Ronald Lynn, a physical oceanographer with the Southwest Marine Fisheries Center of the National Marine Fisheries Service in La Jolla, has revealed that sea surface temperatures through the region have averaged 2 to 3.5 degrees C higher than normal. The pattern is reminiscent of El Niño, a phenomenon whereby a large mass of warm oceanic water accrues in the equatorial regions, affecting oceanic temperatures, disrupting weather patterns and fisheries elsewhere, but in this case, there was no El Niño at the equator.

Most of the planet continued to post near-record high temperatures for the rest of 1996, making the 1990s the hottest decade of the century and 1996 one of the top five warmest years ever recorded. Interestingly, despite this continued trend, one of the premier ocean-atmosphere computer forecasting models, located at the Lamont-Doherty Earth Observatory in Palisades, New York, predicted cool to normal conditions in the central equatorial Pacific during 1997 with only a slight warming trend by year's end. In actuality, the central Pacific spiked a fever during the first four months of 1997, and oceanic temperatures along the west coast of South America climbed so quickly that they took climate experts completely by surprise. By July, sea temperatures were more than 4 degrees Celsius above normal, the result of a growing El Niño event that is predicted to surpass even that of 1982–83, the strongest in this century.

In the opinion of a substantial sector of the scientific community, an ecological catastrophe of unparalleled proportions is looking humanity right in the face. It is no longer a question of *if* it will happen but *when*. A 1995 report from the International Panel on Climate Change, a respected U.N.-sponsored body made up of more than fifteen hundred leading climate experts from sixty countries, has stated that unless the world takes immediate and drastic steps to reduce emissions of heat-trapping gases, the greenhouse effect will increase global temperatures by at least 6 degrees Fahrenheit (2 degrees Celsius) in the next hundred years (which, given the temperature jump in 1995 alone, may be a dramatic underestimation), causing huge areas of densely populated and agricultural lands to be inundated by rising seas, displacing roughly 80 million people. In addition, entire ecosystems will vanish in response to the attendant changes in rainfall and temperature.

And the solution? Most scientists recommend radically slashing emissions of greenhouse gases; switching from coal and oil to natural gas; turning to solar and nuclear energy; stopping and reversing deforestation; and curbing automobile use, some even advocating the elimination of the internal combustion engine entirely and the development of alternative solar-powered and electric-powered transport vehicles. This means that people in the developed world will have to completely transform their societies, and rich countries such as Germany, Japan, and the United States will have to subsidize poor but rapidly developing nations such as China. And this is just to lower emissions to where they were in 1990, the target level of the agreement signed by the participants at the 1992 environmental summit in Rio. To stave off global warming completely, we will have to cut back emissions to where they were in 1920, a virtually inconceivable goal.[5]

And what has been the response of our economic and political leadership to this unsettling news? In the United States, business interests continue to aggressively lobby the political administration, arguing that the kind of pollution cuts urged by the scientific community would wreck the American economy. On December 6, 1996, just two weeks after President Clinton called for an international program to fight global warming, his administration revealed a new plan that would allow polluting companies to exceed allowable pollution standards in the United States if they help foreign companies reduce pollution elsewhere.

This is a most serious error in judgment, because the United States produces 20 percent of the world's man-made greenhouse gases, more than any other country, even though it has just 4 percent of the planet's population. While the politicians and the business community continue to engage in sterile debates about acceptable pollution limits and economic gains and losses, researchers have detected a slight rise in the Indian Ocean around the Maldives, and Pacific Ocean island states are reporting losing low-lying atolls to the sea.

In view of the failure of our political and corporate leadership to come to terms with this most important of issues, an increasing number of scientists are now saying that we should spend what research money there is figuring out what to do when the greenhouse event becomes manifest. It is already too late to do much else, they say.

And what will happen when the crunch comes? The probable scenario is not difficult to imagine. The central issue will revolve around human populations continuing to grow in ever-increasing numbers, with the resultant greenhouse gases continuing to be produced in ever-increasing amounts. Slowly but inexorably, the atmosphere and the seas will warm until a critical threshold is reached. At some point, the snow cover and the polar ice will begin to melt in earnest, and each high tide will get perceptibly higher, with former low tide levels never being quite reached.

An initial rise of several inches the first year will be disturbing. The effect on real estate values in prestigious coastal areas will be immediate, and the coastal cities will attempt to brace for the worst. A rise of several feet the next year will bring chaos as the world's low-lying coastal cities and agricultural areas become flooded, forcing the relocation of billions of people and causing incalculable agricultural losses. Worldwide famine will begin.

A subsequent annual sea level rise of between six and sixty feet, and another the year after that, and the year after that, will quickly and completely inundate the world's ports, including all those involved in the onloading and offloading of oil. Should the slippage of the east Antarctic ice sheet into the southern oceans occur, the height of the resulting tidal wave can be only imagined (estimates of between one thousand and fifteen hundred feet have been hypothesized), an event that could sweep every coastline and take out every port in the world in one cataclysmic incident.

If this should occur, the entire world's transportation system, dependent as it is upon the oil industry, will collapse, and with it, Western civilization. All of the world's peoples living in urban and suburban areas, completely dependent on the long-range transportation of everything they consume, from food and medicine to gas and electricity, will be completely without these products. Lacking either local or long-distance systems of transportation or communication, they will also be completely isolated. Within weeks or months, vast areas of the earth's surface will be completely depopulated of people, their huge populations literally starving *in situ* as the sea continues to rise and rise.

There will be some who last for a while—small, isolated groups of hardy survivalists—but these will tend to disappear in time because of the lack of genetic diversity within their relatively small breeding populations and because of the possible concentration of genetic lethals. It will be a classic genetic bottleneck of immense proportions as the urbanites starve and the small groups of survivors succumb to the hazards of inbreeding.

And who will ultimately survive? Will it be the so-called primitives, the few remaining traditional tribal peoples left out there in the bush? And how many, if any, will be left? This is very difficult to determine.

Many in the scientific community today believe that humanity is about to go through a stage much like an endangered species. The handwriting is on the wall for all to see. If we choose to pursue the path of denial, humankind is in for very serious trouble. In the opinion of many experts, we have at most thirty years, so this is a time for action. In order for humanity to survive, we must do five things, and the sooner the better.

I. We simply must control and reduce our population size. Studies of the contemporary population dynamics in natural ecosystems reveal that species engaging in catastrophic overpopulation inevitably crash. There seems to be no built-in evolutionary mechanism to keep organisms from reproducing too rapidly; that is, there is no built-in safeguard against extinction—and extinction is a real possibility. Our runaway population size is the single root cause of all our problems—economic, political, social, religious, and environmental—and if we fail to address this problem and reverse the trend, we're done for.

2.   We must stop degrading the environment that feeds us. When the Spaniards first discovered the ruins of the Maya cities in the rain forest, they also found the descendants of the Maya living in savagery in the bush. Studies done by contemporary archeologists have revealed the cause—the Maya populations grew too great, and they degraded their environment to the extent that the soil would no longer produce the food needed to survive. When the critical threshold was reached, there was a severe drought, the Maya civilization collapsed. This brings up the issue of sustainability.

3.   We must assess the planetary resource base—water, air, soils, agriculture, livestock, forests, metals, petroleum, energy, and everything else upon which we depend. We must determine the carrying capacity of this resource base. In addition, we must determine exactly how large the human population can be to remain within this limit. To exceed this number means that we are "spending our savings," with the inevitable result—bankruptcy. The universal law of natural selection will not take religious dogma, the rights of special interest groups, or the businessman's profit margin into account when the planetary climatic shift occurs.

4.   I believe that those most capable of determining the nature of the resource base and the management of it are the transnational corporations. These economic giants have created a privately run world economy in which they now control the global flow of materials, energy, and capital. The time has come for them to take responsibility for the survival of the human species. These multinationals simply cannot continue to do business as usual, because if they do, they (and we) will lose everything. There is a design flaw in the way we now do business, but if we correct it, we may yet save ourselves.[6]

5.   We must promote worldwide awareness of these issues

through education. Here in California, we are closing down schools and building prisons. This is not a good sign.

I have come to regard the above as Plan A. It could be much more detailed, and indeed, each of us can fill those details in and begin to take the appropriate action. If Plan A is unsuccessful, there is no Plan B. If Plan A fails, humankind and the incredible world that our technology has brought into being is finished.

All this ran through my mind as I spent the rest of the conference listening to my fellow colleagues split hairs about issues of concern to only a few highly trained professionals. I realized, with some despair, that my confidence in the scientific community's ability to help save the world was dwindling.

In response, my inner mystic emerged to consider the nature of the spiritual reawakening going on in the West. If the scientific, political, and corporate sectors of our society are unable to save humanity, perhaps the spiritual community can.

It was about this time that I began to lead shamanism workshops in my community, events that were bringing me into increasing contact with people involved with the New Age movement. One of the first things I discovered was that there is nothing particularly *new* about this cultural phenomenon. And because virtually everyone involved in it is a seeker of transcendant experience, many prefer to call it the modern mystical movement.[7]

Interestingly, most of these modern seekers are not affiliated with organized religions, nor are they associated with cultlike groups. Rather, they tend to gather in temporary local meetings and work-shops in which they network with each other and acquire information and experience about such esoteric and practically useful subjects as chi kung, Reiki, psychic healing, hypnotherapy, and shamanism, to name a few. They then disperse back into the wider society, where they utilize what they have learned to benefit themselves, their fami-lies, and their communities.

As my connections within the movement deepened, I became aware that those involved hold beliefs and values that differ from those of the general public. I also began to perceive a distinct character profile, reinforcing my growing suspicion that I had stumbled onto something of vital importance to the well-being of Western society.

Firstly, virtually all modern mystics possess a strong sense of social justice and are deeply concerned about the quality of human life at all levels, both nationally and internationally. They feel strong support for women's issues, are concerned with the safety and well-being of children and the elderly, and see human relationships as clearly more important than material gain. Social tolerance, personal individualism, and spiritual freedom are highly valued ideals, and the rebuilding of neighborhoods, communities, and families are major areas of concern.

Secondly, like traditional tribal peoples, modern mystics have a clear understanding of the importance of physical, mental, and spiritual balance and harmony. This is seen as critical to the well-being of the individual and the family, the community and the society, the corporation and the nation-state. It is also understood to be crucial to the well-being of the planet as a whole. It is clear to the modern mystic that human beings must strive to live their lives in ways that contribute to this balance and harmony rather than following lifestyles and pursuing goals that create its opposite. Accordingly, the value of simple, natural living is seen as a high ideal, and the monumental waste being generated by every level of the world capitalist system is regarded with grave concern.

This reveals that modern mystics are both well-informed and environmentally savvy. Like traditional peoples, they feel an active, almost ritual respect for nature. All express a deep concern for the survival of the environment and, by association, ourselves. Many view shamanism as a potential means for increasing awareness of our intimate relationship with nature and reversing the progressively devastating trends of industrialized humanity. All are seriously concerned with stopping corporate polluters, with reversing greenhouse warming, and with discovering the limits to short-term growth so that we can achieve the long-term ecological sustainability upon which the future of humanity depends.

These environmental concerns are reinforced considerably by the understanding that everything and everyone is part of a pattern and thus interconnected, a core belief articulated not only by tribal peoples but also by quantum physicists and Zen Buddhists.

Unlike many of the hardcore environmental activists of the last several decades, however, members of the modern mystical movement are deeply committed to achieving the direct, personal transformative experience of the sacred, and it is really this that defines them as mystics.

Most believe, for example, in the existence of more than one level of reality. In addition to the everyday, objective physical level in which we all live and have families and careers, the modern mystic understands that there are also the nonordinary realities, the subjective dream worlds or spirit worlds, where the laws of physics and cause and effect may not work in the same way.

This belief leads directly into another: that some individuals have the ability to enter or journey into these alternate realities to accomplish certain things and gain help, direction, and knowledge from the inner sources of wisdom and/or spiritual entities that reside there—a belief that reveals why shamanism is a major area of interest. The relative ease with which the shaman's time-tested methods for achieving altered states of consciousness can be learned and practiced, even by nontribal Westerners, stands in stark contrast to the years of rigorous training often required in many of the contemplative disciplines.

This realization leads into another: the belief in the existence of spirit helpers and spirit teachers, who, in turn, are thought to provide the seeker with power and knowledge, protection and support, that one cannot access on one's own. Interestingly, despite the modern mystic's disaffection for and lack of affiliation with organized religions, most profess belief in some form of universal, godlike consciousness, and Jesus of Nazareth is seen as an important teacher, whether or not the seeker is actively Christian.

Another related belief concerns the existence of spiritual or mystical power, perceived by virtually all as an invisible essence or force that pervades everything in the universe and that can be highly concentrated in certain places, objects, and living beings. This power is analogous to the *mana* of the Polynesians, the *chi* of the Asiatic peoples, the *num* of the !Kung San, and the Force of Obi Wan Kenobi. It is understood that everyone can learn how to access, accumulate, and focus this power, and that one's health, well-being, and success in life are all dependent on being able to increase and maintain one's personal supply of it.

There is also a belief in a personal energy body—the aspect of the self that carries this power as life force and which provides the etheric pattern around which the physical body is formed. The ability of some psychics and traditional healers to manipulate the energy body is seen as crucial in accomplishing healing, a skill that many in the modern mystical movement have personally experienced. It is believed that this personal energetic aspect can be perceived by some as an aura, and that it can be enhanced through the energy centers that Eastern thought calls the *chakras*, or meridians.

Most modern mystics also feel a genuine distance from and disaffection for Western allopathic medicine. While all are very much aware of Western medicine's often miraculous achievements, the majority feel that it is failing on many fronts. Elders who are terminally ill, for example, are often kept alive during the last year(s) of their lives by a medical system that is trying to do the right thing, but in the process, their physical suffering is needlessly prolonged while the escalating costs of treatment can wipe out their family's financial resources.

In addition, all see quite clearly how the business-oriented and profit-motivated health maintenance organizations (HMOs) are affecting the quality of health care in an increasingly negative way. As a result, the majority within the modern mystical movement express

strong interest in alternative health care strategies, including meditation as well as shamanic, holistic, Ayurvedic, and herbalist healing
techniques, to name only a few. Most see these strategies as adjunct
to, rather than as replacements for, Western medicine.

As a group, modern mystics perceive quite clearly that the world's
problems are reaching a "critical mass," and virtually all feel that the
ultimate solutions to these problems will be achieved through a general spiritual reawakening expanding ever outward from the personal
to the global. They believe that this growing mystical awareness carries with it the potential to project humankind into entirely new
realms of knowledge, awareness, and experience—realms that will
initiate us into a more expanded understanding of reality as well as of
ourselves and who we are in relation to the greater whole.

In short, this spiritual reawakening is believed to contain within
itself the potential to change the course of world history, and many
feel that without such a major shift, Western civilization is going to
hit the wall.

Taken together, these beliefs and values constitute a new worldview
that is being shared by an increasing number of people. And how
many are we talking about? In the spring of 1996 the preliminary
results of the national American Lives Survey, conducted by sociolo-
gist Paul Ray and sponsored by the Institute of Noetic Sciences and
the Fetzer Institute, revealed that in the United States alone, 44
million Americans fall into this category, representing about 24 percent of the adult population.[8] According to Ray, this group represents a "larger population of socially concerned, environmentally
aware and spiritually focused creative people, who are carriers of more
positive ideas, values, and trends than any previous renaissance period
in history."

The sudden appearance of an entirely new subculture of individuals
who are attempting to construct a whole new approach to the world is
what anthropologists call a cultural revitalization movement. It's what
a culture does when it is willing to face the fact that the old story
doesn't work anymore and that we need to write a new story in which

we explore a whole new set of ways of seeing ourselves, our problems, and their solutions.

Ray points out that this "lurch toward the new" is a very unusual time in history, because such a change in the dominant cultural pattern happens only once or twice in a thousand years. The fact of the approaching millennium change is itself seen as significant in that it is apparently liberating people to try something entirely new at the societal level. The old modernist paradigm is being dismantled by the sciences of quantum physics, holistic biology, and complexity theory, with their discoveries of self-organizing systems, nonlocality, and ecological interdependence. The new transmodern worldview, with its awareness of spiritual realities, mystical power, and concepts such as ecological sustainability, is growing. Yet within our socially and ethnically complex society, its widespread acceptance depends on many factors.

One may be the positions in society held by those who profess the new view. As anthropologist Joan Townsend and others have pointed out, the educational level among these seekers tends to be high and they often are in professional and social positions that make it possible for them to influence the social and political attitudes of those around them.[7]

Like Townsend, I have also discovered that more than half of the people who attend my workshops have children. This is a very hopeful sign. These mystical beliefs represent a wholly different attitude from the me-first competitive paradigm that most of us absorbed unconsciously from our parents, teachers, and friends as we were growing up. If parents can pass these altruistic, spiritually based beliefs on to their children, they will spread rapidly throughout Western society, accelerating the shift.

Another reassuring fact: The prerequisite population base of modern mystics is already in place. Ray's study reveals that although there are a few more "cultural creatives" in places such as California, they are more or less evenly spread throughout the population. This suggests that the modern mystical movement is not a soon-to-be-forgotten fad, but a cluster of major trends, values, and beliefs that carries the potential to radically shift the beliefs of Western society. We should take heart, for in Ray's words, "we are traveling in the company of an enormous number of allies."

I was reflecting on all this as the conference came to a close and I flew back to Sacramento. The mind-numbing immensity of the environmental problems I was considering was offset by my growing awareness that a shift in the consciousness of Western people is taking place, and for some unknown and baffling reason, the media seems to have completely missed it.

Through my connections with the modern mystical movement, on the one hand, and my visionary contacts with Nainoa, on the other, I was rediscovering the ancient truths found within the core of all the world's great mystic and religious traditions, revelations that have shown me unequivocally that the mystic is truly the exploratory consciousness of our species, and that true mysticism leads to action. In this wisdom, I find hope for the future.

My reunion with my family was joyous, a celebration that progressed into a lovely romantic encounter with Jill once the children were asleep. As had so often happened in Hawai'i, I woke in the dark before the dawn to feel the sensations of power expanding within me.

As the phosphenic lights began to dance within my brain, heralding the onset of the deep mystic experience, I wondered why so many religions and spiritual traditions have suppressed the incredible power that our sexuality provides to us, and I understood as never before that there is one vow that the universe does not accept—the vow of celibacy.

As I watched the great grid take form and struggled to breathe in the grip of the ecstatic, paralytic force, I exerted one last effort and managed to touch Jill's hand. Her fingers stirred in her dreaming and briefly caressed mine in response. Then the crescent of light opened and I was off, soaring on a roaring rush of feeling that was simply, magnificently overwhelming.

CHAPTER 14

Seventh Journey: The Enemy

T HE ROCK OUTCROP loomed above him as Nainoa emerged
from the trees. He paused at the hill's summit and looked
down through the hazy light across the cleared fields of the
Kaneohe land division. He had taken to walking to this place for
exercise on a daily basis since his return from the capital. It was early
morning, his favorite time of day, and clouds of mist drifted through
the forest to merge with the smoke of the community's cooking fires.
The omnipresent roosters crowed in the distance.

Off to his right, he saw the spot he had occupied on that first night
of his journey more than a year ago. His eyes skimmed the landscape,
seeking the familiar. All over the estate, people were preparing the
land for the coming rains. In between the long, pale green rows of
the *kukui* groves below, he could see farmers guiding their oxen across
the gentle slope, plowing long parallel furrows in the rich earth while
a second contingent of commoners sowed seed behind them. He

guessed that they were probably planting corn. His gaze drifted across the dark rows of macadamia and avocado orchards to find the reddish scars on the distant hillsides where the woodcutters had cleared new areas of the forest. Bananas or sisal would probably be planted there, or perhaps breadfruit. Columns of smoke rose from these places, and he knew that the wood burners were at work converting the fallen timber into charcoal. Smoke rising from deeper in the forest's interior betrayed the location of the hunters' outlying hamlets. He discerned movement on the north road—a dozen plank-wheeled carts were coming from the town, bearing human waste and refuse to be used as fertilizer in the fields.

A chevron of swans suddenly appeared over the ridge behind him, passing close overhead, their long necks stretched out and their great wings beating in unison. They looked at him curiously as they passed, then they banked and headed down the valley across the bright green banana plantations toward the taro paddies and fish ponds beyond. Nainoa's eyes followed them with delight. Reassured, he sat down on his spot and settled into a light meditation.

As his trance deepened, he felt a shift, and it was then that he became aware of the presence. He could feel it at the edges of his mind, and yet somehow within it as well. He knew instantly who it was and extended a warm greeting. Then he smiled, watching as his memories of recent events unfolded before them both.

His first recollections were of William's departure from the capital. He and the Ennu hunter had become very close, and he had sensed that the older man would be leaving. He remembered a morning when the two of them had been sitting together eating breakfast in the men's house.

"Why don't you stay with us for the coming year, William?" he had said. "You have become a person of power here in the capital. And your life has been anything but lonely."

The Ennu hunter had cocked his head to one side with a wistful smile. Then he had sighed and replied, "I have enjoyed my stay with you and your people, Nainoapak, but my son and I will depart soon.

When the rains come east of the mountains, the game will disperse out onto the grasslands, and my family will break camp to follow them, as we always have."

William's statement had made his departure a certainty, and Nainoa had felt a profound sadness, though at some deep level he had always understood that William would go back to his people.

But then the older man had suddenly grinned at him and said, "Your hospitality has been most generous, and I have especially enjoyed your food and your custom of bathing in hot water. I have also valued your friendship and good company." He laughed with pleasure, then his expression turned serious.

"But I have left my wife Kalvak in the care of our sons, and my daughter Kenojelak also needs to be provided for." He left the thought hanging, then added, "Zaki has left his mother, my other wife, and his sister in the care of his brothers. Our families need us; I can feel their thoughts turning in our direction, and I see them in my dreaming. The time of our return to our wonderful open country filled with animals is fast approaching." Nainoa saw William's eyes brighten at the prospect.

The older man had turned then and looked at him thoughtfully. "Your life here seems to be unfolding in a most positive manner. You have acquired new family ties through your relationship with Maraea. This is very good. A man should have as many wives and as many children as possible. It is in this way that life, and especially old age, will be rich with relationships.

"But there is also something else. You, Nainoapak, will be the river that flows between your people and mine, bringing us into frequent contact. You will come to our lands often in the years ahead. So although there will be sadness at our parting now, I already look forward with enthusiasm to our reunions." He grinned and added, "My daughter will be glad of your company as well."

The light had been increasing steadily, and at this moment a hummingbird had zoomed into the room through the open section of the wall that fronted on the lagoon. It hovered briefly, as if looking the two men over, then streaked off toward the east. William's eyes had twinkled. "You see? My daughter has sent one of her helpers to find us. It was probably outside on a bush the whole time, listening to all that we said. It will now fly back to her with information, and she will know that I am planning to return."

At this moment their host, Chief Wilipaki, had walked by the men's communal dining hall. He had seen them talking and saluted them jovially, then turned to enter the cooking area to check on what the servants were preparing. William had nodded, then glanced at the younger man. "I am leaving you in good hands, Nainoapak. That man is an accomplished spiritwalker. He will assist you in your training."

"Training, William?" Nainoa queried.

"The path of *ungagok* is a lifetime commitment, Nainoapak. In the beginning, it helps to have guidance from an experienced spiritwalker. That man will help you find your way. When you have attained the ability to see and interact with your spirits at will, they will become your teachers, and then you will know what an extraordinary thing it is to be fully alive and fully aware. You are going to have an interesting life, my friend. I can see some of it already forming. There will be much adventure and travel for you, in both the outer and inner worlds."

"What can you see, William?" Nainoa asked.

"Sometimes I am shown things," the older man answered elusively with a wave of his hand as Wilipaki emerged from the kitchen with a wooden bowl of food and approached their table. "I wouldn't dream of spoiling it for you by telling you in advance, and besides, the future is not fixed. It shifts in response to our actions in the here and now.

"But here is something interesting," he finished as Wilipaki arrived at the table. "We have talked about the ability of the spiritwalker to see spirits, even in their waking state of consciousness. Let me share something with you. Since we've been talking, I have sensed another presence in proximity to us. I feel it strongly, even now. It is not your ancestor. I know what his presence feels like. I suspect that it is your spirit helper and that he is watching me right at this moment. And so I, William the hunter, offer him greetings."

At the older man's words, Nainoa became very still, but he had been in his ordinary state of consciousness and had perceived nothing unusual.

Shortly after this conversation there had been a lavish feast in the capital to celebrate the end of William's visit. Special chants had been composed for the occasion, and the community's most accomplished dancers had ceremonially depicted the highlights of William's stay, including his many healings and conquests of the heart, much to the general hilarity of the assembled chiefly families.

On the morning of their departure, thousands of people had gathered along the edges of the harbor. Governor Ruth Kahalopuna had come with all the members of her family, including High Chiefess Lowena and High Chief Wilipaki, accompanied by their daughter High Chiefess Maraea with Ziku on a leash. The white Ennu dog had taken quite a liking to Maraea. William and Zaki had been delighted and had given her the dog as a gift, announcing that Ziku had actually made the choice herself and that it was a most fortuitous omen. Ziku now accompanied Maraea almost everywhere and slept on the floor at the end of her bed.

The party had walked up the gangplank and onto the central platform of the governor's personal flagship, the great double-hulled *wa'a'kau'lua* that had brought her ancestors from the home islands 131 years in the past. Nainoa had heard of this legendary craft, but he had never seen it until now.

The canoe was named after *Kanaloa*, the mythic sustainer of life and the *akua* of the deep ocean. It had been newly caulked before being brought out on rollers from the longhouse where it was kept, oiled and polished, as an object of history and power. Its rigging had been replaced and new sails made for the occasion. Even the roof of the cabin on the main deck between the hulls had been rethatched. More than a hundred feet long, with forty paddlers in each massive hull, the canoe was an object to inspire awe. This was the first time in more than five years that the *Kanaloa* had been launched, and the crowd was silent as the governor's party boarded, aware that they were witnessing a historical event.

The *haku* of the canoe had greeted them formally, and after Zaki tied the other two dogs to one of the two main masts, the *haku* had led the visitors to the place of honor near the craft's high upswept sterns. Then the Ennu and their coming journey had been blessed by a contingent of the oldest and most powerful *kahunas* in the capital, and the governor had made a formal speech of farewell, declaring both William and his son welcome within any of the Hawaiian land divisions from that time forth and presenting them with chief's necklaces made with the customary hook-shaped ivory pendant in the center.

At the ritual's culmination, Lepeka'okalani, a *kahuna* renowned for her ability to work with the weather, had performed a ritual to summon the west wind and speed them across the inland sea. Then the governor and all of her family had embraced the travelers warmly and disembarked with Maraea and Ziku, who whined and looked mournfully at her departing companions as the gangplank was drawn back and the ropes cast off. Nainoa had remained on board to accompany the Ennu and help guide the canoe back to the place on the eastern coast where they would reenter the great forest for their return trek across the mountains.

The *haku* had then given the command, and as the paddlers bent their backs to the task of taking the great canoe out into deeper water, the crowd spontaneously broke into the great Hawaiian song of farewell, an ancient hymn of blessing and affirmation brought down from the past. Tears had flowed freely from every eye in response, and many, many flower *leis* were cast into the water.

As the ship picked up speed, William had turned to him and said, "And how will I tell my family about all I have experienced here, Nainoapak? How can I describe this huge canoe to hunters accustomed only to our reed rafts for fishing and catching waterfowl? And your camp . . ." He gestured toward the sprawling community spread out in all directions along the bay and surmounting the sides of the distant ridges. "How can my people understand all I have seen here?" He shrugged helplessly, then grinned with glee despite his dilemma.

As they had achieved distance from the capital and the song of farewell grew faint, the west wind arrived, and the *haku* ordered the false keels to be set and the long scoop sails unfurled. The *Kanaloa* had surged in response, slicing elegantly across the whitecapped bay at a truly astonishing speed. At that moment, with the water rushing by and seabirds streaming in their wake, it was not difficult to believe that the craft was imbued with a spirit—as though the canoe itself were a living being.

The wind had risen steadily throughout the morning, causing all in the crew to comment on the power and effectiveness of Lepeka'okalani's prayer. The great canoe had raced across the inland sea in record time, achieving the eastern shore by midafternoon. The keels allowed the craft to cut across the wind, and the navigator, who knew of the river that Nainoa had taken into the interior, had guided them right to its mouth.

The keels had then been raised to accommodate the shallow draft of the river, and with eighty strong paddlers, they were able to progress upstream at a rapid pace, by dusk reaching the broad sandbar from which Nainoa, William, and Zaki had emerged from the forest. They had then beached the canoe and all disembarked, camping the night there and having a last feast with the travelers who would depart into the great forest the next morning.

At dawn William had looked thoughtful as he shouldered his gear and supplies. When he had them arranged to his satisfaction, he turned and said, "You remember that chief with the dark shape to his spirit, the one you call Paleko? Watch out for him, Nainoapak. That one is sick in his mind." After another long moment of reflection, he added, "You do not have to worry for your safety, of course. Your spirit helper will assist and protect you. The spirit of the spotted tiger is an ally with many abilities; it is also the master hunter."

Then William's thoughts shifted and his eyes had filled with emotion. "Sometimes when I appear in your mind for no reason, you will know that I am thinking of you, Nainoapak, and you will know that I am sending you strong thoughts. Perhaps we will also visit in our dreaming. Stranger things have happened." He had thrown back his head with the wonder of it. "Heeeeee . . ."

Nainoa had then passed William a necklace of beautiful blue stone beads he had found in one of the capital's many markets. "For Kenojelak, who lives within my heart."

The older man had smiled and nodded. "I will carry your heart feelings to my daughter, and I will hunt for her and her child to be born. Do not worry; my sons and I will take care of them."

Then William had looked deeply into the younger man's eyes and said, "I look forward with joy to your next visit to our camp beyond the mountains. I regard you as my son and closest friend, Nainoapak. I will carry you in my heart forever. Farewell and good hunting!"

Nainoa's eyes had filled with tears as he embraced the older man, and then Zaki had come and clasped his shoulders fiercely, silent as always, but his own eyes flowing with emotion. At last the hunters had picked up their bows, whistled up their dogs, and melted into the green wall of the forest.

This distant barking of a dog brought his thoughts back to the present as his eyes refocused on the fields spread out below him. The *haku* of the governor's canoe had dropped him at the port of the Kaneohe land division before returning to the capital. For the past twenty days he had been working closely with Chief Kaneohe, assisting him with the administrative functions of the estate while putting his own affairs in order. He had also begun work on his written account of his travels during his year away.

His mind returned to William's statement about Paleko. The priest did indeed have a dark shape to his spirit. The man had been coldly polite to him and given nothing away on the surface, but the servants had told him that strange rumors were spreading, suspicions that

Nainoa had used William's assistance to bewitch the governor as well as High Chiefess Maraea, and that he was using sorcery to consolidate his influence over them.

He had discussed these rumors in private with Chief Kaneohe, who had looked thoughtful and replied, "Your success and sudden rise into the hierachy of the chiefly class has elicited the envy of certain parties, who, shall we say, feel threatened and perceive you as an adversary. As we have discussed, there are reasons why Paleko behaves the way he does. Unfortunately, he has powerful connections among the priests. If he is the source of these rumors, we will deal with him when the time is right, but we will have to use caution to avoid dividing the community politically."

Three days ago Chiefess Lowena had arrived from the capital with Maraea and a small party of servants. Officially she had come on a visit in her capacity as *kahuna* healer to determine the progress of Chief Kaneohe's recovery from his illness. Unofficially Nainoa knew that Maraea had convinced her mother to make the trip so that they could be together. And indeed, although the mother and daughter were staying in the chief's guesthouse, Maraea had spent every night in his cottage—with Ziku asleep at the foot of the bed. He smiled to himself.

His thoughts shifted, and his mood grew serious. On the day of their arrival, there had been a ceremony of welcome in Chief Kaneohe's reception hall, during which something unforeseen had occurred. Maraea had brought Ziku into the hall on a leash, and the dog had lain down silently at her feet. When Nainoa had arrived shortly thereafter from a distant part of the estate, the dog had leaped up and greeted him with lavish displays of canine affection in front of the assembled dignitaries. After he had formally greeted Maraea and her mother, he had taken a place beside Chief Kaneohe on the raised platform at the end of the room. Ziku had then lain down again, and Nainoa had put aside his uneasiness at having the big Ennu dog inside with so many people, reasoning that she had become used to being indoors.

All had gone well until Paleko had arrived with a group of his fellow priests. As they approached the visitors to pay their respects, without warning Ziku had lunged at him with a blood-chilling snarl. Unfortunately, Maraea was unprepared for this, and Ziku had jerked the leash from her fingers.

Paleko had lurched backward and stumbled, ending up flat on his back with the snarling dog on top of him as the priests scattered in all directions. Before anyone could react, Ziku had clamped her jaws around his arm, bringing a shriek of pain and terror from the man. Nainoa had immediately called the dog off him using the whispered Ennu hunter's command, but it was too late to salvage Paleko's dignity. The man had risen with blood streaming from his arm, shot a look of pure hatred at Nainoa, and stalked out of the hall without a word.

Nainoa recalled the event with a mixture of amusement and uneasiness as his eyes refocused on the scene below. A man could be seen running along the north road, probably a messenger with information for someone at this end of the estate. He watched the man cut into a field, talk briefly with a farmer, then run back to the road, continuing outward.

What was he to do about Paleko? He thought about William's warning and considered his own personal protection. He looked at the forest surrounding him and recalled the ally to whom William had alluded, the spirit he thought of as the spotted tiger man. All of a sudden he remembered seeing the painting of this entity in the American's home during one of his visionary connections with him, and with the thought, he recalled the presence of the man's awareness within him. If the American was actually in contact with him at this moment, he must be monitoring his thoughts. He wondered what his ancestor would do in his position.

He immediately perceived a shift of some sort within his mind. It was as if there was a response, but one that he couldn't quite grasp. He listened intently, as though trying to hear something—something that was almost inaudible, something distant. And then an idea appeared within his mind. He sensed that he should make an appeal, a supplication to his spirit helper for protection and support. As the thought took form, it was reinforced by a strong sense of confirmation.

He sat very still as he digested what had just occurred. He waited for a moment, then brought up the memory of how the spotted tiger man appeared, and as he did so, he made the appeal—protection and support, protection and support.

The blood began to hiss in his ears as a new presence appeared within him . . . or was it around him? He wasn't quite sure. He looked out into the trees but saw nothing unusual. Yet the presence remained. It was big, and it was powerful. In his mind's eye, there was a sudden glimpse of movement—of swirling lights on a dark field that suddenly shifted, becoming clusters of dark spots on a tawny field that, in turn, began to coalesce around a set of pale green eyes he remembered well. And as those eyes met his, his body surged with a jolt of the power sensations.

He was momentarily taken aback, aware that in some way he had conjured up the spirit he called the spotted tiger man. Moreover, it was here now, with him or within him.

Recovering, he again put out the appeal—protection and support, protection and support. Simultaneously he ran the story of Paleko through his mind. He remembered all of it, from his earliest boyhood connections with this hate-filled individual, using his creative imagination to form a mental image of the priest. Here was the one to be protected against. Here was the one who had taken up the role of enemy, and possibly a deadly one.

Within his mind's eye, the green eyes closed, then opened and closed again, conveying reassurance. The power sensations abruptly increased within his body, as did the rush of sound within his ears. His muscles were shaking with it, and he felt immensely strong. He smiled, a thin, tense grimace of a smile, as he took a shuddering breath and managed to contain the vibrating power within himself. He was aware that the spotted tiger spirit had merged with him, just as it had that night of the healing ceremony for Chief Kaneohe. He felt absolutely, superbly marvelous.

Then his senses shifted outward and his eyes fastened on the runner on the north road. The man paused again to talk to a commoner, then continued rapidly along the track toward the end of the estate. Slowly a premonition appeared, and words in Old English whispered in his mind's ear: "I sense it, too. Something's up and it doesn't feel good."

Without thought or intention to do so, Nainoa got up and reentered the trees, his pace quickening as his sense of urgency grew. He began to run, descending the slope in long bounds. As he ran he thought he saw the spotted tiger running through the trees. He saw it within his mind, as though it was accompanying him, as though it *was* him. He felt its presence as well as a mind-shape that expressed an incisive clarity. He noticed that his vision had become noticeably sharper and his hearing incredibly acute.

He erupted from the forest at the base of the hill and leaped across the exposed boulders in the streambed, executing a series of running jumps that part of his mind registered as quite extraordinary. He ran up the opposite bank, achieving the top without effort. From the edge of the cotton field, he saw the man running in his direction. Even at this distance, he could discern who it was.

It seemed to take only moments for him to cross the field. Milo, Maraea's servant, ran up to him, his face expressing a mixture of relief, physical exhaustion, and fear. The man was quite out of breath.

"Chief Nainoa . . . something has happened. . . . My lady, Chiefess Maraea, has sent me to find you."

Nainoa felt the calm, clear minds nested within his own become focused upon the upset servant. One was an alien, dispassionate mind, utterly devoid of emotion; the other was familiar to the point of intimacy and expressed a mute yet palpable concern. "Breathe deeply, Milo. Calm yourself and tell me what has occurred."

"Chief Nainoa, it is my lady's dog," the man got out. "Chiefess Maraea found her dog unable to walk." The man bowed, lowering his gaze out of fear. "Ziku . . . it was as though the dog could not breathe. She could not get up and walk. She went into convulsions. And within a short time . . . Ziku died." Overcome by emotion as well as exhaustion, Milo began to weep.

Nainoa felt a cold, deep well of anger open within himself, and as the anger grew, the minds within his own watched.

"My lady Maraea," Milo continued between sobs, "is very upset. She believes that . . . that Ziku was poisoned." The servant buried his face in his hands and could say no more.

There was no question as to who was responsible. There could be only one man who would do this unthinkable thing. Nainoa's anger surged into a blinding rage, and all of the outrages he had suffered in his life, all of the abuses and injustices, emerged from within his soul to feed his fury. The hissing rush increased in his ears, and a deep snarl emerged from his lips, causing Milo to look up in alarm. It was not a human sound.

As Paleko's hateful visage emerged within his mind's eye, Nainoa felt the immense *mana* generated by his extreme emotion surge outward toward the priest, and he knew that had Paleko been standing before him at this moment, he would surely have killed him.

At that moment he felt the release. It was as though he was buffeted by a gust of wind—a blazingly hot burst that departed as suddenly as it arrived. Simultaneously he felt his rage cool, subsiding into a dull, bitter anger once again. And with this shift, he regained control of his inner emotional state.

"Come, Milo," he said. "We must return to the hub." He began to run, then slowed to a walk almost immediately. The power that had carried him down the hill was gone. He felt depleted, as though the impact of this sad news had diminished him—as though it had damaged him at the level of his soul. His memories of Ziku now emerged, and with them his anger transformed into a deep, personal sorrow. His eyes filled with tears. He slowed his pace still further and began to mourn for his lost friend. The servant caught up with him, and the two began the long walk back to town.

The administrative center was uncharacteristically silent when he arrived some time later. He went straight to the guest house, but Maraea and her mother were not there. A servant redirected him to Chief Kaneohe's offices, and there he found a solemn-faced group of chiefs, subchiefs, high-ranking servants, and priests. Maraea and Lowena, as well as Chief Kaneohe himself, were among them. On the floor before them, a long *tapa*-wrapped bundle reposed on a platform of *ti* leaves surrounded by flowers. Incense hung in the air. Maraea's face looked wooden. All turned in his direction as he entered. The director spoke.

"Chief Nainoa, I can see by your face that you have received the sad news. Come and join us so that we can have the benefit of your presence, your wisdom, and your clarity."

The chief's words had a calming effect. Nainoa bowed to him and to Lowena and her daughter, then took a place among them and sat down. He withdrew once more into himself, into his sorrow and his pain. He put his face in his hands and drifted deeper through his suffering until he passed into a dreamlike inner silence in which he only half heard the discussion that followed. Paleko's name was mentioned, but in what context, he cared not. Forgotten as well was the presence within his mind, until he heard a soft voice utter a statement in Old English.

"Esteemed descendant, allow me to intrude upon your suffering. Something happened back there at the edge of the cotton field. I am not sure what it was, but I felt our spirit helper depart rather abruptly. I suspect he has gone on an errand—one that does not bode well for your enemy."

Startled, Nainoa felt his awareness shift, and he looked up. Nobody else seemed to have heard the voice. He listened intently, but the voice was gone and he heard only silence. Maraea was watching him. "What is it?" she asked. All faces turned in his direction.

Just then the sound of running feet could be heard outside in the courtyard. A priest entered through the open doors at the end of the room. The man was breathing hard and sweating heavily. He bowed before Chief Kaneohe, and waited for permission to speak, looking with confusion at the *tapa*-wrapped bundle on the floor. The director regarded the man evenly for several moments, then gestured to the priest.

"Chief Kaneohe," the man began, "a most unfortunate accident has happened. As you know, a delegation from our order left the settlement at daybreak to attend meetings that are to begin at the port community tomorrow. When we reached the part of the road that runs along the river, we stopped to answer the call of nature."

The priest paused and gestured helplessly, trembling with emotion as he prepared himself to continue. "We all got back in the wagons and were starting up again when someone noticed that Chief Paleko had not yet returned from the trees. We stopped and waited, but he did not come. We called, but there was no response."

The priest looked nervously at the assembled gathering. Chief Kaneohe glanced at Nainoa with a blank look. Then he turned back to the agitated man before him and said, "Breathe deeply and calm yourself, Eli. Tell us what happened."

"We got down from the wagons again, sir. It was then that we noticed the forest was very silent. We looked at the trees and called again. No response. We sent some of our novices to find Chief Paleko—to see if he needed help. They were not able to locate him. We all began to search. I was the one who found him."

The man went very pale and began to tremble once more. Several of the priests got up to support him. "A tiger, Chief Kaneohe," Eli managed to whisper. "A tiger had taken him and dragged him into the forest. His throat was torn away and his face was crushed. We recognized him only by his cloak and by his bandaged arm, bitten by a dog several days ago. We never heard a thing, nor did anyone see the tiger." The priest began to babble at this point, repeating himself as the tension within him found release in words.

Nainoa became very still as the realization hit him. His eyes continued to watch the distraught man, but his ears no longer needed to listen. From somewhere he heard the director's voice say, "We must track down this tiger who has developed a taste for human flesh. Assemble the hunters who live at that end of the settlement. We will need someone to take them to the exact spot. Assemble the priests. We must prepare a funeral for Chief Paleko."

The smoky incense suddenly seemed cloying, and Nainoa felt the need for fresh air. He rose to his feet, bowed to the assembled gathering, and left the room without a word. Outside, he saw the chief's *heiau* on its stone platform across the courtyard. He felt the need for solitude. The chief had lifted the *kapu* on the *heiau* so that Nainoa could sit in meditation there whenever he so wished. He crossed the compound and stepped up onto the platform, unlatched the gate, and said a small prayer requesting permission to enter. Then he stooped and opened the door, crawling on all fours as he passed through the low entryway and closed it behind him.

In the dusty silence he began to feel better. He rose from his knees and used the pole to open the high windows, admitting light to the dim interior. Then he placed a cushion on the floor before the low altar and sat down. The spirit stone was there, propped upright in its place behind the sand tray. He took a flower from the arrangement of offerings placed on the altar every morning. He smelled it, slowly savoring its scent, then put it on the tray before the stone. Only then did he place his hands upon the stone and ask for its blessing.

He felt light-headed and realized he had had nothing to eat all day. All his anger was gone, and in its place was only a hollow emptiness. He let his thoughts drain out of his mind and listened to the silence until the dreamlike state descended and only his breathing connected his mind to his body. Then he refocused his thoughts, accessed his memory of Old English, and asked the question.

"Esteemed ancestor, have I committed a great wrong?"

He waited. There was a long silence within his mind, and then an answer formed. "The question might better be expressed, 'Did *we* commit a great wrong?' In that moment of extreme emotion I too forgot the presence of our spirit helper. I suspect that it mistook our collective rage for a directive."

"Directive?" Nainoa reacted with confusion to the unfamiliar term.

"A command—*ho'una*," came the answer. There was a long pause. "In perceiving Paleko to be a threat to you, the spotted tiger spirit may have interpreted our anger as a command. If so, it may simply have gone off to do what it does best, believing that it was acting in your best interests, so to speak."

Nainoa digested this information for long moments. "I have used power for destructive purposes. To practice negative sorcery is considered a great crime in my society."

"And in mine," came the answer. "But in this case, you did so accidentally, without clear premeditation. In my culture, a clever lawyer might plead self-defense, even innocence, with success."

"A lawyer?"

"A professional interpreter of the laws of society—what yours once called *kumu'kanawai*."

"Ah."

A noise behind him revealed that the door to the *hale mana* was being opened, and Nainoa's awareness shifted. Chief Kaneohe entered, bowed to the room, arranged a large cushion beside him, and sat down. He uttered a short prayer to the spirit in the stone, placed a second flower before it, then lapsed into silence. For a time neither said a word. When the chief spoke, he came right to the point.

"It seems that your enemy made two serious errors when he decided to avenge himself by poisoning your dog."

Nainoa bowed but said nothing.

"First, in allowing himself to be swayed by his emotional negativity, he forgot about your spirit helper." There was a long pause. "And second, he continued to think of you as a servant, and in doing so, he forgot that you carry your grandfather's *ike*, his spiritual power."

Nainoa remained silent, awaiting the director's judgment. When the chief said nothing further, he gave a brief account of the morning's events and finished by saying, "I did not consciously send the tiger spirit after Chief Paleko, yet he is dead, and I feel I am responsible."

"It seems to me that in this case the responsibility is clearly shared." The director paused again, considering his words. "First we must consider Paleko's responsibility. This consists of his intentions and his actions that set the dynamic into motion—actions that ultimately turned on him and contributed to his demise. This man also had your grandfather's *ike*, but as we have discussed, he used his power in destructive ways, and in the end, that is what really did him in.

"The *kahuna* healers among us know that the ultimate source of our *ike* is the great force or power that pervades the universe. Our personal life force, our *mauli*, as well as our *ike*, are constantly being replenished through the benevolent spirits that connect us to that great source. These powers who protect and support us are also the ones who help us relieve pain and suffering in others. They are not at all inclined to help us inflict pain and suffering. When Paleko turned in that direction, his spirits detached from him, and from that point on, his personal supply of power began to diminish.

"He had a lot of power, of course, and like his grandfather, he inflicted a lot of damage in the last few years of his life, but his supply eventually ran down to nothing. The chances are that he was unaware of this until it was too late. It must have come as quite a surprise when he met the tiger in the forest and discovered that he had no protection."

Chief Kaneohe paused dramatically, then continued. "In my opinion, Chief Paleko was ultimately responsible for his own fate. He has received his just deserts, and there are not many in our community who will mourn him. To the contrary . . ." He let the thought hang.

"And you, my close friend and cousin, have received an important lesson that may ultimately function as one of the most significant of your training. During the past year you have acquired knowledge and power from many sources, and you have stepped onto the path that was predestined for you since before you were born. Now you have discovered that with knowledge and power comes *kuleana*—responsibility.

"The *kahunas* in our society are those gifted individuals who enter into direct relationship with this knowledge and power and use it in a life-enhancing capacity to help others. On the positive side, *kahunas* can enjoy many benefits, ranging from people's respect to their awe and fear. On the negative, the spiritual path entails certain sacrifices and responsibilities that can often be quite burdensome.

"Sometimes these constraints are determined by the nature of the powers associated with us. All among the *kahuna* order know that failure to follow these guiding constraints laid down by our spiritual helpers and teachers results in consequences. These may be suffered not only by the *kahuna* who has strayed but also by those close to the *kahuna*, even extending into the community itself."

Nainoa nodded. "William told me a similar tale before he left."

The chief smiled and eyed the stone before them. "Those who are chosen by the spirits must live their lives differently. But like everyone, we must make choices. These choices are determined by who we are, by our temperaments, and by the circumstances of our lives. The actions that we take, combined with the decisions that each of us makes in accordance with the spirits who are allied with us—these are what draw us further and further along the path of power.

"If our actions and decisions are deemed unworthy by the spirits, they detach themselves from us, and our power, as well as the abilities conferred by our power, are progressively diminished. Our life, how we lead it, is part of our training. It's part of the test. The *kahuna* who abuses power inevitably loses it and is dumped back into life as an ordinary person. Sometimes, as in the case of Paleko, the results can be quite dramatic.

"So you see, Chief Nainoa, your role in his demise has been a rather circumstantial one—but one that may, in the long run, be as beneficial to you as it was detrimental to him."

The chief looked at the younger man with affection. "It is always life-enhancing to reflect on such lessons in depth. It also helps to purify oneself after such a lesson before proceeding on with one's life. I suggest a pilgrimage to the place of refuge—to the *pu'uhonua* in the Pukui land division. The priests of that sanctuary will purify you during your retreat, instructing you in *lokahi*, the ways of achieving inner balance and harmony. I will ask Wilipaki to accompany you. Among other things, this will provide you with an opportunity to get to know him better. I think you will find him a most interesting man and teacher.

"But right now, I think it would be most beneficial if you were to go to Chiefess Maraea, who has suffered a great loss."

Nainoa bowed and prepared to leave.

"You also have my blessing, Nainoa, and my compliments on your coming marriage," the chief concluded. "You have chosen well. You will have a most interesting life, I think."

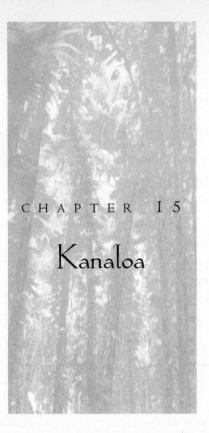

CHAPTER 15

Kanaloa

SHORTLY AFTER NAINOA'S departure from the *heiau*, he dashed a gourdful of water into his face to clear the mood. The shock terminated my connection with him, and as I emerged from the deep state, my own mood was somber. Had I just participated in a murder by the use of sorcery?[1] The thought produced feelings of misgiving, yet I found comfort in the chief's words. I was also very much aware that this extraordinary event had been a lesson for me as well as for Nainoa.

As I lay in my bed in the dark, memories arose in my mind— wraithlike images of people who had passed through my life in the role of enemy or adversary. I watched with concentration as I reviewed each case with reference to the surrounding circumstances in which it had occurred. Even after all the intervening years, my feelings for the individuals involved still ranged from distrust to outright anger. If I had known then what I know now, would I have sent a "power" after

243

those adversaries in a destructive capacity? Probably not, but to be honest, there were a couple of cases about which I wasn't so sure. And now? Could I use my knowledge and power in a destructive way to avenge a wrong or take care of some enemy? The chief's words whispered in my mind, and the answer was clear: To do so would be the beginning of my own undoing.

I felt profoundly moved by these realizations. Little remained of the night, so I got up and brewed a pot of strong tea. Then I walked outside and sat with the stone in my backyard and watched the sunrise as the whole episode ran through my mind again.

A long, busy year followed, and it was during the month of August in 1994 that my next connection with Nainoa was achieved. I always pay particular attention to the context in which these visions occur. This time, I had decided to take Jill and the girls over to the coast for a long weekend in a vacation rental house on the Russian River close to where it enters the Pacific Ocean.

After living most of the year in the suburban sprawl of Sacramento, I found it a great relief to be close to nature once again. I could see seals cruising up the river while ospreys patrolled the sky and grebes and cormorants dived for fish within a stone's throw of the house. In the mornings we took long walks on the many beaches, trudging happily along the interface of land, sea, and sky while the children avidly looked for sand dollars and shells and I scoured the dunes for bones, as usual. We found a favorite café in Bodega Bay where we wolfed down chowder and sandwiches, salad and garlic bread, before heading for yet another beach in the afternoon, where we flew kites and checked on the resident populations of harbor seals basking on the sandbars. In the evenings, we discovered an Indian restaurant that featured spicy tandoori-cooked food reminiscent of the meals I used to eat in the old days in Nairobi.

My subconscious ku was most impressed by all this, to say the least, and I wondered if it would happen.

During the second night in the house by the river, I had a dream in which I engaged in a classic shamanic journey, the first time for this to happen to me in this particular way. It was as though I woke up within the dream and promptly went right into the trance state, during which my body continued to sleep while my conscious mind was quite awake, witnessing all that occurred. The trance deepened and the phosphenes appeared with the now-familiar somatic grip of power sensations and the rushing hiss of sound.

The sparkling light show abruptly became woven into a tunnel-like shape through which I traveled, flying effortlessly through the shimmering darkness in the grip of the ecstasy. I suddenly emerged into a beautiful blue and green world, one that was dark on one side and light on the other—one in which there was an unmistakable presence. It felt huge and solid, yet diaphanous and flowing. It was immensely strong, yet yielding and soft. I didn't actually see this presence, nor did it feel human; rather, it was all around me, as though I was inside of it. As my conscious mind sought for a way to categorize the contact, a way to establish order on the experience, my subconscious *ku* released a series of impressions that were recognizable—impressions of liquid, of water.

With this realization, I heard a curious sigh that deepened, deepened, deepened . . . and then abruptly ceased. The sound then repeated itself in a rhythmic, surging murmur, almost like the breathing of some vast organism. It was a gravelly intake and outgo of sound that rose, peaked, and subsided, rose, peaked, and subsided, establishing a repetition that almost approached singing. The song, if it could be called that, rose in volume and eased off, waxed and waned. I could feel it at the same time I was hearing it.

A swirling mass of bubbles rose toward me through the dark blue-green field, and I became aware that I had, in some way, merged with the river flowing by the house, or perhaps I had drifted out into the ocean. Curiously, I seemed to have no trouble breathing. I recalled Nainoa's memory of Kenojelak's vision, and with that association, an image took shape in the swirling field before me.

It was as though an area of density, a maelstrom of sparkling, prismatic light, established itself within the water. It was less like an objective thing or form and more of a subjective process involving movement, energy, and aliveness—like a huge school of fish, perhaps—but energetic ones. As I struggled to perceive, to understand what was being shown to me, I again felt the awareness—a huge flowing mind-shape that was, without doubt, fastened upon me.

As my mind continued its search for a way to order the experience, a memory was jogged loose within me—a recollection of something that had happened at the place of refuge at Honaunau down on the Kona Coast of Hawai'i, five years before.

It had been one of our last evenings at this magical locale before returning to California back in 1989. It was close to sundown, and Jill was packing up the remains of our picnic supper when I had decided to walk out on the lava flows to the edge of the surging ocean. Ordinarily we always kept a respectful distance, for sudden waves have been known to sweep the unsuspecting off their feet and into the deep water, from which they often did not return. On this evening, however, the sea had been calm, so I walked right out to the end of the lava flows, where the black rock wall drops off abruptly into the watery realm.

I had always had a strong sense of connection with the ocean during our four years on the island and had fallen into the custom of addressing it by using the Hawaiian name for the spirit of the deep sea—Kanaloa. I did so at that very moment as the waves lapped gently around my ankles, explaining that my time in the islands was coming to an end and that I was going to have to leave for reasons that were not altogether clear to me. I had stared out across the darkness of the ocean and felt pangs of sadness arise within me. The thought of leaving this place had been wrenching.

I had made a strong affirmation that I would return someday, that I would come back to this place of power, and I asked the spirit of the deep sea to bless me and my journey as I went out into the world of humanity once again. I asked that Kanaloa remember me in its great dreaming, and that it provide a strong assist in whatever came to be.

This ritual had settled me, and I began to feel better. I had said my farewell to the great *akua* of the ocean, and now I could leave. I felt sudden gratitude well up within me. It was as though I had just received something of great value, and I felt the need to give something in return—an offering to clinch the deal, so to speak.

I had searched in my pockets. All I had were my car keys and my Swiss Army knife, an expensive one to which I was very attached. Like an old friend, the knife had traveled with me for a long time and had twice been to Africa. As I remained perched at the edge of the vast ocean, I looked at the knife in my hand and realized that it was *because* I valued it so highly that it made the perfect offering. Without further hesitation, I said aloud, "Great Kanaloa, ancient progenitor and sustainer of life, remember me," and tossed the knife into the water. It disappeared into the blue depths without a sound.

I had turned then and had barely begun to head back across the frozen flows of black stone when I heard a familiar sound behind me. I looked around just in time to see the wave as it hit me. It wasn't a big one, only thigh deep, but the tremendous power of the surge swept me off my feet. On the white coral beach in the distance, I saw Jill start up in alarm as she saw me fall into the rushing water. I waved reassuringly. The water was carrying me toward the beach across the hundred yards of lava shelf. As I struggled to regain my footing, pain scratched across my ankle from the sharp stone below, and I kept my feet up after that, treading water and going with the flow.

I had been deposited in a tide pool close to our picnic spot under the palms. As I stood up and waded out of the receding water, there on the sand was a beautiful cowrie shell in pristine condition. I knew it hadn't been there when we arrived, so it must have been carried up onto the shore by the same wave. I picked it up and turned it over in my hands. It was a really nice one. At an earlier time in my life, I would have thought of this as pure coincidence, if I thought of it at all. Now I regarded the shell as a gift.

All this flashed through my mind in that instant as I hung there within the blue-green void in the visionary state. At that moment it was as if the sun had suddenly come out from behind a cloud above the surface of the sea. Long undulating shafts of light coalesced around me, their source in the unmeasurable distance above, their destination in the unimaginable depths below. I just floated there, entranced, suspended in the blue world of the ocean, surrounded by the brilliant green and gold columns of light. Words emerged within my mind: "Great Kanaloa, ancient progenitor and sustainer of life, I remember you and I greet you with *aloha*."

As if in response, something flickered down toward me out of the light, drifting in and out of the swirling shafts of color. Reaching out, I caught the shell in my hands. With that act, my consciousness shifted, and I awoke, wide-eyed, in my bed in the house beside the river.

We went to a friend's house for dinner our last night on the coast. Her domicile was perched on the edge of a bluff right over the water, with the windows looking out toward the sunset across the dark ocean's undulating surface. We enjoyed each other's company over wine and food in the fading light, and at one point our hostess gestured toward a huge outcrop of stone, shaped like the hump of some gargantuan camel, buried in the sand right at the edge of the water below the house. "That rock is not an ordinary rock," she told us. "The healers of this region say it's a stone of great power. They bring people here to visit it."

I descended to the beach after our meal and approached the mono-lithic stone. As I got close I did indeed feel something, but I had drunk quite a lot of wine, and I was in my ordinary state of consciousness, so whatever it was, it was just there, undefined—a sense of presence, perhaps.

The tide was out and the base of the huge rock was exposed at the edge of the tideline. It was about thirty feet high and appeared to be fairly symmetrical—roughly pyramidal in form with a blunt top. I asked permission, then climbed a short way up its wet flank. The light was fading and the rock was slippery, so I desisted and climbed back down again. At its base I saw a shallow depression, a natural bowl scooped out of the stone, filled with seawater from the last high tide. Curious, I approached it and looked in.

There in the bottom of the bowl was a dark pebble, a flat, smooth lens of stone about the size of a fifty-cent piece. I picked it up. It was a jet black, dense basalt and jogged loose a memory of Hawai'i—a recollection of our last afternoon on the beach when I found a small stone adze blade.

I looked around carefully in the dying light as I examined the smooth pebble closely. The time of day, the finding of the stone at the water's edge, the stone itself—all were similar to the event that had happened in Hawai'i. Even the fine-grained basalt was identical to that of the adze—so similar, in fact, that it could easily have come from the same source. This was impossible, of course. The beach I was standing on was separated by almost three thousand miles of ocean from Hawai'i.

I remembered my visionary meeting with Kanaloa the night before. I searched in the pockets of my jacket and found another stone, a smooth piece of Sierra granite that I had picked up in the mountains several years before. I had been carrying it around ever since, a small token that reminded me of the place I had found it. Despite my feelings of attachment for it, I put it in the stone bowl. Then I tucked the newfound pebble into my pocket and walked back to the house. I didn't see any other black basalt pebbles on the beach, none at all.

It was well after midnight when we got back to the house on the river and tucked the children into bed. Stimulated by the evening, Jill and I stayed up and talked for a while, so it was very late when we finally turned out the lights and prepared to go to bed. In a sudden change of mind, I walked out through the sliding glass doors onto the long porch that fronts the river. There I saw something truly wondrous. There was no moon, and the night sky was both very clear and totally dark. The constellation known as the Big Dipper hung low in the heavens just above the water. Much to my amazement, the river's glassy surface reflected a second Dipper, upside down, so that the two were almost touching. It was as though I could see into two different levels of reality simultaneously . . . as above, so below.

We withdrew to bed, where Jill drew me into her embrace and we had a joyous marital encounter, fueled by the wine and by the great affection that we felt for each other. I wasn't surprised when the surge of power slammed into me in ecstasy's aftermath, rendering me completely paralyzed in an instant. The darkness of the bedroom was suddenly lit by flashes of light—like heat lightning during a summer thunderstorm far in the distance. I recalled the Dipper as the phosphenes appeared and began to coalesce into the grid and the opening crescent of light. I plunged through it into the dark hall of the zone of silence.

CHAPTER 16

Eighth Journey:
The Place of
Refuge

THE RETREAT CENTER in the Pukui land division was a place of great natural beauty located on a wide bay with expansive views of both the lagoon and the mountainous ridges across the water. The shallow harbor had been cleared of mangroves, providing a suitable ship landing as well as a rich place to sieve for shrimp. Chief Wilipaki's double-hulled canoe was beached there along with several other craft belonging to the center. On the other side of the bay, isolated from the center by a long stretch of forest, could be seen the port settlement of the Pukui land division, with its harbor filled with sailing craft and its elevated administrative hub in the center of the sprawling town.

The sacred area of the center was delimited from the outside world by a tall earthen wall faced with stone that ran inland from the shore in a great semicircle breached only by one large gate with tall wooden doors. Beyond the wall was the commercial center, which included a small open market whose stalls were surrounded by the houses and shops of the artisans, merchants, woodcutters, weavers, fishermen, farmers, hunters, and others who served the priests.

Inside the great wall, the living quarters of the priests were arranged in a random fashion among a dense grove of coconut palms that ran right down to the beach. Some fish ponds had been excavated in the central area, and to one side of them rose the long stone platform of the main *heiau*, crowned at one end with the large multiroofed hall for meetings and spiritual practice. On the platform's other end stood the house of power, in which sacred relics were kept. Next to it on one side was a smaller drum house as well as an oven house. In the platform's center stood a cluster of carved post images that symbolized the powerful ancestral spirits associated with the center. Among them rose a single tall, uncarved monolith of stone, the tangible symbol of the *aumakua*, the spiritual aspect of the self, to which this *heiau* was dedicated. Below the standing stone was an altar upon which sat an arrangement of freshly cut flowers and a stone bowl filled with water.

Several other stone platforms rose among the trees, each crowned with a building capped by a tall thatched roof. Nainoa sat with Wilipaki on the *lanai* of one of these, listening to the light breeze rattle the palms. It was early evening and the two had just returned from the main hall, where they had partaken of the *kahunas'* sparse meal of grilled fish and boiled taro greens washed down with spring water, followed by fruit and coffee.

Nainoa was chewing the end of a short stick, working the fibrous, well-frayed end around his teeth and gums. His eyes watched a large storm passing through the burnished copper sky over the purple ridges in the distance. The summit of the towering mass of cloud was pink with the sunset while its dark innards disgorged an impressive curtain of rain on the distant slopes. A brief flash of lightning lit up the roiling mass, and after several seconds the rumble of thunder rolled across the intervening waterway. The rainy season had begun.

The two men had been guests at the center for ten days, participating in the daily life of the priests and their novices while Nainoa was ritually cleansed of any residual negative forces associated with the recent conflict within his lineage. He thought about his lineage as his gaze rested on the storm.

His relationship to his grandfather, the sorcerer whose name no one would speak, had now become generally known. This had created considerable social distance between him and the general populace, a distance that had been reinforced by what had happened to Chief Paleko. From the day of his arrival at the place of refuge, he had been treated with formal deference by all except the Kahuna Nui, a large, jovial high chiefess known for her great psychic power and intuitive wisdom. She was named Kahu Sala Kahalopuna, and she was a distant relative of the governor.

As director of the center, the Kahuna Nui presided over the cere-mony of the great prayer that was offered to the sunrise at dawn and to the sunset at dusk. At these times, she was remote, her mind focused on the mystery to which she had dedicated herself as a student for life. During the daytimes, however, Kahu Sala, as all called her, was a warm, personable administrator and a witty conversational-ist known for her great sense of humor and robust belly laugh. She had been present at the capital when Nainoa had recounted the story of his year in the interior, and he had felt some relief at not having to repeat his tale in detail yet once again.

On the day of their arrival, Nainoa had met with the Kahuna Nui to discuss the events that had brought him to the place of refuge. She had listened, saying little until he had concluded his story, whereupon her eyes had twinkled merrily.

"Chief Paleko was a priest of great power and considerable ability," she volunteered, "although, speaking frankly, when we heard what had happened to him, more than one of us said, 'That malevolent piece of excrement had it coming.'" She laughed heartily. "Others have ob-served that after all the trouble and bad medicine he created, he's in his true element now—compost." She chortled again, then her mirth subsided as her demeanor shifted into a more formal mode.

"Long ago, I knew Paleko as a child and saw the darkness in him even then. In those days, I came into contact with many families because I myself was in the life stage of raising my own children. As I came to know both parents and offspring, I learned something very interesting. I discovered that many children who came from families within which there was disharmony and imbalance were often quite positive and filled with light. Yet just as often, I saw the opposite, where positively focused, light-filled parents produced children whose souls were filled with negativity and darkness.

"In time, I came to understand that each of us comes into life with a certain *ukana*, a distinct package that has nothing to do with who our birth parents happen to be. This *ukana* is reflected in our personality, positive or negative, courageous or fearful, powerful or powerless, revealing what is prominent in our *aumakua*—our personal spiritual aspect.

"Paleko's spirit always reflected the negative because he was carrying part of his grandfather's dark nature. But here is something curious. Power that is consistently and persistently misused ultimately diminishes the one who abuses it. This is especially true of the *kahuna* who has turned bad. Such a person can do a lot of damage for a while, but he or she fails to perceive that while there is great power in the negative forces, it is necessary to transmute them by balancing them with the positive—and in equal proportion. Failure to do so results in disaster.

"Quite frankly, I'm amazed it took this long for Paleko to fall from grace, but all of us have been aware that it would happen sooner or later. The fact that you, the carrier of the same grandfather's spiritual *ike*, should be the catalyst for his downfall is rather mythic, don't you think?"

She had concluded, "One hopes that people like Paleko wake up before they come to the end of their lives, short or long. Power is just power. It's not good or bad; it's the way it's used or misused that creates positive or negative effects. And realizing this, one comes to understand that only by changing one's intentions and lifeway is it possible to shift one's personal destiny and start accruing positive *hoalona lanakila*—lofty measure. Interestingly, it's when this realization is achieved that the true ascent to power really begins."

At the end of the interview, he had thanked the Kahuna Nui and had settled into a guest house in which he and Wilipaki occupied separate rooms. Long days and nights had then been spent in the meditation hall practicing *lokahi*, reflecting on all aspects of the episode in which he had played a part. The goal was to come to terms with the deed—to cleanse himself and rebalance his *wa*, his inner harmony. Only in this way could closure be achieved.

Kahu Sala had also provided him with various mental exercises designed to enhance his awareness of the different aspects of himself and how they functioned, thus increasing his own self-realization. His long periods of solitary introspection were interwoven with informal interviews with her twice each day to discuss his progress. She had been a powerful teacher in this inner quest, providing clear guidelines to follow. Nainoa understood with some amazement that his training as a *kahuna* had begun.

Nainoa's introspection was interrupted as he suddenly perceived the watchful presence within himself. Although he was not in an expanded state of awareness, he listened intently and was not surprised when a question formed in his mind. He smiled as he turned to the older man seated next to him.

"Chief Wilipaki, we have discussed my relationship and occasional connections across time and distance with one of my ancestors. If this man and I are really manifestations of the same spiritual *aumakua*, or source self, what does this relationship reveal about the nature of that source, as well as about who we are and what we are doing here?"

Nainoa had learned that this was the sort of question that Wilipaki loved. He felt anticipation as he watched the older man's eyes narrow speculatively.

"First of all," Wilipaki mused, tugging at his trimmed white beard with a lean hand, "it must be understood that the relationship between a living person and their *kupuna*, their ancestors, is a close one. I

255

don't so much mean our immediate living family members but rather the etheric matrix of departed ones who came before us—their spiritual essence.

"Each of us is like a knot along a cord that includes an immensely long succession of knots that, in turn, are woven into the living, spiritual net-like matrix of humanity. Each string of knots is a continuously reincarnating lineage that grows and changes as it travels through time. This spiritual lineage represents our spiritual *ohana*—our spiritual extended family, so to speak. Our personal *aumakua* is our knot within this lineage, and it is through the dynamic of countless lifetimes spent here on the physical plane that our *aumakua* grows and the lineage is increased.

"What we do and become here on the physical plane determines the level of development of our *aumakua* in *Po,* the spirit world, for our spirit source self is always there, even when we as physical beings are manifested here. Do you understand? Good. It is through decisions and actions made during our past lives that our spirit aspect has already reached a certain level of achievement and awareness.

"It follows then that our relationship with our personal *aumakua* is an intimate one. On the one hand, this aspect functions as our spirit teacher, and as such, it is the source of information, dreams, visions, ideas, and intuition that we receive during our lives here on the physical level of existence. In communicating with us in this manner, it is responsible for guiding us to a great degree. I suppose you could call it a personal guide or guardian, but it is actually considerably more than that.

"The *aumakua* is also the spiritual source from which we as individuals are manifested when we are born, and it is the spiritual destination to which we retire after the death of the physical body. In the intervals between each successive lifetime, we exist purely as *aumakua* in a state of deep meditative awareness. Under this circumstance, our sense of the personal, so strong while we are physically manifested here, is subsumed into the greater collective whole of the human spirit."

Wilipaki rubbed his hands briskly together, cracking his knuckles and warming to his topic. "There is thus a cyclic relationship between ourselves, our spiritual aspect, and the realm of the *aumakua* spirits, which, in turn, is a specific place in the dream worlds. This level can be a great source of information, because it also functions as a reposi-tory, if you will, for the collective essence, awareness, and wisdom of all humanity.

"Each of us, through our personal *aumakua*, is in connection with this great collective spiritual-essence-plus-wisdom, which, in turn, changes and grows in response to what we become in the here and now. The same is true for every manifested life form. The spotted tiger *aumakua*, who seems so fond of you, is the collective spiritual-essence-plus-ability of all spotted tigers: the hummingbird *aumakua* is the spiritual source of all hummingbirds." Wilipaki lapsed into silence as a small sparkling bird zoomed up and hovered around their heads, then disappeared into the growing dusk. His white teeth flashed as he gestured toward the departing bird.

"Eventually we will all achieve levels of experience and awareness that allow us to remain merged with the source," he continued. "When we reach that stage, we no longer need to return to life on the physical plane. Such highly evolved ancestral spirits often take on the task of guiding human destiny to some degree with their collective will, so we are still in relationship to them in a way. Each of us is actually in relationship to a cluster of such soul spirits, and we confer with them many times during that period when we are in the spirit world between lives. Ultimately, of course, it is through the rest of us, through those of us who keep returning, that our evolution into the higher regions of spirit is accomplished.

"This is our *kuleana*, our responsibility—to grow in beauty and wisdom positively and deeply so that we can contribute to the greater good of the human spirit. It's really quite marvelous, when you think of it. As your friend William used to say, our minds and spirits are in the process of becoming the greater mind-spirit of humanity, which, in turn, is part of the still larger collective mind-spirit of our world."

"In turn, part of the great mind-spirit of our star," Nainoa murmured with a smile.

"Exactly," agreed the older man. "And knowing this, our *kuleana* is clear. We are responsible for the evolution of the mind-spirit of our star, and as our connection with this great creator being grows and deepens, it becomes possible to connect with the still greater collective mind-spirit of the vastness of the universe." His words drifted into silence as his gaze lifted into the darkening sky. The first stars were just appearing.

"On a more immediate level," Wilipaki went on, "your ancestor, the one you call the American, is a distant member of your lineage. Part of your life force and your *ike* is derived from his. It is through this etheric matrix of shared power that the connection between the two of you is enabled. As William said, there are two yous in this dynamic." He laughed with the pleasure of the thought. "I've never had this experience myself, but there are others who have. Like you, they describe deep visions of great realism accompanied by bodily feelings of power or force. Some of the dreamer *kahunas* among us have actually connected with more than one ancestor, and some go in the other direction and connect with descendants. Such people are rare, but they exist."

Wilipaki became pensive and looked down for a moment, then smiled. "I like William's term for such people—spiritwalkers."

Moving points of light among the palms revealed that torches were being lit, lending a festive appearance to the retreat center. Wilipaki fell silent as a servant carrying a bundle of torches climbed the stairs of the house platform and approached the *lanai* on which they were sitting. Nainoa had gotten to know the man and greeted him by name. The servant placed two torches in stone brackets at each end of the *lanai* and lit them off the one he was carrying before disappearing silently into the growing darkness.

"Can you connect with your ancestor at will?" Wilipaki asked.

Nainoa shook his head. "It still seems to be a largely spontaneous phenomenon. I do not know for certain what initiates it, nor can I control it." Nainoa paused and reflected briefly, then came to a decision.

"I am almost always aware when his mind enters into connection with mine. A sense of his watchfulness and presence appears suddenly within me. You might find it interesting to know that such a feeling occurred when we were watching the storm only moments ago. It may well be that he is here right now."

Wilipaki eyed him owlishly. "You mean that he is *here*? Right now?"

"I believe so. I can feel his mind, although I cannot communicate with him directly unless I am in the deep trance state. Sometimes I perceive his will at work, accessing my memories for information. If he wants to look at something tangible, the way our walls or wagons are built, for example, I will find myself going over to a wall or wagon to observe it closely, for no apparent reason of my own.

"The American is a historian. He's interested in very long reaches of time. In fact, his knowledge spans millions of years of the past instead of mere hundreds or thousands. He occasionally travels to an exceedingly dry place halfway around the planet on the land mass known to us from our ancient maps as Africa. None of us has ever been there, of course, but I now know for certain that such a place exists. Amazingly, it takes him only two or three days to accomplish the journey, because he utilizes airships to get there. I have seen some of his memories of these machines, as well as memories of his life in Africa. He goes there to dig in the ground, searching for the bones of humanity's most ancient ancestors. There are exceedingly dark-skinned people who live there in his time."

The older man raised his eyebrows and nodded in amazement. There followed a long silence while Wilipaki looked at him closely, then asked, "Has your ancestor actually handled the bones of ancestors who lived millions of years ago?"

Nainoa nodded. "He works with a group of other historians, all of whom are involved in investigating various aspects of the great mystery of our source. They find the bones buried in ancient lakebeds or streambeds that are now dry. The bones are not like those of humans of today but are those of an earlier form that was somewhat similar to the hairy forest people."

"Really?" said the older man with surprise.

Nainoa nodded. "It makes sense, of course. Our mythology reveals that the ancestry of all life, including humanity, lies within the great spiritual matrix of nature. Of all the other animals, the hairy forest people are the ones most like us, so I suppose in the distant past, we could have looked more like them. We can see this pattern everywhere. Some things are simple; others are complex. Jellyfish are very simple creatures compared to the sea turtles that eat them. My ancestor believes that this progressive increase in complexity is characteristic of the great pattern, of which all manifested forms are simply different aspects."

Wilipaki watched him carefully for several moments, then said, "You are recovering lost knowledge of the past from this man's mind when you are in connection with him."

Nainoa nodded again. "I am. He lives in the time before the fall of the American civilization, and his knowledge is vast. His world is filled with miraculous things." Nainoa's eyes rested on one of the burning torches. "The American people have a most amazing method of creating light at night, for instance, but I have no way of truly understanding how it is done. In some manner, they discovered how to harness the power of the sun and direct it through ropes of metal to objects of glass and metal that then glow with the sun's power." He shook his head as he searched for words to describe what he had seen.

"Ropes of metal," Wilipaki muttered. "We find such ropes in the farmers' fields, and the histories confirm that the Americans had immense amounts of metal."

"They did indeed," said Nainoa. "But the American's mind reveals that their metal was dug from deep within the earth—so deep, in fact, that machines were required to accomplish the task. They had so much metal that it is possible that they could have exhausted their sources of supply." As darkness fell in earnest, Nainoa recounted a small portion of the growing store of knowledge he was acquiring from the mind of the American.

The sharp report of a slit drum sounded, calling them to the meeting hall of the main *heiau*. As the two rose to their feet, Wilipaki said, "Perhaps you can enter the trance state during the evening's meditation. Perhaps you will be able to speak with your ancestor."

"Perhaps." The younger man smiled.

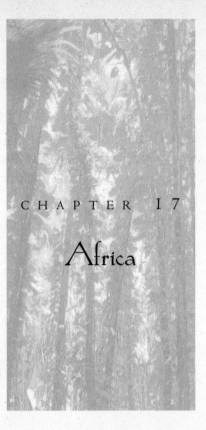

CHAPTER 17

Africa

S OMETHING OCCURRED AT that point, shifting my awareness back to my body lying in bed in the house on the Russian River. I felt intense disappointment as I opened my eyes. The connection with Nainoa had been a brief one, and I would very much have liked to have had a longer talk. I sat up in bed and wondered what had disrupted the contact, but whatever it was, it eluded me.

I felt thirsty from the previous evening's wine and got up to get a drink of water from the kitchen. On impulse, I walked over to look out the big windows at the river below the house. The tide had turned, and the water's surface was now rippled and nonreflective. I looked up at the stars blazing away in the darkness and saw that the Big Dipper had set. This glance triggered a recollection of something extraordinary that I had just seen through Nainoa's eyes.

When his gaze had followed Wilipaki's out into the starry sky above the palms, his eyes had sought out the direction of true north.

As my own mind registered what he was seeing, I had suddenly realized that he was not looking at Polaris, the North Star, but rather in the direction of another star cluster, the constellation Cepheus, beyond the Little Dipper and above the arch of Draco.

The moment had passed as his eyes and his thoughts had shifted to other matters, but I was left with a sense of wonder at what had just been revealed. Over the approximately five thousand years that separated Nainoa's world from mine, the earth's orbit had wobbled and I had just seen the results of that wobble reflected in the position of the stars, or rather, in the new position of the axis of our planet—a fact confirming once again that I was indeed perceiving a slice of the future.

Science has shown that the earth is not a perfect sphere, but is actually somewhat flattened at the poles, causing the equatorial regions to bulge slightly by comparison. The moon's gravity affects the earth's axis, tilting it perpendicular to the moon's orbit—an axis that is also, to some extent, affected by the gravity of the sun. These two gravitational forces, combined with the earth's asymmetry and gyroscopic spin, cause the planet's orbit to wobble, or precess, slowly in a clockwise direction opposite to that of the earth's spin. This means that as the earth orbits the sun, year after year, millennium after millennium, the tilt of the planet's axis shifts slightly, so the poles change the position of their "point," sweeping across the heavens from star to star in both the northern and southern skies in a great circle that takes almost twenty-six thousand years to complete.

The rental house on the river had a large collection of back issues of *National Geographic*, and I had noted one with a map of the heavens just the day before. Excitedly I turned on a light, retrieved the issue from the pile, and studied the star map carefully. There was Polaris, the North Star, at the end of the Little Dipper. I made a rough calculation and drew a circle on the map. Five thousand years ago, one of the stars in Draco had to have been the North Star, and five thousand years from now, it would be located in Cepheus, as I had just seen through Nainoa's eyes. Roughly thirteen thousand years from now, the earth's axis will place Vega at polar north.

How had I missed this important piece of information from all the previous encounters I had had with Nainoa? When I recalled how many times he had looked out at the stars, my first impulse was to berate myself for not paying closer attention. I figured I had been taking mental notes or thinking about something else at the time, but then I began to wonder. Perhaps I simply hadn't registered the position of polar north in his time as unusual because Nainoa hadn't, either.

I turned out the light and got back into bed. Dawn was close, but I was too excited to sleep. I lay beside Jill, listening to her breathing, thinking about all that I had just experienced. Once again I had eavesdropped on a conversation about the nature of the human higher self—our personal spiritual aspect, which the Hawaiians call *aumakua*. I wondered what my personal *aumakua* looked like. I had come to understand the nature of my relationship to this immortal spiritual aspect, but I had never actually seen it.

We headed back to Sacramento the next day, and classes for the fall semester started soon thereafter. Just days before my first class, I got a call from Tim White at UC Berkeley. He was ready for me to join his expedition in Ethiopia as soon as my teaching responsibilities were finished in December. He was sending me a plane ticket, a visa application, and some malaria tablets. A month later, he and several colleagues published a scientific paper in the British journal *Nature* describing a new species of human, *Australopithecus ramidus*, the earliest and most primitive form of the human lineage ever discovered.[1] I would be one of a team of specialists working at this early hominid site, dated at nearly four and a half million years old.

As the semester came to an end, I celebrated an early Christmas with my family, packed my bags for a month's safari into the African bush, and soon found myself on the night flight from San Francisco to Frankfurt. From there I took another flight down into Ethiopia.

The morning after my arrival, I was picked up at my hotel in downtown Addis Ababa by Dr. Berhane Asfaw, an Ethiopian physical anthropologist who had brought a Land Cruiser in from the field camp to get me. We spent the morning loading the car with food and supplies as well as attending to business at the Ethiopian National Museum. By noon, I was heading north across the stark beauty of the Ethiopian highlands in the company of Mesfin Asnake, a geologist from the Department of Mines who would be working closely with me on my research project for the next month. We made our descent into the Rift Valley late in the afternoon and spent the night in a frontier town at the edge of the lands of the Afar people.

The next morning we made contact with an Afar woman who would serve as our first guide. We filled our dozen jerry cans with gas, tied them to the roof rack, then left the paved road behind and headed east into the Rift on a graded gravel track. It felt absolutely wonderful to be back in Africa once again. Having spent many years out in East Africa, I knew most of the birds, trees, and bushes like old friends, and every moment elicited happy memories.

Two hours later, the Afar woman indicated that we were to turn off the road and drive north through the bush. I put the car in four-wheel drive and followed her directions, weaving through the thorn trees until we arrived at a rather bleak collection of corrugated iron buildings, which constituted a road camp where workers and machinery for maintaining the road were housed. As we got out of the car we were greeted by half a dozen lean-looking Afar men, all of whom had Kalashnikov machine guns slung over their bony shoulders as well as the ubiquitous curved Afar short sword strapped around their waists.

They looked me over carefully while the introductions were made. I smiled and shook hands, whereupon an elder man named Mohammed Gana stepped forward and revealed himself as our escort. He was the chief of the road camp and a man of great influence and power in this part of the world. We got back in the car, and after protracted farewells to those remaining behind, we headed off across the Afar lands, Mohammed Gana sitting beside me, staring fiercely out at his domain with his Kalashnikov propped between his knees.

After descending a couple of steep escarpments in first gear, we crossed the Arso River, then drove out across the flat, thorny desert of the northern Rift. Immense vistas opened in every direction, shimmering in the heat. A massive volcano called Ayelu loomed to the northeast. All day long we churned along in four-wheel drive, throwing up a plume of dust as we crossed silty floodplains that would be completely impassable in the event of rain. Sometimes I was able to follow the track that had been made by the car coming out of the field several days before, but more often than not, the faint tire marks disappeared entirely as we crossed gravel flats or traversed dusty plains where herds of livestock had obliterated all traces of the route. Although we couldn't speak a word of each other's language, Mohammed Gana guided me with sparse gestures of command to turn here or go straight there, and I realized quite clearly that without him, I would never find Tim White's field camp.

The Afars are Muslim pastoralists who live a lean existence with their herds of camels, goats, and cattle in a harsh, dry land unsuitable for agriculture. Occasionally we would stop in one of their villages, whose inhabitants and camels would flock around the car, staring curiously at me as Mohammed Gana carried on lengthy discussions about issues of local concern. I let my eyes drift across the Afars and perceived them as a proud, dignified people whose men are formidable warriors and whose women are among the most beautiful in the world.

This last point was brought home repeatedly that day as many young Afar women approached the car, dressed only in trade-cloth skirts and brightly colored trade beads. They were long and lean, with beautifully braided hair styles and flashing smiles. They reminded me of the Ennu women, expressing the same style and grace of movement and exuding that same wild freedom. Throughout that day, I thought often of Kenojelak, and deep within my soul, I realized that I missed her.

Although the Afar lands are within the political boundaries of the nation-state of Ethiopia, no one enters their territory without their knowledge and permission. Each clan is led by a chief called the *balabat,* and the clans are frequently at odds with each other. This point was brought home at midday when Mohammed Gana quietly slid ammunition into the magazine of his machine gun, then deliberately had me steer a wide berth around a large village in the distance. As we passed, several angry adolescent boys ran after us and threw rocks in our direction.

In another incident, we passed close to an isolated compound with a single dwelling, from which an Afar boy emerged and threw a stone at the car. Mohammed Gana immediately motioned for me to stop. He got out of the car and unslung his Kalashnikov. The youngster apparently hadn't seen the old chief riding beside me and stopped dead in his tracks as Mohammed Gana approached him and began to speak in an imperious tone. Mesfin leaned out the car window and watched the two with great concern for long moments. Then he relaxed and laughed as the older man turned and came back to the car, telling me that Mohammed Gana had informed the boy that if he ever threw stones at another vehicle under his protection, he would shoot him. The Afar chief got back in the car with a short glance in my direction and motioned for me to drive on.

It was late afternoon when we came up over a rise and finally spied a cluster of sun-bleached tents huddled in the shade of a long line of flat-topped acacia trees in the distance. As I parked in a cloud of dust I saw that the trees were growing along the edge of a sand river, a dry riverbed, which Mohammed Gana informed me was known as Ganduli. The arid, pastel landscape surrounding the field camp was of very low relief, and the cloudless pale blue sky seemed immense.

Tim got back to camp with his crew toward dusk. He seemed glad to see me, showed me which tent was mine, then went to get cleaned up for dinner. As darkness fell, one of the graduate students started a field generator, activating a string of electric lights strung between the thorn trees. I unpacked my gear and arranged it in my tent, then wandered around the camp, introducing myself to anyone and everyone I met. With the exception of Tim, all were new faces.

There were four Ethiopians from the highlands working as cooks in the field kitchen. Meals were taken sitting outdoors in canvas folding chairs arranged along both sides of several long tables placed end to end under the largest of the acacias fronting the sand river. All our food had to be brought in from Addis, and in the days that followed, breakfasts consisted of oatmeal, toast, jam, peanut butter, tea, and coffee. Lunches were usually taken in the field and included peanuts, canned meat, bread (baked daily by the cooks in camp in Dutch ovens), peanut butter, cookies, and Kool-Aid. Dinners began with soup followed by a main course, usually pasta or rice with meat sauce, canned vegetables, and coleslaw (if we had any fresh produce). Dessert consisted of cookies and fruit, and was followed by coffee or tea.

When the dinner bell was rung on that first evening, I looked our gathering over. In addition to the dozen or so scientists from the United States, France, Belgium, Turkey, and Ethiopia, there were thirteen Afar men of the Alisera clan in our camp, all of whom were toting machine guns and swords. Their job was to keep an eye on things and protect us from the rival clans, with whom we (and they) didn't have an alliance. From the look of them, they meant business. We were far from the well-beaten path traveled by most tourists seeking adventure in Africa.

During dinner that evening, I watched Tim interact with his fellow scientists and his Afar hosts. He approached relationships with a guarded, crotchety gruffness that could erupt into icy Clint Eastwood–like anger or a wacko sense of humor, depending on circumstance. He is also an acknowledged expert in his field who knows precisely how to plan and run a field expedition. As the day's work was discussed, I learned that very few fossils had been recovered during the six weeks the group had been in the field. I scanned the assembled scientists. Faces were long and people looked frayed. The long days of hard labor in the hot sun had taken their toll, and most had that peculiar vacant look that belied their weariness at the soul level.

When dinner was over, the plans for the next day's work were outlined, then all dispersed into the darkness. Tim and several graduate students went to the work tent to sort and catalogue the day's finds. I followed and looked over their shoulders as they turned on solar lamps and mulled over bone fragments that to the uninitiated would be totally meaningless. Tim's knowledge of comparative osteology is formidable, and we all listened enthralled as he picked up a succession of unauspicious-looking fossils and proceeded to read them like books, revealing their secrets as he deciphered their codes.

Eventually I walked out into the darkness away from the camp and climbed a nearby hill. I turned off my flashlight and just stood there in the warm African night, staring out into the starry universe. The north star, Polaris, was just visible above the black wall of trees across the sand river. The constellation Orion was well up in the eastern sky and the Pleiades were directly overhead. Across the great void, the cloud of our galaxy stretched like a misty river in the sky. I thought of the immense collective mind composed of all those stars and felt awed by the revelation that the evolutionary destiny of humanity was to join it someday, to be part of it . . . to *be* it. And here I was in the place the human journey had begun.

The night wind arose, bringing the dry, dusty scent of the desert. I felt profoundly moved to be out here again, and on impulse I bowed to the four directions, inviting their powers to approach and interact with my body and mind. My thoughts turned to the leopard man, and I put out a request, asking for his company and assistance in this wild place where his lineage and mine had evolved in relationship over immense amounts of time. One by one I sent warm greetings to each of the powers that function for me as spirit helpers, and as always, I wondered if my spirit teacher was out there, too, listening to my thoughts, monitoring my life. For the thousandth time, I wondered what my *aumakua* looked like.

And then there was the *dorajuadiok.* Was that awesome spirit out there, too, watching me, watching the camp?

I felt tired from the arduous two-day drive as well as the eleven hours of jet lag, so I bowed to the great void filled with starry creators one last time. As if in response, one of them moved, dropping down out of the night sky and heading right toward me. I stared, astonished, only to see it wink out, then wink on again before zooming right over my head—a lightning beetle. I smiled in the darkness. The universe had responded.

I clicked on my flashlight and walked back to camp. I went to bed in my small tent on the levee above the sand river and slept soundly until the middle of the night, when my bladder demanded I get up and have a pee. The generator was off now, and as I stood in the darkness, relieving myself, my eyes turned again to the stars. And there in the eastern sky, the constellation Leo had risen, the lion in the sky, following Orion, the hunter.

My days in the field camp took on a regular pattern almost immediately. I would awaken before dawn and sit in meditation in my tent for an hour or so until I heard the first birdcall. Then I would emerge, put on my boots, and walk to a high place across the sand river to watch the sunrise. This was always a magical time for me—the time before shadows. As the light grew, the endless expanse of the Rift valley floor was revealed, stretching away in all directions, filled with a vast, monumental silence.

When the sun finally crested over the eastern horizon, I could see the dark escarpment of the Rift wall to the west with the blue hills of the Ethiopian highlands beyond. In the skies to the south rose the massive cone of the volcano Ayelu. Twenty miles to the east lay the Awash, a muddy, crocodile-infested stretch of river that was the source of the camp's drinking water. To the north, the Rift opened into the dry country that would eventually meet the shores of the Red Sea. Somewhere out there was Hadar, the now-famous fossil beds where Don Johanson and his student Tom Gray had found the 3.2-million-year-old partial skeleton known as "Lucy" twenty years before.

Each of the dozen or so scientists had various chores to perform each morning, such as filling canteens for the day's water supply or filling the sun showers for our sparse bath at the end of the day. Solar lamps would be placed to charge during the day; field equipment and tools would be mobilized and packed in one of the seven vehicles; the day's plans would be gone over in the work tent as everything came together. I often did my laundry at this time, washing and rinsing my grimy clothes in a bucket, then hanging them to dry on a line next to my tent.

When the breakfast bell was rung at sunup, all would gather and eat quickly, finish their tasks, then climb into one of the vehicles and head out to the site for the day's work. One of the Turkish scientists, a paleontologist named Gerçek Saraç, was interested in micromammals and had decided to work with Mesfin and me. The three of us took on the task of providing firewood for the camp kitchen, and so every other day or so we would get in our truck after breakfast and make a foray into the thorn scrub along the dry river searching for deadwood, with which we would fill the truck bed and return to the camp before heading out to our own work in the fossil beds.

South and east of White's camp was a long, low range of hills. Among them, the ancient banks of a paleoriver are slowly being exposed by the wind and the seasonal rains. It is from these riverbank sediments, dated by the potassium-argon method at 4.4 million years old, that the fossilized bones of animals are eroding out, and this was where fragments of the new hominid species were being recovered. Each of the localities that has yielded fossils has been given a number and a name, usually derived from an Afar place name.

The localities currently being excavated by White's team were named for the Afar village of Aramis, and for the next three weeks, we surveyed these areas for prospective sites, crawling on hands and knees, our eyes inches from the surface as we picked up every scrap of bone for identification and later analysis. When Gerçek, Mesfin, and I found a promising place, we dug samples of sediment and filled a dozen large sacks, put them in the truck, then returned to camp, where we extracted water by the bucket from beneath the sand river with a hand pump. We then "washed" our sediments, passing them through fine metal screens to reduce their volume, as the clays and silts passed through. The fine gravels and sands from the screens were then "picked" under a microscope for the fossilized teeth and jaws of small mammals.

Unlike the large mammals, such as elephants, giraffes, or gazelles, which live relatively long lives and have relatively large home ranges, micromammals, such as rodents, bats, or shrews, live lives of very short duration in very small home ranges. They also tend to be very habitat-specific. Some species live only in forests, while others like patchy environments, and still others inhabit grasslands of various kinds or are found only in arid biotypes or deserts. The majority of the sub-saharan micromammals haven't changed much in the past several million years. This meant that if I could find them, I could compare the bones and teeth of the fossil forms with those of their modern descendants, determining not only their taxonomic affinities but also their habitat preferences.

These fossil micromammals thus had the potential to reveal a great deal about the immediate environment around a paleontological site at the time it was laid down, enabling me to reconstruct the paleoecology of the ancient sites from which the bones of humanity's earliest ancestors have been recovered.

The tricky part is finding the fossils. In the 1970s I had spent three field seasons in the Omo Valley in southwestern Ethiopia, a collective nine months of hard work, during which I had screen-washed over twenty tons of sediment, producing less than three hundred tiny specimens, mostly single molar teeth not much larger than grains of sand—hardly a monumental sample.

So as I went to work with Gerçek and Mesfin, I was hopeful but realistic in my expectations. There was also considerable excitement. This ancient Pliocene riverbank was the place where bits and pieces of the new hominid species, *Australopithecus ramidus*, had been found— several skull bases as well as a handful of isolated teeth and limb bone fragments, seventeen fossils in all that demonstrated the hallmarks of humanity and yet were incredibly primitive.[2]

On my first morning in the field, Tim took me on a tour of the geological beds, familiarizing me with the stratigraphy of the Aramis localities. Then I joined one of the multinational survey crews fossil-crawling one of the outcrops, reprogramming my eyes with the discrimination skills essential to the success of such work. As the morning progressed and the temperature rose, the specialists went to work on a hillside from which one of the team had found several *ramidus* teeth eroding out only the previous day. It was there that I suddenly detected a feeling I knew well.

Something was watching me.

I stood up slowly and looked around, but I saw only the stony, arid hills dotted with acacias. I squatted down again and continued my work, sifting through the umber sediments looking for fossils. But the feeling continued and remained throughout the day. In my mind there was absolutely no doubt that I was being observed by something that I couldn't see. I was fully focused on doing science now, however, and the long, hot days that followed were filled with arduous, sometimes mind-numbing work that required my full attention.

The nights were another matter.

It was during my second or third night in the camp that something awakened me. At first I thought it was merely my full bladder, but after taking care of that problem, I remained awake, watchful and listening for whatever might come.

Near dawn I was drifting between wakefulness and sleep when I felt a surge of the power sensations in my body. Simultaneously my conscious awareness detached itself and drifted up toward the ceiling of my tent. I became instantly awake. I remembered having such experiences years before in Africa, and I watched, thrilled, as I slid through the tent screen without having to open it. With a rush that took my breath away, I found myself ascending, flying up and over the camp, looking down on the cluster of trees and tents below me and gasping with wonder. I was aware that a *kahuna* mystic would say that part of my *aka* body had detached from my physical body, carrying my awareness with it, producing what I thought of as a flying dream.

Although there was no moon, I could see quite well. It seemed as if each tree and tent was outlined, or perhaps suffused, with a curious greenish glow.

I saw two or three moving puffs of the same glowing luminescence crossing the wide bed of the sand river below me and zoomed down to have a look. They were jackals, and amazingly, the wild dogs could see me and immediately darted into the cover of the thick bush at the edge of the sand river. I wondered if all animals could do this, which, in turn, led me to wonder if humans had been able to do it too while we were still very much part of nature. Perhaps we had lost the ability through lack of use in our modern societies.

All this passed through my mind in a flash as I hovered over the camp. I thought about making an extended foray across the Rift, then thought better of it. I was new to this part of the world. What if I couldn't find my way back to the camp? This thought produced feelings of concern, which, in turn, caused me to descend suddenly and merge back into my physical body, which jerked as the contact was achieved.

I sat up in bed, excited beyond words. This "flying dream" was virtually identical to the ones I had had in Africa many years before. As I sought the cause, the answer was immediate and two-pronged. On the one hand, my *ku* was happy to be back in the bush again and was responding by opening the inner window. On the other hand, something or someone else was providing assist. I knew this for a certainty, because I had felt its presence strongly during my brief soul flight. Who or what could it be?

My old friend the leopard man was a prime candidate. My inquiries to the Afars had revealed that there were leopards around, still taking the occasional goat or cow. But could it be someone (or something) else, and if so, who (or what)? No answer was forthcoming, but during the next day and the next, the sense of being watched grew stronger.

In the final weeks of the 1994–95 field season, several extraordinary events occurred. They began in an interesting way. Late in the afternoon on the day before Christmas, Tim and I walked up the sand river and cut down a small tamarisk for the camp Christmas tree. We carried it back and set it in a large bucket filled with sand next to the dinner tables and decorated it that evening with ornaments brought from America. Berhane Asfaw and Yonas Beyene, two of the Ethiopian scientists working at the site, arrived from Addis before dark, bringing a case of beer for those of us who drank alcohol. I don't recall if we sang carols, but the mood was definitely up as the moon rose and old stories of past field seasons were recounted.

On Christmas morning I walked up to Tim before breakfast and held out my closed fist. Curious yet guarded, he held out his hand. I dropped a small cloth bag into his palm. His eyes narrowed as he felt the bag, trying to determine its contents. Then he untied the top and reached into it with his fingers. He withdrew a Zuni fetish, a coiled stone rattlesnake with turquoise eyes I had found in a Native American trading post just before leaving California. It was a magnificent piece of work, and at the moment of seeing it, I had known it was for Tim. I grinned at him and said, "Gift." He studied the piece for long moments, then smiled and said, "This is going in the hominid box"— his way of saying how much he valued it.

It was about this time that a monumental discovery was made at a fossil locality called Aramis 6. Intensive survey of the site's crumbly surface had already revealed a fragmentary *ramidus* shinbone or tibia, and over the final eighteen days of the field season, a full-fledged excavation was begun at the site. Bone after bone of a single individual began to be uncovered. It appeared that we had discovered a partial *ramidus* skeleton.

The fact that this one was almost one and a half million years older than Lucy, a different species called *Australopithecus afarensis,* made the find exceedingly important. Up until now, Lucy and the formidable sample of fossil evidence Don Johanson and his colleagues have amassed over the past 20 years had provided the best set of evidence yet for humanity's earliest stage. Tim and his team were working on a much older species of protohuman, one that lived in that magic slice of time between four and six million years ago that DNA researchers have designated as the age during which our lineage must have separated from our African ape cousins. Exposed fossil-bearing sediments are rare from this range of time, and up until now, only bits and pieces—a few teeth and jaw fragments and a few other bones—were known from this period.

The long, hot days were filled with tension and excitement as the site was excavated by Tim and his skilled crew. Because of time constraints, many bones were taken up in blocks of sediment and would only be fully exposed in the laboratory in Addis. But some of the bones revealed features so primitive that we began to wonder if this could be the famous "missing link" between apes and humans that none other than Charles Darwin had predicted would eventually be found.

The missing link—the very thought of it was mind-blowing. The search for such a link had been the holy grail of anthropology for well over a hundred years.

Miraculously, Mesfin, Gerçek, and I were equally as successful, sifting the sediments of the *ramidus* sites and extracting an almost endless succession of micromammal fossils that were unbelievably rich in their species diversity. Quite suddenly I found myself a primary investigator of a world-class site—one of the most important that had ever been discovered.

It was during this exciting time that I was awakened toward dawn one morning by the chorusing of jackals from across the sand river. Suddenly I heard a loud snuffling and snorting outside my tent; concerned that it could be a hyena, I took hold of my rock hammer and shone the flashlight out through the tent screen, revealing a huge crested porcupine frozen in its tracks. The bizarre creature looked at me with startled beady eyes, then rattled its long quills at me warningly before turning and trotting off into the darkness.

This incident rendered me quite awake. I had gotten to bed early the night before and had already had almost eight hours of sleep. I felt rested and refreshed and wondered if I could induce a deep trance experience. I recalled my last connection with Nainoa and my chagrin at its termination before we had had a chance to talk. My thoughts moved backward across the whole series of expanded-state connections with him, and an odd coincidence appeared for my consideration.

About six years before, while I was at a Zen Buddhist *sesshin* at a retreat center on the island of Hawai'i, I had had an altered-state connection with Nainoa while he was at the spirit hills out on the arid grassy plains of what is today western Nevada. Now here I was, out in the arid thorn scrub of Eastern Africa, while Nainoa was at a retreat center, or he had been the last time I saw him. The similarity seemed just a little too close.

I clicked on my flashlight to check the time—a quarter to four. I glanced down at the floor of my tent, and something caught my eye. It was a Zuni fetish I had been carrying around in my pocket for over a year—a small stone mountain lion. This particular piece was interesting in that it had been made of leopardstone serpentine, giving it an unmistakable resemblance to my spirit helper. I had brought it along for company and had stood it on a flat river cobble next to my bed.

I reached over and picked it up, rubbing it affectionately. Then I clicked off the light and settled back into my sleeping bag as comfortably as I could. I relaxed my body and erased the screen of my mind. For long moments I rested in that emptiness, feeling its peace. Then I formed a thought—an intention to connect with my descendant at the place of refuge, where I had last seen him. I wanted to have that dialogue.

The intention deepened. Perhaps I could summon Nainoa's conscious awareness to me in the same manner that mine had been conveyed to him at the spirit hills. Perhaps there was a *dorajuadiok* residing out here in these dry, empty landscapes who could provide an assist, or perhaps the leopard man could do so, if he was around.

I held the small stone animal in my fingers and put out the call, invoking the aid of my spirit helper, summoning Nainoa. I held the thought . . . held the thought . . .

Wham! The sensations of power appeared within me with a hissing rush of sound. As the inner doorway opened, my body stiffened and my hands began to inflate, dropping the fetish. The feelings were incredibly strong, as strong as I had ever felt them. I felt myself surrendering into the power as flashes of light began to illuminate the darkness, and my eyes sought the door of my tent.

I watched entranced as the stars began to fall. Then there was a sudden lurch sideways, as though an earth tremor had struck. My body began to vibrate, to shake uncontrollably. Again I looked toward the doorway, but there was no doorway now. The stars were there in the tent with me, streaming past me in zigzag patterns as I gasped for breath and my gaze fastened on the great luminous grid that was forming in the darkness.

There was a brilliant flash that momentarily blinded me, and when my vision came back again, I seemed to be high in the air. As I looked downward, the arid landscapes of the Rift once again became manifest around me, but the stark vistas were quite distinct from the ones with which I was familiar. The trees looked strangely geometric and their ordinarily dark foliage appeared light and somewhat orangish. The normally sun-bleached desert substrate looked bluish and dark.

I realized with amazement that a reversal phenomenon had occurred and everything had shifted into its complement, or color opposite. I had traversed the barrier between worlds and was now flying in some level of the spirit world—or, to be more precise, I seemed to be in the dreamtime equivalent of the place in which I had been spending my days looking for fossils.

As I continued to scan the fantastic landscape below me, my mind marveling, three things happened virtually simultaneously. First, I picked up a quick glimpse of my spotted familiar lying on the branch of a tree near the sand river. Second, I saw a huge form in the near distance that I remembered well. The *dorajuadiok* looked somewhat different here. And third, I felt a familiar presence become manifest. I wondered where he had just been, and vivid memories began to flow within my mind.

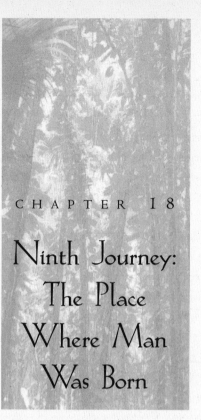

CHAPTER 18

Ninth Journey: The Place Where Man Was Born

I T WAS EVENING and Nainoa was practicing *lokahi* in the main hall of the place of refuge, attempting to establish inner balance and harmony in an exercise given him by Kahu Sala.[1] Suddenly a sense of tension and urgency invaded his inner calm. This was not part of the exercise. Whatever it was, it had seemed most insistent.

The feeling abruptly decreased, then disappeared. He wondered what it had been—a thoughtform, perhaps, directed at him by someone, or something? His eyes swept the hall. The few students and priests who were present seemed deep in meditation. Even the novice near the door looked rapt.

He looked over toward Wilipaki's place in the dim light. The older man was not there. Then he remembered. The chief had arranged to have a *lomi* session and had gone to the building where the steam room and massage tables were located.

He closed his eyes and sought the emptiness that had been disrupted moments before, attempting to reach the innermost central place within himself, but it eluded him. His stomach growled, and a thin smile crossed his face. After the celebrations of the harvest season, replete with all those sumptuous feasts, the spare diet at the retreat center was rather lean by comparison. He thought about breadfruit, and his stomach moaned again. He knew then that *lokahi* would elude him this evening. Perhaps the steam room would settle his inner disharmony.

He rose silently, gathering his cloak around himself, then bowed to the low altar in the center of the room. It was graced by a tall black stone standing on its end in a flat wooden tray filled with sand. The stone had come from the home islands of Hawai'i and had a *lei* of small red flowers wrapped around it. A stone lamp burned to each side of the stone, while before it was placed a flower arrangement and a bowl of water. He glanced at the student near the door as he left, but the boy gave no sign that he noticed Nainoa's passage.

He emerged onto the *lanai* facing the central courtyard and looked up at the night sky. The fog had begun to drift in off the lagoon and no stars could be seen. In the courtyard's center was a long rectangle of raked sand occupied by nine large rocks that had been placed there by the founders of the center over one hundred years ago.

He studied them carefully in the torchlight as he slowly walked along the narrow wooden deck that ran around the inside wall of the courtyard. He felt strongly drawn to the group of dark monoliths. He recalled the *dorajuadiok*, the immensely powerful spirit he had encountered at the spirit hills in the company of his ancestor, and wondered if his attraction for the standing stones was related. One of the tall, dark shapes definitely resembled that awesome being. He paused for one last look, then turned, retrieved his sandals from the rack on the wall, and descended the stone stairs of the *heiau* platform.

He slipped on his sandals and walked along the path that crossed the palm grove to an adjacent building. He passed several commoners tending a fire in a rock-lined pit, heating the stones that were used to maintain the temperature of the steam room. He nodded to them as he passed through the gate, then slipped off his sandals again and placed them in a wooden rack under the overhang of the roof. He stepped up onto the wide *lanai*, from which a row of closed doors revealed the presence of the small rooms where *lomi* was practiced. At the end of the wide veranda was the door to the steam room.

An elderly woman with white hair falling loose around her ample shoulders emerged from one of the doors, carrying a stack of thin cotton blankets. Her eyes widened in surprise as she bowed, "Chief Nainoa. What a delight to see you this fine evening." He bowed to her respectfully in return and whispered, "Kahu Merelina."

The *kahuna* studied him in silence for a moment, then said in a quiet voice, "I was going to work on our esteemed director this evening, but Kahu Sala is temporarily inundated with administrative duties. Why don't you go sit in the steam room for a while, and then I will come fetch you? I perceive something hovering around the field of your *aka* body. *Lomi* might be just the thing to assist in finding out what it is."

Nainoa recalled the inner disruption that had just occurred and nodded thoughtfully. The woman handed him several blankets and gestured toward the end of the *lanai*. He bowed to her again, then entered a small foyer and disrobed, hanging his cloak and pants on a wooden wall hook. He wrapped his lower body in one of the cotton blankets before pushing open the heavy wooden door at the back of the room.

The dim interior of the steam room was lit only by a single stone lamp placed near the door. The room was filled with heat. He closed the door behind him and sank gratefully onto one of the benches arranged along the walls. He was alone, the sole occupant of the steam room.

He had just begun to settle when the side door opened and two burly servants brought in a wooden barrow filled with newly heated rocks. They placed them in the pit in the room's center, removed those that had cooled, then withdrew in silence. Nainoa raised himself on an elbow, took a wooden vessel of water from a cistern, and poured some on the stones. They hissed and popped as the room filled with searing steam.

He closed his eyes again and let the heat seep into his muscles. He thought of Kenojelak, and her beautiful face appeared in his mind's eye as he heard her merry laughter in his imagination. He missed her. He wondered if William and Zaki had made it back yet. Forty days had passed since the Ennu hunters' departure. He remembered them in their camp below the strange scarred mountain.

He tried to picture Kenojelak here in his world and shook his head gently. She would never fit in. He remembered her in the midst of her family and friends. That was where she would flourish and grow. That was her *kuleana*, her rightful place. He wondered for the thousandth time if she was with child.

His feelings for the Ennu woman caused his *mana* to flow, raising gooseflesh on his arms and legs. He continued to build the energy with his intentionality, to build it until it began to surge. Then he felt his heart connection to Kenojelak open and he sent her the *mana* in a loving capacity, releasing and sending his *aloha* to her.

Abruptly several things happened all at once. He felt a sudden shift within his body, like a hot wind blowing through him. In his mind's eye he saw an open, dry landscape, much like the Ennu lands to the east, but it was different somehow. It was as if he was floating in the air looking down at a strange place, a wide dry river with a patchy fringe of woodland running along its sides. There were curious colored objects partially concealed below some of the trees. He couldn't see them clearly and wondered what they were.

Something attracted his attention to the fringe of trees along the dry wash. For long moments he perceived nothing unusual, and then he saw a spotted tiger lying along a thick branch, partially concealed by other thorny branches. It seemed relaxed and was looking directly at him. Before he had time to react, a low, hollow knocking sound was heard, and the scene dimmed.

Tok—tok—tok. Kahu Merelina knocked on the door again, summoning him to the massage. He blinked and looked around in the hot, dark room. He was streaming with sweat, and his heart was pounding. He felt light-headed and rather dreamy. He must have been in the steam for some time, yet it had seemed like only moments. He rose and pushed open the door. The *kahuna* was waiting. She looked him over again and her eyes brightened. "Yes, something is calling you. Follow me, Chief Nainoa."

He entered one of the small rooms and lay down on his stomach on a table padded with several woven pandanus mats that were covered, in turn, by a cool, smooth cotton blanket. The air was fragrant with the scent of the night-blooming coffee trees planted along the building's periphery.

The *kahuna* rubbed him down, briskly drying his body and wrapping him in a blanket to hold in the heat. He closed his eyes and felt himself relax as his *ku* responded to her touch. She sat on a tall stool at the table's end and took his head into her strong hands, her fingers probing his neck beneath the base of his skull. For long moments there was just her touch and the silence. And then she began.

As she worked, Nainoa surrendered to the deep sense of physical satisfaction he felt in response to the *lomi*, relaxing into that private inner place that he had been trying to access in the hall. As he became still, his awareness of her touch receded.

He recalled the brief vision he had just had in the steam room. In response, his awareness expanded, and the sensations of power appeared within him at very low levels. It was as if they were being channeled through him, flowing from one of the *kahuna*'s hands to the other. He was just about to open his eyes when Kahu Merelina whispered, "Relax, Nainoa. Keep your eyes closed and pay attention."

He sank once again into the *lomi*, and the sensations increased dramatically. The grip of force seized him, causing him to draw in his breath sharply as his body stiffened and his ears filled with a rushing hiss. He felt a peculiar pulling high up between his shoulder blades and wondered what the *kahuna* was doing. It was as though she had grabbed him by the soul and was pulling at it, attempting to free it from his body. Spots of light began to appear around him in the dark, heralding the onset of a deep state. As the lights began to stream past him, there was a distinct pop at the base of his neck, and the table seemed to fall out from under him.

His mind raced. He was falling through the darkness, and all around him were the brilliant fibers of the grid, forming a vast net stretching in all directions. One of the lines curved up toward him. He fell toward it, the fibers blurring as he picked up speed. Then he was flying through a series of luminous holes in the darkness, plummeting through a tunnel delimited by rings of light. He thought of the American and wondered if he could visit within the man's body again. And with the thought, he passed through the place of silence.

His next impressions were of excitement and of a dull ache. It felt as if the muscles in his arms and back were sore. His left knee felt tender. Before he had a chance to find out why, he was seized by astonishment. Below him in his visual field was a dry, open landscape dotted with brushy, flat-topped trees. And there among them loomed the towering shape of the *dorajuadiok*. It was glowing much like a candle flame or metal heated to the point of softness. He recalled the en-counter at the spirit hills, but this place looked different, and the spirit did not have exactly the same shape. As he wondered where he was, words in Old English appeared in his mind.

"Greetings, descendant."

He gathered his wits and replied in the archaic language, "Warm greetings to you, ancestor." For long moments wonder was perceived in silence within the minds of both.

"Where are we?" came Nainoa's question.

"We are in Africa, in a place where the ancient bones of our most distant ancestors are buried. We are in the place where humankind was born."

Long silence.

"How did I come to be here, merged with your awareness?" came Nainoa's thought. There was a brief pause. "And why is the *dorajuadiok* here?"

"I was resting in my tent when the deep state came on," answered the American. "I decided to see if I could invite you to visit—if I could summon your awareness into connection with mine with my intentionality. I am currently in a place very similar to the spirit hills, and you, I believe, are at a *pu'uhonua,* a place of refuge. The dynamic is much the same as the time when I was at a retreat center in Hawai'i and was summoned to join you out in those arid wastes."

"Dynamic?"

"An interaction or encounter, a situation, a *kulana* when many things may occur." There was a pause. "I have been here for many days looking for ancient bones with my fellow historians, or rather prehistorians, for we are investigating a range of time long before the advent of written history. I have felt something watching me from time to time. I sense that this something is our tall friend out there among the trees. But why it has come, I do not know."

There was silence in the minds of both as they watched the monolithic spirit among the trees. Although it was stationary, it had a quality of movement to it, as though its edges were shimmering or flickering. A curious tone of sound could be heard, a high-pitched ringing.

"It appears different to me," came Nainoa's thought. "It looks more like a huge triangle."

"Or a pyramid," observed the scientist. "I believe it is watching us. Perhaps it is waiting for us to acknowledge its presence."

With the thought, the power sensations touched them with a blazing flash of blue light, rendering them mute as well as blind. The blast was accompanied by a feeling of polite curiosity. For a brief moment they were connected with the awesome being, then the light dimmed and they could see once more. The American recovered first and ventured a response.

"Greetings, great spirit. And to what do we, my descendant and I, owe the honor of your presence?"

The sense of enormous power swept over them both once again, and a thought-feeling appeared within their merged yet separate awarenesses—one that conveyed friendly greeting, and that same sense of curiosity. Both understood and reacted with amazement.

The American then created and released a long stream of thoughts, revealing his identity and the nature of his research in this desolate place. There was a brief pause, whereupon Nainoa did the same, saying something about himself and his time and place—a mental statement that concluded with a memory of the *dorajuadiok* at the spirit hills, and a question: Was the entity before them the same as the one they had encountered before?

Nainoa heard the American add, "And I would be grateful for any information that you might provide on the nature of humanity's earliest ancestors—the ones whose bones we are currently excavating here at Aramis."

The thought was never finished. Their merged yet distinct consciousnesses were drawn into connection with the bright being's monumental mass with a blast of sensation that rendered them empty, vacant, nonexistent. When a sense of the personal reemerged much, much later, the American recovered first once again.

"Great spirit," he began, "we simply cannot absorb the full power of your presence all at once. Please decrease the strength of the connection so that we may maintain the integrity of our selves."

It was then that the stream of memories began—their recollections of what had just been perceived. The answer to the first question, whether the entity before them was the same as that seen at the spirit hills, was ambiguous, suggesting the *dorajuadiok* didn't understand the question. The American concluded that the entity didn't have a sense of singularity versus plurality, an insight that suggested that the *dorajuadiok* could be a manifested representative of a larger collective, a singular facet of a much larger composite whole. As this probability passed through his mind, there came an answer: a thought-feeling that conveyed a sense of definite affirmation.

As the American wondered about the second question, the one about the nature of humanity's distant ancestors, imagery began to move through their minds—imagery that took on flesh and came to life. A sound of flowing water was heard. They seemed to be high in the air, looking down from the branches of the crown of a tall tree. Below them was the green mosaic of the forest canopy, an emerald world traversed by a wide chocolate-colored slice of river.

Could it be? the American thought excitedly. Could they be seeing the place of the campsite along the sand river as it was during the Middle Pliocene? If so, it had changed dramatically. The river below them appeared to be part of a large meander bend filled with muddy brown water, with crocodiles basking on a distant sand bar. The river's banks were bracketed by an extensive forest, many of its trees festooned with vines. Movement was seen in the crown of a nearby forest giant. It appeared to be occupied by a troop of multicolored monkeys. They looked like large *Colobus* monkeys. Moments later, a loud, grating call from their direction confirmed this suspicion.

As their gaze traveled inland, they saw that the landscape was essentially flat, with wide floodplains choked with verdant tropical trees giving way to a low range of hills far to the west. Or was it east? There was no way to be sure, unless the "hills" were actually the Rift escarpment, or its beginning. Some distance from the river, they saw what appeared to be a large swamp, an isolated oxbow of the river surrounded by dense forest. They could see standing water reflecting the sunlight through the trees. Perhaps the river had recently flooded, inundating the nearby forest.

Nainoa monitored the American's mind as it raced. Once again the man wondered if this could be the ancient site they were currently excavating, but at the time it was laid down. And if so, could they actually gain a glimpse of the earliest protohumans who inhabited this wild landscape?

It was then that they looked down and saw the hands gripping the tree limb. They were dark-skinned hands with long, curved fingers and furry wrists and forearms. The thumbs seemed very small by comparison. Nainoa felt the American react with astonishment. Was it possible that they were looking through the eyes of a *ramidus* ancestor?

Nainoa felt shock accompanied by a sense of numbness as this concept passed through the scientist's mind. Suddenly there was a pulse of doubt, or was it scientific skepticism? Whichever it was, the scene abruptly dimmed, and the tropical forest evaporated, to be replaced once again by the glowing immensity of the shimmering pyramid standing in an open area among the acacias.

It seemed taller and narrower than a typical pyramid. The huge form was also without any surface features and appeared flat, with no sense of three-dimensional depth. Perhaps Nainoa's term, *triangle*, was a more appropriate description. Its presence continued to generate a feeling of enormous force, and there was always that curious ringing sound in their ears. As their collective attention fastened on the sound, it suddenly increased dramatically into a surge of insistent vibrational tension accompanied by a tremendous increase in the sensations of power. The stream of memories within their minds reappeared. Perhaps the informational matrix was being carried or transmitted by the sound.

Much of what was then perceived was seen symbolically. The information came at incredibly high speed, almost as though it was transmitted all at once in a single chunk, a multidimensional and many-leveled mass that was both informational and experiential in nature—at this level of interaction, there was no difference. Astonishment swept through their minds accompanied by a clear rational sense that they had just received an incredibly large volume of data; that this extraordinary information was now in storage within their memory banks; and that this body of knowledge would take considerable time to excavate, let alone comprehend.

"We are getting too much information all at once," thought Nainoa as he struggled to maintain a sense of the personal.

"Perhaps we can adjust the focus," replied the American with effort.

"Focus?"

"To pay attention in a closely directed way. Let us try to get the *dorajuadiok* to answer a single question on a very specific topic. Let us request information about its identity—let's ask about the nature of this strange entity."

As soon as the thought was formed, impressions began to flow within their minds in response—conceptual ideas that were formless, yet carried a clear meaning that the *dorajuadiok* was not really an entity, nor did it have any manifested equivalent form on the physical level of existence. It was/is a dense concentration of energy associated with awareness—a field of power expressing an enormous, multileveled form of intelligence.

"And what do you know of your origin, if I may ask?" the scientist inquired.

Another clear response: The *dorajuadiok* had always existed and it always would. It was a primordial force that was, is, and always would be a part of the manifested structure of the universe. It was part of the source, the creative foundation of the all.

"Are you alive?" the scientist asked. "And if so, what is your function, your reason for living?"

Thought-feelings flowed toward them, utterly alien in shape, yet once again clearly discernible. The immense energy field before them was indeed alive, and among its many functions, it was an activator and conductor of power that could also serve as a source of information and ideas. As such, the *dorajuadiok* could function as a bridge between the worlds, a connection between the levels of action and the levels of information, a doorway into the endless vastness of the great void. In all of these capacities, the *dorajuadiok*'s field was, is, and forever will be an expression of the generative state of being.

"Do you have emotions?" asked Nainoa, watching the immense form uneasily. "And if so, what is the nature of these feelings?"

The two men could feel the awareness of the great being resting upon them both. The spirit expressed a form of consciousness that was completely devoid of emotion, suggesting to the two men that once again it didn't understand the question.

There was a momentary pause, followed by a confirmation of this insight. The brilliant field did not possess feelings, nor did it understand the nature of what humans call values. The *dorajuadiok* was completely nonjudgmental, utterly innocent of human values such as good or bad, or emotions such as love or fear.

For the *dorajuadiok*, the experience of being in harmony, in balance, and in connection with everything, everywhere and at every time in a positive, growth-enhancing potential was opposed to the condition of disharmony, the experience of imbalance, the state of being disconnected in a negative growth-inhibiting capacity.

For a brief span of time the two men watched the great spirit before them with awe as they digested what had just been revealed. Then there was a staccato, crackling rumble of thunder, and the scene before them dimmed.

It was at this moment that Kahu Merelina lifted her hands from Nainoa's body and he felt an abrupt diminishing of the power sensations. The brilliant, geometric prism of the huge spirit faded from his sight, shifting into a dark, monolithic shape as his conscious awareness returned across the boundary between the spirit world and the ordinary state of consciousness. This image too began to fade, and he felt his contact with the American dissolving.

In a last, almost desperate effort, Nainoa reached out, expressing an urgent invitation: "Return with me, esteemed ancestor. We need to talk!"

There was a distinct pop as the connection with the *dorajuadiok* was severed, and then Nainoa was fully back, lying on his stomach on the massage table, blinking his eyes as he raised his head and looked at his hands. They were his hands, no doubt about it.

He felt a surge of excitement at what had just happened. He had made connection with the American in a most extraordinary set of circumstances. He turned over and looked at the older woman looming over him in the dim light. He wondered if the American's awareness was still connected with his. Had he managed to bring him into his level of reality and time in the same way that his ancestor had summoned him to Africa?

Nainoa listened, but there was only silence. Throughout the entire visionary encounter, he had heard a curious high, ringing sound. It was gone now. Abruptly he threw an arm over his face and closed his eyes. He sighed deeply and thought of Maraea. He felt the need to tell her about the incredible experience he had just had. He wondered when Kahu Sala would declare him purified and send him back to the capital.

An image of Maraea sleeping in her bed appeared in his mind's eye, shifting his awareness still further and grounding him firmly to his world once again. He understood immediately. His new best friend and lover was to be a major figure in his life to come. She was to be his wife and the mother to his children. He felt a sense of eager anticipation as he wondered what his life with this interesting woman would bring. He knew with absolute certainty that he would find out.

His reflective mood departed as he lowered his arm and opened his eyes. Kahu Merelina sat with her hands folded, watching him with interest.

"*Hea'hea*, Chief Nainoa." The older woman smiled. "A hospitable welcome back."

"*Kia'ola*," he responded. "Upright life."

"And where have you been these past few moments?" the *kahuna* asked him quietly. "Or should I ask," she continued, "in whose company you have been traveling?"

Nainoa marveled at the older woman's intuition and asked her, "Do you believe it is possible to travel across time?"

The *kahuna* looked at him for a few moments, then smiled and said, "There are no limits. What is possible for each of us is determined only by our beliefs." Nainoa watched her carefully, saying nothing.

"Sooner or later," she continued, "each of us learns that there are only two great tasks that confront us in each lifetime. There are many missions and life goals, of course, but all of them can be combined into two primary objectives." Nainoa watched the older woman and sensed the presence of another listening. He smiled, waiting for the wisdom he knew was to come.

"As we pass through life," the *kahuna* said, "each of us creates the reality in which we live." She paused as if to see the effect of her words. "And each of us is responsible for creating the self that lives in that reality."

For long moments there was only the silence as the two Hawaiians considered the implications of this statement. Then the thunder cracked again, breaking the mood. The evening rains began to patter on the roof, and Nainoa sighed with pleasure as the woman took one of his feet into her strong hands. Her fingers began to probe the arch of his foot, and the second stage of the *lomi* began. He sank into the place of utter relaxation and deep healing as the rain intensified.

Lokahi had been achieved.

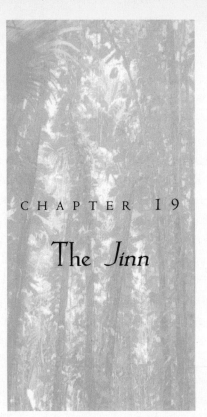

CHAPTER 19

The *Jinn*

M Y DISCONNECTION FROM both Nainoa and the *dorajuadiok* occurred suddenly and was accompanied by an enormous decrease in the power sensations. The high ringing sound in my ears abruptly ceased as well. Why the contact was severed at this point, I don't know. Perhaps it had been the thunder and the rain.

The dawn was breaking outside my tent as I sat up dazzled with *kahaha*, as Nainoa would say—stunned with wonder and astonishment. I looked at the riverbed through the tent screen. It was still dry and the sky was clear. I was definitely back in my canvas abode under the thorn trees.

I suddenly felt the need to ground myself, to reestablish a sense of what was real. I pulled on my pants and shirt and emerged from my tent. I checked my boots for scorpions and looked down at the dusty sand as I put them on. There, overlying my own footprints from the previous evening, were jackal tracks. There had been two of them, and they had come in the night. There were the porcupine's prints as well. I perceived movement above me as I stood up. A beautiful blue and green bird took flight with a flash of lavender from the thorny branch that overhung my tent. It was a lilac-breasted roller, one of my favorites.

I walked across the dry riverbed and climbed to a high point, from which I could look down and out on the camp. I sat down on the hilltop and began to pick through the incredible quantity of information that had just been injected into my memory banks by the *dorajuadiok*. I had no idea what much of it was about, nor did I have a clear sense of how long it would take to review it all or to get it down in note form. I did know that the long hot days here in the Middle Awash part of the Rift would be filled with work from here on out. There was much to be done, I knew, and there would be perilously little time to write. My note taking would have to wait.

This prediction proved true. Over the next ten days, Gerçek, Mesfin, and I screen-washed large volumes of sediment, working until late each day to increase our sample of fossil micromammals from the *ramidus* sites until we had over four hundred identifiable cranial and dental specimens and vial after vial filled with limb and other bones, right down to tiny toes. It was a very respectable sample for only three weeks' intensive work.

Tim White's team continued to excavate the hominid site at Aramis 6 until ninety-five skeletal elements had been recovered, all from a single individual. This sample included the bones of the feet, legs, and hip so critical in determining if this early ancestor had been bipedal. We had the bones of the hands as well, and of the forearm. Some of the bones were badly crushed, and I knew it would take many months of painstaking preparation under the microscope to clean and reconstruct them and put them back together. Until then, crucial questions about body size, proportions, and manner of walking would have to go unanswered.

One magical morning I was present on the site when Tim exposed the left half of the lower jaw with the teeth still in their sockets. For much of the morning I watched him work, carefully reinforcing the fragile specimen with a syringe of glyptol as he freed the bone from its entombing matrix. He had the patience and the skills of a world-class neurosurgeon, and, using my Nikon, I shot several rolls of slide film as more and more of the jaw became visible.

As the days passed and more and more of the skeleton was found, everyone in the camp was mad with joy over the discovery. All of us were aware that we were participating in a truly great event. These bones were "going to open up worlds of possibility for scientific analysis," to quote Tim, and when the analysis was done, the published results would most likely make headlines all over the world.

Throughout all of this excitement and work, I continued to be aware of the watchful presence of some unseen entity, but I had no further contacts with Nainoa or the *dorajuadiok*. There were the winds, however.

One morning I was working on a south-facing slope being baked by the sun when I idly thought how nice it would be to have a breeze. And much to my surprise, the breeze arrived. I didn't think much about this coincidence until it happened several days in a row.

It was also during this time that a whirlwind began to appear near the camp on a daily basis—a tall, spinning vortex of hot air filled with dust that came dancing down the sand river, picking up clouds of debris as it approached. When it reached the level of the camp, it inevitably stopped and waited. My team and I were usually screen-washing sediments under a big acacia somewhat upstream from the tents, and we watched the big dust devil curiously. After long moments of watchful intensity, the whirlwind cut directly into the camp, ballooning the tent flies and blowing any unattached items, such as drying laundry, up high into the air, where some inevitably ended up in the thorny branches of the trees.

After the first day, the whirlwind appeared every afternoon at about the same time, moving up the sand river until it reached the camp. There it would pause dramatically before cutting through the camp, wreaking havoc with everyone's laundry. I began to joke with Gerçek, who was both Turkish and a Muslim, that we were being visited by a *jinn*, a mischievous genie that was having fun with us out here in the desert.

In pre-Mohammedan Arabia, the *jinn* were known to be powerful spirits made of "subtle fire" that lived out in the empty desert wastes, inhabiting old wells or canyons or abandoned caravanseries. Normally invisible, but capable of taking on form at their own pleasure, the *jinn* were known to come in three basic types: those that walked on the land, those that flew in the air, and the ones that lived in the water. They were regarded with a good deal of respect and fear, and it was known that dealing with them was unpredictable. These spirits were so well known that the Prophet Mohammed himself admitted in the Koran that the *jinn* were real.

After the whirlwind appeared several days in a row, it became annoying to have my socks and underwear end up in the trees, so on impulse one afternoon, I stepped out of the shade onto the surface of the sand river and raised my voice as the whirlwind approached. "Hey, genie!" I yelled, drawing an appreciative laugh from Gerçek. "Would you please try to bypass the camp from now on?" I shouted. "It's a drag having to retrieve my laundry from the thorn trees, and everyone's tents are getting filled with dust!"

Much to my surprise, the dust devil stopped dead in its tracks and remained dancing for several moments right in the middle of the riverbed. Gerçek laughed again and called, "The genie hears you and obeys. . . ." Immediately the whirling air mass pounced upon me like a cat, sucking my hat from my head and carrying it high into the air. Eventually the hat came down and we all had a good laugh about that, but interestingly, the whirling vortex didn't cut through the camp that day, nor did it ever again, although it continued to appear each afternoon at about the same time.

The abundance of hominid bones at Aramis 6 seemed to come to an end at about the same time that we ran out of food, heralding the end of that season's fieldwork. I got up at dawn on the last day and climbed to the high point above the sand river to watch the last

sunrise. I waited in the deep silence with the vast, dry African landscape for the sun to touch the boundary between the earth and the
sky, and when it did, the omnipresent jackals began to chorus, first
from the south, then from the east, then the north and the west, until
the whole landscape seemed to be singing, greeting the dawn with a
high, shrill paean to the creator. Profoundly moved, I stared into the
sun's brilliant disk and bowed.

Breaking camp was hectic, with all of us working to take down the
tents, watching for scorpions and snakes beneath them, cleaning and
rolling them and packing them into their tent bags. We took down
the large tent flies that had been used to create shade, collapsed the
tables and chairs, took apart the camp kitchen, and began to load the
vehicles. The trove of fossils was packed in wooden boxes filled with
sand, and carefully placed in Tim's car for the rough journey back to
the capital.

When we were finally ready to depart, close to noon, we were
delayed for another half an hour by the Afars, who, after three months
in the camp, suddenly had endless numbers of important things to
discuss with us. I found it sad to part company with them. For a time
we had worked and lived together, and strong friendships had formed.
I knew they would talk about us endlessly when we had gone, recounting stories of the things we had done, mimicking each one of us to the
delight of all listening. They had given all of us nicknames in their
own language. Because of my research specialty, mine was Dr. Han-
tuta—Dr. Mouse.

As the palaver between Tim and the Afars stretched into an hour, I
wandered down to the sand river and left an impromptu offering for
the spirits of the place, thanking them for their hospitality and their
help. When I thought of what had been accomplished in the last three
weeks, it was tempting to speculate that there had been spiritual
assistance. I looked up at that moment and saw the lilac-breasted
roller watching me from the branch above where my tent had stood. I
bowed to her and left an offering there as well, then walked back and
got in the truck.

As our convoy finally got rolling, I commented to Gerçek, sitting beside me, that the genie would not find us at the sand river today. He laughed, and agreed, saying that it was too early in the day for *jinn*. At that very moment a dust devil touched down immediately in front of the truck. It remained there, just in front of us, dancing along the track for the first quarter mile or so, until I leaned out the window and shouted goodbye, whereupon it suddenly evaporated and was gone.

We drove in convoy all the rest of that day as we crossed the Afar lands, and I watched immense whirlwinds tower above the plain shimmering with heat. Sometimes there were four or five of them in attendance, the largest among them reaching thousands of feet in altitude. We churned across the floodplains, throwing up our own plumes of dust behind each car until we were all the color of the earth, Africans and Europeans alike.

When we stopped beside the Arso River for a bite to eat late in the afternoon, I walked along the water, looking, as always, for interesting rocks and possibly fossils. I was some distance from my colleagues when I came across a small muddy patch near the edge of the water. There, impressed into its sticky surface, was a clear pug mark. There was just one, but there was no mistaking it. It was the footprint of a leopard. So he had been around after all. I scanned the dense groves of green tamarisks fringing the river. Was he out there right now, watching me with pale eyes? As if in answer, I was startled by the distinctive yodeling shriek of an African fish eagle, and looked up just in time to see the majestic bird fly right overhead, then tuck its wings and drop into the trees upstream. This seemed like an answer, so I dropped the memory of the moment into my pocket, to relive it through the years to come.

It was not until nightfall that our loaded vehicles slowly climbed the steep, rocky escarpments out of the rift. We dropped Mohammed Gana back at the road camp as the moon began to rise, then we headed west toward the highlands and left the Afar and their *jinn* behind.

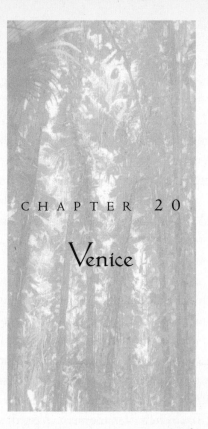

CHAPTER 20

Venice

A WEEK LATER I was on my way home, looking out the window of the aircraft at the distinctive sun-blasted desert landscapes of upper Egypt as we flew down the Valley of the Nile. There wasn't a cloud in sight as my gaze roved across the vast vistas, and my thoughts moved back over the past few days.

It had been a hectic week in Addis. We had all put in long days at the National Museum, where we cleaned and inventoried the expedition's equipment, putting everything into storage in preparation for the next year's field season. Those of us involved in paleontology had catalogued our newly discovered finds into the museum collections, making notes and preliminary identifications where we could. Most of us had to return to teaching responsibilities for the next semester, so the detailed analytical studies would have to await our return to Ethiopia.

I had spent much of the week curating the Aramis micromammals, but at every opportunity I wandered into the hominid room, watching Tim White as he began the arduous task of freeing the ancient bones of the partial hominid skeleton from the rock that surrounded them. Mostly he was silent, totally absorbed in his paleo-Zen practice. But occasionally he emerged from his task, expressing his amazement and wonder about this most important of discoveries.

As we wound up our work at the week's end, Tim placed the Zuni rattlesnake fetish in the museum safe with the fossil skeleton. He grinned at me as he closed the steel door. "Guardian," he said. I had no doubt that humanity's ancestor would be safe until his return.

As the plane passed over the Giza plateau west of modern Cairo late in the afternoon, I looked down at the Sphinx and the Great Pyramids and was awed at the monumental mass of the ancient structures. The eastern walls of the pyramids were in shadow, triggering the memory of the pyramidal *dorajuadiok* perceived in the field camp only two weeks before. For a moment it seemed as if I was observing three immense spirits on the desert below—four, if one counted the Sphinx. Then the moment passed and we jetted on, passing over the Nile Delta toward the dark, wrinkled mass of the Mediterranean. I got out my notebook and began to access the mass of information injected into my memory banks at Ganduli by the powerful spirit.

Something truly wonderful happened in the next twelve hours. Those of us returning to the United States had decided to break our two-day journey and stay overnight in Venice, and it was late afternoon when we landed at the airport. We took speedboats across the dark lagoon past San Michele, the island of the dead, to enter the labyrinth of canals, winding through the ancient waterways as we headed for our hotel. As I observed this dreamlike city built on the sea with water for streets, I found it as fantastic as anything I had perceived in my visionary states. I wondered what Nainoa would think of it.

We checked in at our hotel, then I did a bit of shopping, buying gifts for my family—carnival masks for my daughters and some beautiful earrings made of gold and orange coral from Sardinia for Jill. Then I wandered the streets, watching the tourists and the changing winter light, until darkness fell and we all met at Harry's Bar for dinner.

It was mid-January, so it was very cold and very dark when we walked back to the hotel, but I was warmed internally by endless Bellinis, a drink for which Harry's Bar is famous. Perhaps it was the Bellinis, perhaps it was the waterways, but I couldn't sleep, and at two in the morning I got up, showered and shaved, and put on all my clothes, layering myself against the winter cold outside.

Then I walked out of the hotel into the silent, deserted streets of Venice. Water lapped at the dock where we had disembarked late that afternoon. For long moments I just stood, staring at the water, wondering what I was doing out here in the middle of the night. I didn't know, but I sensed I had to walk—and walk I did.

Throughout the rest of that night, I wandered restlessly through the ancient city streets, accompanied only by Venetian cats and perhaps by the unseen Venetian mice for which the cats were searching. Often I got lost, but I continued on, crossing bridges, traversing canals, turning first one corner and then another. The dark stone city was a far cry from the sun-drenched plains of Africa I had just left, and I was thoroughly chilled by the time I found myself at the famous Piazza San Marco close to dawn.

I drifted around the massive, multidomed basilica crouched in the dark, seeking refuge from the cold. On the building's north side I saw a light, and under it a small door open for early worshipers. This gathering place for tourists during the daylight hours was also, and above all, a church.

I walked inside. Only a few lights were lit. The place was utterly silent. I sat down in a chair before an archaic icon of the Madonna and her child, a power object that had been a focus for spiritual practice for the best part of a thousand years. I chafed my hands to warm them and looked around in the dim light. I was alone in the huge building, but I sensed presences in the dark—awarenesses that had watched and waited through the centuries as endless visitors had passed through this old building.

When I had warmed up a bit, I recalled the walking meditation of the typical Zen retreat, so I got up and slowly strode around the inside of this most holy of places, one fist inside the other, inner thumb tucked in, calming my mind as the eyes of the Christian saints watched me from the darkness of the ceiling.

My own eyes were cast down as I walked, and there, on the floor, were mosaics arranged in designs that reminded me of the phosphenes I saw during my visions. As I studied them with alert interest, it was obvious to me that the builders of this edifice had known about mystic states. I felt a connection with them across the ages, and with it came a shift in my awareness. The daydreamy light trance state descended upon me, and when I arrived back in front of the Madonna, I lit candles for her and those of my lineage who now exist in spirit. Then I sat before the icon, achieving inner silence and sinking effortlessly into deep meditation as I looked into her dark eyes.

How long I sat there before the image of the Virgin, I don't know. At some point I heard human voices chanting a singsong refrain that sounded vaguely familiar. Some part of my mind recognized the language as Latin. I emerged from the deep state and looked around. The sound came from my left, from an open door that led into a small side room.

I got up from my chair and looked in. A priest with short-cropped hair, wearing a green robe, was conducting an early mass for a small congregation of Venetians. I saw an empty chair near the door and sat down. As I listened to the ancient language, I closed my eyes and sank back into the trance state. I do not remember clearly what happened next, but I recall sensing presences watching me, and in my mind's eye I saw again the eyes of the saints focused upon me in the darkness.

I emerged at some point to discover that holy communion was being celebrated, and for the second time in my life I received the sacraments, the body and blood of Jesus of Nazareth. There before me was the silver chalice of wine and the wafer stamped with a Christian symbol. Startled, I looked up into the priest's pinched face, and he gave me a surprised expression in return. Did he suspect I was a recovered Episcopalian turned evolutionary biologist and paleoanthropologist? There was no way of telling. But intuitively I sensed his awareness of me as an intruder.

This realization snapped me out of my mystical state. I was an outsider here in this Catholic stronghold, and when the ritual came to an end, I retreated. As I slipped out of the basilica into the cold winter dawn once more, something decidedly strange happened.

Instead of exiting directly out toward the street, something drew me to my left, pulling me inexorably along the series of closed wooden doors under the overhanging archways of the church until I turned left at the corner and approached the main entrance that led into the basilica from the piazza. The massive carved door was closed now and locked, and as I wondered why I was there, I chanced to look up at the ceiling above, and my heart skipped a beat.

There, above me on the archway, was a cherubim rendered in exquisite early-thirteenth-century mosaics against a glittering gold background. This wasn't one of those benevolent babylike cherubs from Raphael's paintings. This was a full-fledged cherubim, as large as myself, with a haloed face placed firmly in the center of several sets of wings—two stretched upward and two pointed downward, with the other pair extended sideways, the entire composition forming the approximation of a cross. The spirit's expressionless face revealed nothing—neither benevolence nor condemnation. There was just its gaze, flat, utterly neutral, staring down from the ceiling.

As I stared openmouthed at the compelling form, my vision expanded, and I realized there were four of them, one at the center of each of the four arches above the main entrance to the cathedral—one for each of the four cardinal directions. For more than eight hundred years, every single soul that had entered this place of power had passed directly beneath their watchful visages.

Something deep within me shifted, and without intention to do so,

I bowed to the cherubim—deep Buddhist bows all the way to the cold stone floor. I bowed four times to the east, four to the north, four to the west, and four to the south. Then I stood once more and just observed them, reveling in the insight that emerged within me at that moment.

There, on the ceiling above me, were four magnificent depictions of the *aumakua*, the eternal ancestral spirit self composed of wings and eyes. I suddenly understood that the wings were symbolic expressions of dynamic and immortal energy and that the eyes revealed fully awakened awareness. Did those four pairs of eyes shift in my direction as I stood there gaping? I do not know, nor do I remember how long I remained rooted to the spot. In those moments of deep insight, I felt I had truly stepped outside of time, and there was only myself and the four great spirits watching me.

Eventually I became aware of the pale winter sunlight creeping across the piazza. Venetians were starting to pass by, heading for work, muffled against the cold in heavy overcoats and scarves. I silently bade farewell to the winged forms above me and requested their blessing for myself, my family and friends, and my future endeavors. Then, profoundly moved, I left the basilica.

I began to cross the piazza, heading in the direction of my hotel, when with my peripheral vision I perceived a large, dark mass moving in my direction. I quickly looked up and saw a prodigious flock of pigeons heading straight for me. It was obvious that they had collectively decided that I was the tourist who was going to offer them breakfast. There were hundreds of them, and as they closed in, I shut my eyes, shielding my face with my hands and hunching my shoulders, expecting them to land on me, as I had seen them do with countless tourists in the past.

Curiously, the birds never touched me, but their hundreds of wings beat the air all around me, producing a most amazing sound. In the darkness of my closed eyes, I perceived the first winged spirit that I had just seen on the ceiling. The sound of wings increased in volume, and the spirit's eyes stared directly into my own. Suddenly it seemed to move, the static form coming to life as the hair rose all over my body. Time and space merged in that instant as I found myself surrounded by beating wings, looking right into the eyes of my "bird man," my *aumakua*.

For a long moment there were only wings and eyes, energy and awareness, all around me and within me. An inner light switched on, a gentle golden radiance that filled my being with feelings of peace and my mind's eye with luminous beauty. Within the golden light appeared a circular blue field, and within that field, the winged, birdlike being floated, the wings appearing as radiant, shimmering clouds of energy.

I felt an enormous surge of the sensations of power, and I realized that my *aumakua* was now within me. It had merged with me, or I with it, and in that instant its awareness was my awareness, and its energy was my energy. The sparkling phosphenes appeared within the radiant energy surrounding the misty form before me, and as I looked into its eyes, it seemed to smile, projecting a timeless patience, profound and enduring wisdom, boundless compassion, and an unconditional acceptance and love that was beyond the power of words to describe. I now knew with certainty the source of the enormous power that seized me in my moments of deep trance when I connected with my descendant self. The spirit before me was the interface, the go-between, and it was my spirit, of which I always had been a part and always would be.

As if from a great distance, I heard the pigeons begin to disperse, disappointed at my failure to offer them bread crumbs. As the sound of their wings diminished, the vision began to fade. I opened my eyes, blinking back tears produced by emotions that emanated from the core of my being. On the one hand, I was stunned by what I had just seen. On the other, I knew that my bird man was still within me and that it would never fully leave me again. In the instant, the world returned to its ordinary state, and I became aware of the cold once more. Stuffing my hands in my pockets, I began to walk.

I returned to my hotel as though in a dream and entered the dining room to find my colleagues engrossed in breakfast. They stopped eating as I came through the ornate doors. I wondered why they were staring at me, then did a quick scan of my outer appearance as well as my inner state. My face was flushed with the cold and my hair was wild. I still felt the inner light suffusing my being. Was it shining out of my eyes? I didn't know, but I confess that I felt a little like Moses after his first meeting with God. Tim White looked at me narrowly, his face expressing his unasked question.

"Couldn't sleep," I said. "Walked all over the city throughout the night and ended up attending an early mass at the St. Mark's Cathedral."

Nobody moved a muscle as they digested what I'd just said—that one of their company, and an evolutionary scientist at that, had just been to mass.

Tim chuckled, breaking the spell. "Lucky you didn't fall in the canal."

Before leaving Venice, I popped into a store near the hotel and bought a carnival mask of the face of the bird man for myself, then found another, more feminine one for Jill. Then we headed back through the city by speedboat and sped off across the lagoon for the airport. The image of the cherubim stayed in my mind's eye as I stared into the dark water rushing by, and much to my surprise, the etheric form suddenly appeared there on the reflective surface. It was as though it had been projected out of my mind, its winglike energy field in motion and its eyes looking into and through my own. Once again I saw its smile.

As I took my seat on the plane, I knew that it would be a very long day. For the next twenty hours I would fly across the sky like a bird, or a god, and at the end of this miraculous journey I would sleep in my bed beside Jill in California.

Abruptly, and for no apparent reason, Nainoa appeared in my mind. My pulse quickened. Was he here? Would he be able to witness everything that would happen this day through my eyes and my awareness? Would this man from the future have the experience of being able to cross the planet in a flying machine in a single day? As the plane took off and ascended rapidly into the sky, I felt a startling surge of astonishment that was not my own.

I continued to feel a pervading sense of wonder for a half hour as the plane gained altitude and I studied the receding landscapes below. The winter air was quite clear, and I could see the snowy range of the Alps to the north, the huge forms prompting a memory of the pyramids seen the previous day. The monumental form of the *dorajuadiok* flickered briefly in my mind's eye.

I took my notebook from my shoulder bag and read what I had written the day before. It was a beginning. I smiled and mentally asked for input from my esteemed friend. Then I picked up my pencil and began to write.

NOTES

CHAPTER 2

I. See Jeanne Achterberg, *Imagery in Healing: Shamanism and Modern Medicine* (Boston and London: Shambhala Books, 1985).

CHAPTER 3

I. See, for example, Matthew Bronson, "When As-if Becomes As-is: The Spontaneous Initiation of a Brazilian Spiritist Medium," *Anthropology of Consciousness* 3, nos. I–2 (1992): 9–16; Stanley Krippner and Alberto Villoldo, *Healing States* (New York: Fireside Books, 1985). There are also the widely read Seth books written (channeled) by Jane Roberts.

2. Mircea Eliade, *Shamanism: Archaic Techniques of Ecstasy,* Bollingen Series LXXVI (Princeton: Princeton University Press, 1964).

3. Those interested should contact the Foundation for Shamanic Studies, P.O. Box 1939, Mill Valley, California 94942; telephone (415) 380–8282.

4. Those interested should contact Westerbeke Ranch, 2300 Grove, Sonoma, California 95476; telephone (707) 996–7546.

5. Sandra Ingerman, *Soul Retrieval: Mending the Fragmented Self* (San Francisco: Harper, 1991). She is also the author of *Welcome Home: Following Your Soul's Journey Home* (San Francisco: Harper, 1994) and *A Fall to Grace* (Santa Fe: Moon Tree Rising Productions, 1997).

CHAPTER 5

1. Many people have asked me to clarify how I determined that Nainoa lives five thousand years in the future. One of the first things I learned during my initial visionary connection with him in the spring of 1986 (see my book *Spiritwalker,* chapter 2) was that his society measures the passage of time in relation to chiefly lineages rather than from an arbitrary point in the past such as the birth of Jesus of Nazareth. From Nainoa's memories, I learned that 247 generations have passed since the collapse of Western civilization. If one accepts that a generation equals 20 years and that there are roughly 5 generations in 100 years, then 247 generations can be translated into 4,940 years. Five thousand years is thus a rough estimate, for neither I nor Nainoa know exactly when the collapse occurred.

2. Tom Cowan, *Fire in the Head: Shamanism and the Celtic Spirit* (San Francisco: Harper, 1993), p. 30.

CHAPTER 6

1. This place is, I believe, the multipeaked volcanic massif in California's Central Valley known today as the Sutter Buttes. In Nainoa's time, it is an island and the mountains are covered with tropical forest. It is unfortunate that I perceived Nainoa's visit there only through his recollections. Had I been in connection when he was actually there, I might have been able to make a rough estimate of how far the ocean rose to isolate it as an island.

CHAPTER 7

1. Her spiritual teacher was an Englishman named Paul Brunton, also known to his students as PB.

2. See Jeffrey Moussaieff Masson, *My Father's Guru: A Journey Through Spirituality and Disillusion* (New York: Addison-Wesley, 1993). Like myself, Masson grew up in the 1940s and 1950s with this celebrated mystic, Paul Brunton, as a frequent visitor in his home.

Notes

CHAPTER 9

1. For an important review of this interesting phenomenon, see P. M. H. Atwater, *Future Memory: How Those Who See the Future Shed New Light on the Workings of the Human Mind* (Birch Lane Press, 1996).

2. For a review of these events, see R. Monastersky, "Seismic Sunday: Recent Jolts Boost Southern California's Hazard," *Science News*, August 1, 1992: 72–74.

3. Interestingly, this same fault seems to have become active again in 1995, producing a series of quakes in late August and September in the China Lake area west of Ridgecrest, a desert town about a hundred miles north of Los Angeles. A magnitude 5.8 quake on September 20 was followed by four hundred aftershocks, including several in the 4.3 range. Based on the size of the mapped fault segments, seismologists are predicting possible further quakes in the 6 to 6.5 range.

CHAPTER 11

1. Once again, let me inject a notation about vocabulary here. As I have mentioned in *Spiritwalker*, the Hawaiians in Nainoa's settlement speak a language completely different from any spoken today, a kind of pidgin or patois unlike the pidgin I have heard in Hawai'i, the Caribbean, or West Africa. In this narrative, I have chosen to include certain Hawaiian words still used today to give the narrative vitality and to facilitate cross-referencing with contemporary books on Hawaiian spirituality. The actual word for the energy body used by Chief Kaneohe was closer to *genaga*, pronounced with hard g's. The term is similar to the contemporary *kino'aka*, from which it is most likely derived. In the same vein, the word used by Nainoa's people for the immortal, spiritual ancestral aspect of the self is *ammagua* or *ommagoa*, a close approximation to the classic Hawaiian word *aumakua*, derived from the Tahitian *aumatua*. Because *aumakua* is still currently in use in the islands, I have chosen to use that term in this account and in *Spiritwalker*.

For those interested in Hawaiian spirituality, I recommend Serge King's many books, including *Kahuna Healing* (Quest Books, 1993); *Mastering Your Hidden Self: A Guide to the Huna Way* (Quest Books, 1985); *Urban Shaman* (New York: Simon and Schuster, 1990). See also Scott Cunningham's *Hawaiian Religion and Magic* (Llewellyn, 1994) and Laura Kealoha Yardley's *The Heart of Huna* (Honolulu: Advanced Neuro Dynamics, Inc, 1990).

2. This and other accounts of *kahuna* healing are to be found in Julius Scammon Rodman, *The Kahuna Sorcerers of Hawai'i, Past and Present* (Hicksville, NY: Exposition, 1979).

3. For those interested, see the volume resulting from this conference: E. Vrba et al., eds., *Paleoclimate and Evolution, with Emphasis on Human Origins* (New Haven: Yale University Press, 1995). My own contribution is chapter 25: "Of Mice and Almost Men: Regional Paleoecology and Human Evolution in the Turkana Basin."

4. For a graphic glimpse into the ramifications of this find, see Kenneth Weaver, "The Search for Our Ancestors," *National Geographic* 168, no. 5 (November 1985): 606–7.

5. Bruce Chatwin, *Songlines* (Picador, 1987), 280–85.

6. For an overview of these and other theories, see Ian Tattersall, *The Fossil Trail: How We Know What We Think We Know About Human Evolution* (New York: Oxford University Press, 1995).

7. Scientists are still debating how speciation—the appearance of new species— actually works. The controversy centers on whether there must be an accumulation of many small genetic mutations, or whether speciation is possible with only a few major genes undergoing big changes. A handful of studies, including one published by Dr. Toby Bradshaw and his colleagues in the August 31, 1995, issue of the British journal *Nature* on the monkeyflower (genus *Mimulus*) suggest that new species can arise largely through mutations in only a handful of genes.

CHAPTER 12

1. The word for "chief" used by the settlers in their everyday speech is *jif*, a close approximation to the English term. The classic Hawaiian word *ali'i* is still used for more formal speech and is sometimes shortened to *ali.*

CHAPTER 13

1. See Olga M. Johannessen, Martin Miles, and Einar Bjorgo, "The Arctic's Shrinking Sea Ice," *Nature* 376 (August 3, 1995): 126–127.

2. An excellent overview of this event, including the views of the various scientists involved, is in Walter Sullivan, "New Theory on Ice Sheet Catastrophe Is the Direst One Yet," *The New York Times*, May 2, 1995: B9. See also Dick van der Wateren and Richard Hindmarsh, "Stabilists Strike Again," *Nature* 376 (August 3, 1995): 389–91.

3. A review article on this study, "Satellite Detects a Global Sea Rise," was published in *Science News* 146 (December 10, 1994): 388.

4. See Nicholas E. Graham, "Simulation of Recent Global Temperature Trends," *Science* 267 (February 3, 1995): 666–71; Richard Monastersky, "Tropical Trouble: Two

Decades of Pacific Warmth Have Fired Up the Globe," *Science News* 147 (March 11, 1995): 154–55.

5. Michael D. Lemonick, "Heading for Apocalypse," *Time*, October 2, 1995: 54–55.

6. See Paul Hawken, *The Ecology of Commerce: A Declaration of Sustainability* (New York: HarperCollins, 1993). It contains the seeds of survival of both the business community and ourselves. It is required reading.

7. A number of investigators have written interesting review papers about this movement. See, for example, Jeffrey L. MacDonald, "Inventing Traditions for the New Age: A Case Study for the Earth Energy Tradition," *Anthropology of Consciousness* 6, no. 4 (1995): 31–45; Joan B. Townsend, "Neoshamanism and the Modern Mystical Movement," pp. 73–85 in Gary Doore, ed., *Shaman's Path: Healing, Personal Growth and Empowerment* (Boston and London: Shambhala, 1988).

8. See Paul H. Ray, "The Rise of Integral Culture," *Noetic Sciences Review*, Spring 1996: 4–15. For information about the Institute of Noetic Sciences, their membership services, opportunities, conferences, travel program, etc., please contact them at 475 Gate 5 Road, Sausalito, California 94965, telephone (415) 331-5650, fax (415) 331-5673.

CHAPTER 15

1. On a semantic note, let me say that I am aware that many use the term *sorcery* to describe a form of traditional spiritual practice devoted to the gathering and use of mystical power in the stage of life sometimes called "the way of the warrior." In a like manner, many use the term *witchcraft* to describe the positively focused spiritual practice devoted to healing associated often with the "wise women" of Europe. In a similar vein, the term *witch* is often used to describe such medicine people and healers.

In anthropology, the term *shaman* has been specifically chosen to describe certain individuals within traditional societies who function on behalf of members of their group as spiritual healers and gatherers of power in the positive mode. The terms *sorcery* and *witchcraft* are used to describe the practice of magic with the intent to inflict harm or misfortune on others. *Magic* refers to the ability to access the realm of the sacred in order to control, influence, or persuade supernatural power to assist in achieving some given end in ordinary reality. Sorcery is distinguished from witchcraft in the sorcerer's use of material substances—the classic voodoo doll or juju object, or the bone pointing of the Melanesian peoples. Witchcraft normally does not utilize material aids but operates solely within the psychic levels of reality, accomplishing the same ends through intention combined with ritual and energy *(mana)* gathered and released with the intent to inflict harm. In this sense, Nainoa's inadvertent use of power resulting in the death of his adversary would technically be called witchcraft.

Semantic bickering over which terms should be regarded as positive or negative, with honor or dishonor, and so on frequently results in confusion and negative effects. In my opinion, the terms *shaman* and *shamanism* lack such negative associations. The adoption of these terms with reference to the spiritual healer, spiritual healing work, and other positively focused, life-enhancing, community-oriented activities would seem to be a way of resolving such academic disputes.

CHAPTER 17

1. For those interested: Tim D. White, Gen Suwa, and Berhane Asfaw, "*Australopithecus ramidus,* a New Species of Early Hominid from Aramis, Ethiopia," *Nature* 371 (1994): 306–12.

2. This fascinating species has now been given a new genus name, as it expresses exceedingly primitive features that distinguish it from other species in the genus *Australopithecus.* Its correct scientific name is now given as *Ardipithecus ramidus.*

CHAPTER 18

1. On a last semantic note, the word used by Nainoa's people for this practice of achieving inner balance and harmony is more on the order of *logai* or *rokai.* It seems to have several meanings, the most common of which is "peace" or "unity." The contemporary Hawaiian word for this is *lokahi,* and since that term is in usage today in the islands, I have chosen to use it in this narrative.

Glossary

HAWAIIAN TERMS

aka	The primordial energetic "stuff" out of which everything in the universes is made; in contemporary usage, its meaning is shadow, image, or reflection.
akaku	Vision.
akua	In the outer tradition, major supernatural deities or "high gods" of old Hawai'i; in the inner tradition, aspects of the self.
aloha	Love, compassion, greeting; another literal meaning is to be in the presence of the "divine breath" or "divinity."
ao aumakua	The place in the spirit world occupied by the human aumakua spirits.
aumakua	Personal ancestral spiritual aspect; high self, god self, angelic self; immortal, spiritual source self.
awa	Ceremonial Polynesian drink also known as *kava*.
bonsho	Raincape made of netting with broad leaves attached.
ganakolao	Hairy forest people; chimpanzees.

Glossary

gocheka	A board game played with white and black pieces, possibly a combination of checkers and go.
ha	The breath; an aspect of the self released upon the death of the physical body.
haka	Trance mediumship in which the medium serves as a channel for a spiritual entity.
haku	Master or captain (of a voyaging canoe).
hale mana	The "house of power" used in containing power objects and sacred relics; usually located on temple platforms.
heiau	Sacred place of power and spiritual practice; usually surmounted by a temple platform including sacred buildings and symbolic images of deities and/or aspects of the self.
hoalona lanakila	Lofty measure, high merit.
ho'omana	The spiritual knowledge and practices of the mystics and shamans of Hawai'i; literal meaning: "to empower," "to place in authority," "to worship."
ho'oponopono	Traditional Hawaiian method of conflict resolution.
ho'ounauna	To send spirits to (someone), to send healing energy to.
ho'una	To command, to send on an errand or direct to work.
huna	Literally, "hidden," "secret," "to hide" or "to conceal"; colloquial term often used by non-Hawaiians for *ho'omana*.
ike	Spiritual power.
kahu	The honored attendant, keeper or caretaker of a *heiau* or sacred object.
kahuna	Literal meaning, "expert"; in colloquial expression, a priest, shaman, or mystic.
kahuna kupua	*Kahuna* mystic, shaman, master of spirits.
kahuna la'au lapa'au	Medical *kahuna*, herbalist, master healer.
kahuna pule	Priest or ceremonialist, master of prayer.
kamea'mana	Power object.
Kanaloa	In its outer aspect, the *akua* of the ocean; in its inner aspect, the fully awakened or enlightened human state in which all aspects of the self are fully formed, fully aware, and fully experienced.

Glossary

Kane	In its outer aspect, one of the four major *akua* of old Hawai'i with over seventy recorded names, the creator god; in its inner aspect, the dual-natured god self (*kanewahine*) or high self of the individual, *aumakua* (the personal ancestral spirit).
kapo'e'aumakua	The collective gathering of all the human *aumakua* higher selves; the composite human spirit.
Kapohaku'ki'ihele	The spirit stone; literally, "the stone that travels."
kapu	Forbidden, taboo, sacred.
ke'aka	Literally, "the shadow"; the formidable, dark spirit that functions as the guardian at the threshold into the spirit worlds.
kealakupua	The shaman's path or way of the mystic.
kino	The physical body.
kino'aka	The energy body; includes what Westerners would call the etheric body and the astral body.
koko'aka	The great energetic grid or net formed of *aka* substance, within which everything in the manifested universe is interconnected across space and time; the great pattern.
Ku	In its outer aspect, the *akua* of rain, fertility, sorcery, war, and business; in its inner aspect, the subconscious mind or body mind of the individual; also known as *unihipili*.
kukui	Candlenut tree; light.
kulana	Rank, position.
kumu	Foundation, beginning, main trunk of a tree; teacher.
lanikeha	The spiritual Upper Worlds of the major gods, goddesses, heroes and heroines, and spiritual teachers; the place of the human *aumakua* spirits; heaven or paradise of the Judeo-Christian-Islamic traditions.
lei	A wreath or necklace of flowers.
lono	In its outer aspect, one of the major *akua* of old Hawai'i, the *akua* of agriculture, medicine, navigation, and science; in its inner aspect, the conscious mind; the thinker, inner director and decision maker, the intellectual aspect of the self, also known as *uhane*.
makalapua	Flowering, maturing, opening.
makana	Gift.

mana	Supernatural or mystical power.
mauli	Life force.
Milu	The spiritual Lower Worlds to which the traditional shaman or *kahuna* mystic journeys to make contact with mystical power and the spirits of nature.
mo'o	Water spirit.
noho	Spirit possession.
oki	Alcoholic drink made from *ti* roots.
ola'hou	Reincarnation.
Pele	The spirit who currently lives within the active volcanos of the island of Hawai'i.
Po	The spirit worlds.
pohaku	Stone; literally, "lord or master of the spirit worlds."
pohaku kupua	Spirit stone.
siti	A word for "city"; probably borrowed from Old English.
tapa (kapa)	Bark paper or bark cloth.
taro (kalo)	Starchy tuber that is a staple crop in Polynesia.
ti (ki)	Plant whose broad leaves are often used to wrap ritual offerings.
uhane	Literally, "spirit," "soul," or "ghost"; another term for the conscious mind, the intellect or *lono* aspect of the self.
ukana	Baggage.
unihipili	Spirit of a deceased person or one able to be conjured up by a sorcerer; alternative term for the *ku*, the inner subconscious or body mind.
wa	Term used by Nainoa's people to signify internal balance and harmony; probably of Chinese origin.
wa'a'kau'lua	Double-hulled canoe.
welina	A greeting of affection, similar to *aloha*.

ENNU TERMS

baton	Stick; spear thrower.
bushivak	The spotted tiger or jaguar.

Glossary

dorajuadiok	Spiritual entities of vast intelligence; composed of pure awareness in association with dense concentrations of energy or universal power; function as activators and conductors of power and are without material, physical form; able to help the shaman accomplish various tasks.
dordok	Spirit helpers.
egimag	Throwing spear; javelin.
kumonek	The inner light; enlightenment.
odiok	The name soul; possessed only by humans.
oma	Heart.
shumonadok	Ethics.
ungagok	The spiritwalker; the shaman, mystic, and master of spirits.
zakray	Holy; sacred.
ziku	White; snow or ice.
Zilatu	The spirit of the air.

OTHER TERMS

nierika	Huichol Indian term (Mexico); the inner doorway or opening into the spirit worlds; often expressed symbolically as an object, a mirror with decorated margins, or a mandala.
phosphene	Visual hallucinations perceived in the initial phases of trance; frequently appear as flashes or spots of light, rows of dots, lines or meandering curves, nested sets of curves, zigzags, vortices, or grids; entopic phenomena that can be seen with the eyes open or closed.
sesshin	Japanese term for the Buddhist retreat, usually lasting seven days.
therianthrope	Literally, "beast-man" (from the Greek *therion*, "animal," *anthropos*, "man"); term used for the power animals or spiritual entities perceived in the deeper levels of trance; the blending of animal and human characteristics into composite form; the perceived merging of a shaman in deep trance with a spirit helper.

319

Acknowledgments

Many of my teachers and students, family members and friends, have contributed knowingly and unknowingly to this book. First and foremost among these are my wife, Jill Kuykendall, and our daughters, Erica and Anna, who stayed with me during a dark time in my life when I had lost virtually everything else.

Others who contributed to this book include Kahu Nelita Anderson, Francisco Arce, Mesfin Asnake, Michael Baldwin, Jeanne Blackstone, Michael Fleck, Sue Anne Foster, Anne Getty, Michael Harner, Ingrid and Reuben Hills, Sandra Ingerman, Lucia and Rocky Ka'iouliokahihikolo'Ehu Jensen, Bokara Legendre, Nina and Kahu Hale Makua, Megan Mitchell, Tina Nappe, Carolyn Lee Precourt, Gerçek Sarac, Molly and Don Toral, Bill Tsuji, Sue Pulk and Chris Wesselman, and Tim White.

There is also Ali'i Nainoa Kaneohe.

Homage and deep gratitude are also offered to Brian Tart, my editor at Bantam Books; to my literary agents, Candice Fuhrman and Linda Michaels; and to my publicists, Cate Cummings and Cor van Heuman.

To all of them, I offer my blessings and my very warmest aloha.

Shamanic Training Workshops

Information and schedules of training workshops in core shamanism and shamanic healing with Dr. Michael Harner, Sandra Ingerman, and their associates are available from:

The Foundation for Shamanic Studies
P.O. Box 1939
Mill Valley, California 94942
Telephone (415) 380-8282; fax (415) 380-8416
Web site: www.shamanism.org

Interest in Dr. Wesselman's schedule of lectures, presentations, and workshops can be directed to:

SharedWisdom
P.O. Box 2059
Granite Bay, California 95746
Web site: www.sharedwisdom.com

About the Author

Anthropologist Hank Wesselman has worked with an international group of scientists for the past twenty-five years, exploring the ancient fossil beds of East Africa's Great Rift Valley in search of answers to the mystery of human origins. In the 1970s, while doing fieldwork in Africa alongside such worthies as F. Clark Howell, Don Johanson, and members of the famous Leakey family, Dr. Wesselman began to experience spontaneous altered states of consciousness similar to those of traditional shamans. Years later, while living with his family on a farm on the island of Hawai'i, he began to experience a series of classic visionary episodes that continue to this day.

His book *Spiritwalker: Messages from the Future* (Bantam Books, 1995), presents an autobiographical account of how these experiences began and how they represent a turning point in Dr. Wesselman's career, providing an entirely new direction in his investigation of the human species—the evolution of consciousness.

Dr. Wesselman has taught at the University of California at San Diego, the University of Hawai'i at Hilo, and California State University at Sacramento. He currently teaches at American River College and Sierra College in northern California.